Play Therapy Interventions
with
Children's Problems

Play Therapy Interventions

with

Children's Problems

GARRY L. LANDRETH, ED.D.

LINDA E. HOMEYER, PH.D.

GERALDINE GLOVER, PH.D.

DANIEL S. SWEENEY, PH.D.

JASON ARONSON INC.
Northvale, New Jersey
London

Production Editor: M'lou Pinkham

This book was set in 11 pt. New Baskerville by Alpha Graphics of Pittsfield, New Hampshire, and printed and bound by Book-mart Press of North Bergen, New Jersey.

Library of Congress Cataloging-in-Publication Data

Play therapy interventions with children's problems / Garry L.
    Landreth . . . [et al.].
        p.   cm.
    Includes bibliographical references and index.
    ISBN 1-56821-482-0 (alk. paper)
    1. Play therapy—Abstracts.   2. Play therapy—Case studies—
Abstracts.   I. Landreth, Garry L.
RJ505.P6P546 1996
615.8'5153'083—dc20   95-49478

Manufactured in the United States of America. Jason Aronson Inc. offers books and cassettes. For information and catalog write to Jason Aronson Inc., 230 Livingston Street, Northvale, New Jersey 07647.

Contributors

Garry L. Landreth, Ed.D., Regents Professor, Department of Counseling, Development and Higher Education and Director, Center for Play Therapy, University of North Texas

Linda E. Homeyer, Ph.D., Assistant Professor, Department of Educational Administration and Psychological Services, Southwest Texas State University

Geraldine Glover, Ph.D., private practice, Santa Fe, New Mexico

Daniel S. Sweeney, Ph.D., Assistant Director, Center for Play Therapy, University of North Texas

Contents

Introduction   **xii**

1   Abuse and Neglect   **1**
Processing Physical and Emotional Abuse through
    Puppet Play, 2
Overcoming the Effects of Severe Deprivation,
    Dehydration, and Coma through Play Therapy, 5
Play Therapy and Disclosure of Abuse, 7
The Impact of Play Therapy on Self-Concept and
    Self-Mastery in Sexually Abused Children, 9
Play Therapy with a Severely Neglected Emotionally
    Abused Child, 12

2   Aggression and Acting Out   **15**
Play Therapy with an Aggressive Child, 16
Play Therapy and Video Feedback of Play Sessions
    with Oppositional Disordered Children, 19
Play Therapy as an Intervention for Acting-Out
    Children, 22

A Group Play Technique for Rewarding Social
    Responsibility, 25
Play Group Counseling as an Effective Intervention
    for Children with Behavior Problems, 28
Brief Play Therapy for a Preschooler with Severe
    Temper Tantrums, 30
Play Therapy for the Institutionalized Child, 33
Play Therapy for Behavior Problems Centered
    around Issues of Anger, Fear, and Control, 35
Psychoanalytic Play Therapy with an Acting-Out
    Child, 38

3   Attachment Difficulties   **41**
Child-Centered Play Therapy for Problems Associated
    with Attachment, 42
Cognitive, Reflective, and Psychodynamic Play Therapy
    Techniques for Promoting the Attachment Process
    in an Adopted Boy, 45

4   Autism   **49**
Psychodynamic Play Therapy with a High-Functioning
    Autistic Child, 50
Treating Autism with Psychoanalytic Play Therapy, 53

5   Burn Victims   **55**
Multimodal Treatment of a Burned Child, 56
Development of a Preoperative Play Program for Burned
    Children, 58

6   Chronic Illness   **61**
Play Therapy with an Asthmatic Child, 62
Filial Therapy with Parents of Chronically Ill Children, 65

7   Deaf and Physically Challenged Children   **69**
Sand Play with Hyperkinetic, Epileptic Children, 71
Play Therapy with Preschool Deaf Children, 73
Treating a Deaf Child with Play Therapy, 75

8   Dissociation and Schizophrenia   **79**
Jungian Play Therapy with a Schizophrenic Boy, 81
Play Therapy with a Dissociative Child, 84

Play Therapy with a Regressed Schizophrenic
    Adolescent Girl, 87
Group Play Therapy with Psychotic Adolescent
    Girls, 90

 9 **Emotionally Disturbed Children**   93
Developmental Play Group Counseling with Emotionally
    Disturbed Children, 94
Play Therapy Treatment of Emotional Disturbance
    and Trichotillomania in a Child with Mild
    Microcephaly, 96
Group Play Therapy with Emotionally Disturbed
    Children, 98

10 **Enuresis and Encopresis Problems**   101
Play and Drama Therapy for Enuresis and Acting-Out
    Behaviors, 102
Cognitive-Behavioral Play Therapy in the Treatment
    of Encopresis, 105
Psychodynamic Play Therapy with an Encopretic
    Child, 108

11 **Fear and Anxiety**   111
Extreme Anxiety in a Primary-Grade Child, 112
Play Therapy with a Child Who Had Pulled Out All
    of Her Hair, 114
Use of Structured Play to Discover the Cause of the Fear of
    Being Kidnapped, 116
Home Play Therapy and Toilet Training, 119
Brief Play Therapy for Stammering, 122
Brief Play Therapy: Pinocchio and School Phobia, 125
Focused Play to Resolve Separation Anxiety, 127
A Behavioral Approach Using Play Therapy to Change the
    Interaction Pattern between Mother and Daughter, 130
The 'Squiggle' Drawing Used to Overcome Anxiety in a
    New Client, 133

12 **Grief**   135
Sandplay Therapy with a Grieving Child, 136
Puppets in the Treatment of Traumatic Grief, 139

Group Play Therapy with Bereaved Children, 141
Child-Centered Play Therapy with a Grieving
    Child, 143

13 **Hospitalization**   145
Therapeutic Play with a Hospitalized 5-Year-Old
    Boy, 146
Treating Hospital Fear Reactions with Play
    Therapy, 148
Brief Puppet Therapy for Children Facing Cardiac
    Catheterization, 151
The Effects of Play Therapy on Hospitalized
    Children, 153
Helping Young Children Master Intrusive Procedures
    through Play, 156
Therapeutic Play for Anxiety Issues, 158
Treatment of Hospitalized Children for Acute
    Illness, 160
Play Therapy in a Pediatric Hospital Department, 163

14 **Learning-Disabled Children**   167
Play Therapy for Children with Learning Disabilities, 168

15 **Mentally Challenged (Handicapped)**   171
Group Play Therapy with Mentally Challenged
    Children, 172
The Effect of Play Therapy on IQ and Emotional and Social
    Development of Mentally Challenged Children, 174
Play Therapy with Mentally Challenged Institutionalized
    Children, 177

16 **Reading Difficulties**   179
Teacher Use of Play Therapy Procedures for Poor
    Readers, 180
Brief Client-Centered Play Therapy to Increase Reading
    Skills, 183
Play Therapy as an Intervention for a Reading
    Problem, 185

17   Selective Mutism   **189**
Nondirective Play Therapy with an Elective Mute
    Child, 191
Individual and Sibling Group Play Therapy with a
    Selective Mute Child, 193
Psychoanalytic Play Therapy with an Elective Mute
    Child, 195

18   Self-Concept and Self-Esteem   **199**
Play Therapy Increases the Self-Concept of Poor
    Readers, 201
Filial Therapy as an Effective Intervention for
    Increasing Children's Self-Concept, 203
Activity Play Therapy to Increase Elementary Students'
    Self-Concept, 206
Child-Centered Group Play Therapy as an Intervention to
    Increase Sociometric Status and Self-Concept, 208
Filial Therapy as a Treatment Modality to Improve
    Parent–Child Relations and Increase Self-Esteem
    in Young Children of Incarcerated Fathers, 210

19   Social Adjustment Problems   **213**
Group Play Therapy as an Intervention for Children with
    Peer and Sibling Relationship Problems, 214
Self-Directive Play Therapy as a Treatment for Socially
    Immature Kindergarten Children, 216
Play Therapy for Children with School Adjustment
    Problems, 218
Group Play Therapy as an Intervention Modality for
    Modifying the Social Adjustment of Primary-Grade
    Boys, 221
Development of Self-Control in Bilingual Children through
    Group Play Therapy, 224

20   Speech Difficulties   **227**
Nondirective Group Play Therapy to Facilitate Speech and
    Language Development in Preschool Children, 228
Treatment of Emotionally Based Delayed Speech with Play
    Therapy, 230

Play Therapy Intervention for Regression of Speech in a
    Young Child, 232
Theraplay with Articulation Disorders, 235
Group Play Therapy to Improve Speech, Social Skills,
    Personality Attributes, and Intelligence, 237

21   Traumatization   **241**
Sand Play as an Intervention for a Child Whose Family
    Situation Changed Dramatically, 243
Child-Centered Play Therapy with a Neglected Child
    Traumatized by Hospitalization, 245
Intensive Play Therapy with Child Witnesses of Domestic
    Violence, 248
Psychoanalytic Play Therapy with a Child Suffering from
    Traumatic Neurosis, 250
Racial Differences Cause Extreme Rejection in Play
    Therapy: An Issue for Therapist and Child, 253
Traumatic Birth Symbolized in Play Therapy, 256

22   Withdrawn Children   **259**
Child-Centered Play Therapy with an Extremely
    Withdrawn Boy, 260
Use of Operant Conditioning in Nondirective Group
    Play Therapy with Withdrawn Third-Grade
    Boys, 262
Teachers Providing Play Therapy for Withdrawn
    Students, 265
Behavioral Learning Theory Applied to Play Therapy
    as an Intervention with a Withdrawn, Noneating
    Child, 267
Child-Centered Play Therapy with a Withdrawn
    Child, 270

Introduction

Play therapy is not an approach based on guess, trial and error, or whims of the play therapist at the moment. Play therapy is a well-thought-out, philosophically conceived, developmentally based, and research-supported approach to helping children cope with and overcome the problems they experience in the process of living their lives. This book is unique in play therapy literature in that for the first time the existing findings of play therapy research studies and case reports have been brought together in one volume. As the reader will note, the popular myth that play therapy requires a long-term commitment for many months is dispelled by the findings of many of the studies reported in this book.

The focus of this book is on interventions and methodologies that have been helpful in alleviating problems of children who have been referred for play therapy. Concise digests of play therapy procedures based on case studies and research reported in the literature highlight the results achieved. These digests provide the reader with a concise reference text to the most difficult, as well as the most common, problems encountered by play therapists in their work with children. In addition, this book contains play therapy approaches based on a variety of theoretical positions for dealing with a broad range of specific problems experienced by children. This practical reference book provides quick access to documented studies that demonstrate the effectiveness of different theoretical models of play therapy and a wide variety of play therapy approaches, such as individual play therapy, group play therapy, sibling group play therapy, sand play, puppet play, structured and nonstructured procedures, "theraplay," and activity play therapy in a variety of settings including private practice, agencies, hospitals, elementary schools, prisons, and homes.

The research studies and case reports included in this volume are the result of an exhaustive literature search and the comprehensive holdings of the Center for Play Therapy Library at the University of North Texas, which includes more than 2,000 journal articles related to the field of play therapy. In addition, extensive use was made of the references in *The World of Play Therapy Literature: A Definitive Guide to Authors and Subjects in the Field* by Landreth, Homeyer, Bratton, and Kale (1995), published by the Center for Play Therapy.

The purpose of this book is to make available to mental health professionals and students in the field of play therapy research-based play therapy procedures that have been demonstrated to be effective with a myriad of specific children's problems. In fact, this book contains every research study and case report with definitive results that we could locate in the literature.

Our experience in training and supervising play therapists has shown that they often begin to doubt themselves and the effectiveness of play therapy when they are not familiar with substantiated results. This book aims to rectify that problem by providing research to encourage and nurture confidence. When practitioners know that what they are doing is based on research, they are more likely to be consistent in their approach and thus more effective.

In this day of accountability demanded by lawyers in courtroom experiences and by managed care providers, play therapists must increasingly be able to document the effectiveness of play therapy procedures. This book should prove a significant asset to those who are required to justify their recommendations for play therapy services.

The reader will note that at the end of each study or case report there is a listing of possible *DSM-IV* diagnoses. In many instances the case report or research study did not provide the detailed criteria necessary for actual diagnosis. Therefore, the suggested diagnosis is provided only to assist the play therapist in exploring possible options.

Abuse and Neglect

The typical approach to child abuse is to remove the child from the home, but in such cases the inner dynamics of the child's reaction to the abuse still exist. The emotional dynamics resulting from abuse must be matched by an equally dynamic therapeutic process, such as that found in the play therapy relationship. Children who have been abused cannot be expected to verbally describe their experience and their reaction because they lack the cognitive-verbal ability to do so. Abused children come from inconsistent environments. The play therapy relationship provides them with an absolutely consistent environment, for without such the child cannot feel safe; it is this dimension of predictable safety that allows children to express, explore, and resolve through play deep-seated emotional pain. Abuse and neglect cause serious inner conflicts and relationship problems for children, and play therapy provides the modality necessary for children to develop adaptive and coping mechanisms on their own terms and at their own emotional pace.

PROCESSING PHYSICAL AND EMOTIONAL ABUSE THROUGH PUPPET PLAY

AUTHOR: **Charles A. Burch**

FOCUS: *Puppet play is used as a technique in play therapy to assist a 13-year-old boy in dealing with physical and emotional abuse.*

INTRODUCTION: Abused children often have very high levels of anxiety. The use of puppet play to distance the self from the content of the play, and thus the anxiety, is used with Carl. Therapeutic issues for Carl involved his ethnicity, abuse and neglect, and abandonment by his birth parents; death of his adoptive father; and rejection by his adoptive mother who wanted to "unadopt" him.

CASE STUDY: Carl was born to an unmarried teenage mother. At the age of 4 months he was placed with a foster family. Although the investigating social worker found evidence of frequent, severe, and abusive physical punishment by the foster parents, Carl was allowed to be adopted. Four years later, after the family had moved twice, the adoptive father died. The adoptive mother indicated that her husband's last wish was that Carl be "unadopted." While seeking a placement for Carl, the adoptive mother indicated that Carl was stupid, mean, jealous, stubborn, and had "bad blood." Carl was then placed in a foster home but continued to have regular contact with his adoptive mother and sister.

INTERVENTION: Increasing social and school problems resulted in Carl's initial involvement in therapy. He worked with a female therapist for a year. When the female therapist left the clinic, Carl was referred to the author because of the recommendation that a male therapist would be appropriate, given Carl's entry into adolescence.

Carl was seen in a play therapy setting. During the early stages, Carl revealed conflicts regarding his African-American identity and his rage about being abandoned. He wanted to discover what was wrong with him and get the right medicine to be cured. A strong therapeutic alliance was developed during this initial stage.

During his seventh session, Carl selected two hand puppets: an aggressive-looking parrot and a woodpecker-like red bird, which he used to ask the therapist questions after a verbal patient–therapist interchange resulted in a high level of anxiety. He asked the therapist to have these puppets available for subsequent sessions.

In the next session Carl immediately sought out the puppets and asked that the play be recorded. After the puppet play was finished, the tape was played and Carl and the therapist discussed various points in the play.

There was significant puppet play during the next four sessions, each followed by a time for listening to the audiotape. The first puppet play revolved around a baby bird (Carl) who hatched after the mother bird left. The baby bird had no one to feed it, and even had no name or understanding of what kind of bird it might be. A neighbor bird came and took the baby bird to its home.

The second puppet play continued to reveal Carl's need to understand why he was abandoned, even though the reason was demeaning to his view of himself. The play also indicated his fantasy that he had his father's name.

The third play focused on a meeting between the red bird (Carl) and his biological mother (the parrot). Although excited about meeting his mother, when she expressed the desire to take him home he stated that she was "too late" and he wanted to stay with the birds who had taken care of him. The play continued to reveal that Carl still desired to be with his adoptive mother, although rejected by her and abandoned, through his death, by his adoptive father.

The final drama revealed Carl's view of the inevitability of abuse from parental figures. During this puppet play, his current foster parents mistreated, threatened, and abused him. The play ended when his biological mother came to the rescue and took him away to live in a pleasurable setting. Carl still hoped to have his birth mother be the perfect parent he had never had.

According to the author, the puppet play revealed how severely Carl had suffered and how he viewed himself as bad, rather than viewing his birth, adoptive, or foster mothers as not meeting his needs. The author indicated that he worked with Carl to develop insight within the metaphor of the puppet play. This allowed Carl the opportunity to work through his view of himself and his feelings toward parental figures.

COMMENTARY: Carl reportedly was very spontaneous regarding development of the puppet play; this activity clearly offered insight into his past and his hopes for the future. The play provided the means through which he was able to replay and master his childhood traumas. By requesting that the puppet play be audiotaped and then played, Carl allowed the therapist to participate in the process at a deeper, more active level.

SOURCE: Burch, C. A. (1980). Puppet play in a thirteen-year-old boy: remembering, repeating, and working through. *Clinical Social Work Journal* 8(2):79–89.

POSSIBLE *DSM-IV* DIAGNOSES:

300.02   Generalized Anxiety Disorder
309.21   Separation Anxiety Disorder
995.5   Physical Abuse
V61.20   Parent–Child Relational Problem

OVERCOMING THE EFFECTS OF SEVERE DEPRIVATION, DEHYDRATION, AND COMA THROUGH PLAY THERAPY

AUTHOR: **David Friedman**

FOCUS: *A severely neglected child participated in play therapy after hospitalization and placement in a foster home.*

INTRODUCTION: Six-year-old Sean had been deprived of all fluid by his mother during a heat wave in an attempt to "cure" his enuresis. His 2-year-old sister died from the same deprivation. Sean was comatose when hospitalized for severe dehydration. After his release, he was referred for therapy. Sean was hypervigilant to his environment. He did not speak during intake sessions but responded by shaking his head.

CASE STUDY: From a self psychology perspective, Sean was conceptualized as a child who had learned to serve as his own hypervigilant self-object, risking disintegration if he did not meet his mother's needs. Repression of his own developmentally appropriate narcissistic needs resulted in a lack of pleasure, of activities, and of initiative. Self psychology believes that reflecting, or mirroring, the child's needs not only validates these needs, but also facilitates the developmental process of integration for the child.

INTERVENTION: When Sean began play therapy, he displayed no affect, appeared almost mechanical, was nonverbal, and did not play. Play was initiated by the author through the use of stimulating toys and food. To help relieve Sean's anxiety about being close, the author played by himself until eventually Sean, who responded only to the most indirect invitation to play, was able to join in.

After four months of weekly sessions, Sean finally was able to ask for a toy or food. Continued reflecting was needed to maintain contact with him. The author indicated that the slightest response that was not in touch with Sean's subjective world disrupted the fragile therapeutic alliance: Sean would look bewildered and immediately withdraw.

After seven months an important change occurred. Sean's flat and monotonous play became animated and filled with affect. Sean's play with a mother and baby doll revealed a baby who was able to smash the "bad mommy" doll into the wall. This play continued for fifteen minutes. Subsequent play included the now-labeled "baby man," who built prisons where the "bad mommy" could be kept without escaping.

Sean's play was now spontaneous and filled with strong emotion. However, the author indicated that the reflections, or mirroring, still had to be focused on the baby. If direct questions were asked, Sean retreated to the previous behavior of bewilderment and withdrawal.

Change was seen outside of therapy as well. Sean was able to be assertive, even to the point of saying "no" to authority figures. The play therapist also assisted Sean's foster parents in facilitating Sean's developmental needs and his emerging self.

COMMENTARY: Long-term, severe deprivation results in the need for long-term therapeutic intervention. Deprivation, or child neglect, often results in children who are unable to play. Many experts agree that the first step to remediation is to help the child learn to play. Once this key developmental task is accomplished, the child is able to use play in an expressive, healing manner.

SOURCE: Friedman, D. (1983). A self-psychology perspective. *Association for Play Therapy Newsletter* 2(3):6–8.

POSSIBLE *DSM-IV* DIAGNOSES:

313.89   Reactive Attachment Disorder
995.5   Neglect of Child

PLAY THERAPY AND DISCLOSURE OF ABUSE

AUTHOR: **Patricia R. Klem**

FOCUS: *A case study describes how a child used the dollhouse in a play therapy session to disclose physical and sexual abuse and produce healing solutions.*

INTRODUCTION: The case study presented is that of James, a 6-year-old boy referred for counseling due to substantial emotional and behavioral disturbance. Play therapy offered James the freedom to overcome his developmental delays and fear so he could disclose sexual abuse by a sibling. The reenactment of physical abuse in the play eventually forced James's mother to admit to physical abuse by the father.

CASE STUDY: James, a developmentally delayed boy who lived with his mother, father, and four siblings, was described by school personnel as disruptive and destructive. He was also preoccupied with death. When he was discovered exposing himself and attempting to touch other boys at school, James told police officers that "my brother does it to me." The family was referred for family therapy and marital counseling, and James was referred for play therapy.

INTERVENTION: In the first play therapy session, James appeared very interested in the dollhouse but would not initiate playing with it. When the play therapist indicated that the dollhouse could be played with and suggested that it could be moved to the middle of the room, James began to explore it with great interest. As he rearranged the dollhouse, he described his own house in detail and selected just the right number of dollhouse figures, labeling them with the names of his family. He quickly went on to describe and act out the nighttime physical and sexual abuse by his older brother. He laid the James doll down on the bottom bunk bed and said, "I'm sleeping now." Then the brother doll came in the bedroom, hit the James doll and touched it in the crotch. Before the brother doll left the room, it said, "If you tell, I'll kill you." This same sequence of interaction was repeated three times before the mother doll called the children dolls to wake up and get ready for school. James then described a typical day's routine and repeated the nighttime abuse again. The entire scenario was played out three times in the first session. James did not want to leave the playroom when the time was up. He left only after reassurance that he could play with the dollhouse during the next session.

In the second and third sessions James continued to act out the abuse with the dollhouse figures. He also introduced an unnamed male who would hit the James doll, throw him against the wall, and pull him by the hair. When the play therapist asked James to identify the new male doll, James answered, "I can't tell you, and you can't make it stop."

The father was away on business and did not attend the family therapy sessions. When the therapist told the family about James's abuse and asked who might have abused him, no one in the family would reveal any information.

During the fourth play therapy session, James placed the James doll on the top bunk of his bed and announced, "I feel safe on the top now that you know the secret." James told the play therapist that the night invasions had stopped but the brother still threw him against the walls and yelled at him during the day.

Only after the father physically abused James in public did the mother, fearing Child Protective Services might remove James from the home, act to protect him. She revealed the long-term physical abuse of James by his father and stated that the older brother had also been physically and verbally abused by him. The mother took the children and left the home.

COMMENTARY: James was able to use the safety of the play therapy sessions and the availability of concrete play (especially necessary, given James's developmental delay) with the dollhouse to act out his abuse. Manipulating the doll figures to repeatedly reenact his abuse gave James the ability to communicate the threats made against him and his fear of being attacked with no internal or external sources to protect him. Through continued play, James was quickly able to develop a sense of control and place himself in a position of safety.

SOURCE: Klem, P. R. (1992). The use of the dollhouse as an effective disclosure technique. *International Journal of Play Therapy* 1:69–73.

POSSIBLE *DSM-IV* DIAGNOSES:

995.5   Physical and Sexual Abuse of Child
V61.8   Sibling Relational Problem

THE IMPACT OF PLAY THERAPY ON SELF-CONCEPT AND SELF-MASTERY IN SEXUALLY ABUSED CHILDREN

AUTHOR: **Charles Lee Perez**

FOCUS: *Individual and group play therapy in the treatment of sexually abused children. Mediating variables of gender, age, type of abuse, and living arrangements were examined.*

INTRODUCTION: As the need to provide treatment for sexually abused children increases, questions regarding the most effective treatment model also increase. In this study individual play therapy and group play therapy were used to determine the most effective treatment modality for sexually abused children. Age of the child, gender, type of abuse, and living arrangements (whether at home or in foster care) were examined as possible factors affecting the child's response to therapy.

Sexual abuse forces children to experience behavior for which they are not developmentally or emotionally prepared. This disruption of the typical developmental process often directly affects a child's self-concept and self-mastery. With this in mind, this study measured the change of self-concept and self-mastery over the course of treatment.

RESEARCH METHODS & DESIGN: Fifty-five children who had been verified by social services, police, or both as having been sexually abused took part in this research. The children ranged in age from 4 to 9 years. They were carefully screened to ensure there had been no previous therapy and that no more than six months had elapsed since the disclosure of the sexual abuse.

Severity of abuse, degree of exposure, type of sexual activity, length of time exposed to abuse, number of incidents, other physical abuse, and emotional response of the child after disclosure varied with each child. The sexual abuse was both incestual and extrafamilial (babysitters, teachers, day care providers, strangers). The abusers were primarily males.

The Primary Self-Concept Inventory (PSCI) and the Locus of Control Scale (LCS) were used to measure self-concept and self-esteem both before and after treatment. Analysis of variance, analysis of covariance, and multiple regression analysis were used to analyze the resulting data.

INTERVENTION: The children were divided into three groups. The first received individual play therapy and the second, group play therapy in once-a-week sixty-minute sessions for twelve weeks. The third group, the control group, received no therapeutic intervention.

Both individual and group play therapy followed the relationship model developed by Moustakas[1] and used Bixler's[2] limit setting. In addition, structured techniques, such as art projects, role playing, mutual storytelling, literature, and snack time, were included. Each group comprised three to five children of the same gender and ranged from 4 to 6 or 7 to 9 years in age. One purpose of the group play therapy was to facilitate the development of a pseudofamily in which the children could unconsciously relate to the therapist as a parent and other group members as siblings.

The play therapists were four social workers who were part of a local sexual abuse treatment team. They received twelve weekly sessions of training and supervision regarding the principles and methodology of play therapy.

RESULTS: The results indicated that play therapy benefits sexually abused children regardless of gender, age, type of abuse experience, or current living arrangements. The results of both individual and group play therapy were statistically significant ($p > .05$) when compared to the control group. There were no significant differences in the effects of treatment between individual and group play therapy.

Play therapy gave the children the opportunity to reorganize the negative events of sexual abuse, gain self-control over these events, and begin developing a positive self-concept. The measured self-concepts of the children receiving play therapy increased ($p < .05$) while the children in the control group actually scored lower at the posttest.

---

1. Clark Moustakas, *Children in Play Therapy* (Northvale, NJ: Jason Aronson Inc., 1973).

2. Ray Bixler, "Limits Are Therapy," *Journal of Consulting Psychology*, 13, pp. 1–11.

Self-mastery is a key therapeutic issue for sexually abused children. The violation of physical and emotional boundaries results in their believing they are not entitled to privacy and exist merely to be used by a more powerful person. These children thus come to believe they have no control, or mastery, over their environment. The self-mastery scores of the children in play therapy rose significantly (p<.05) while those of the children in the control group dropped and their sense of helplessness increased.

COMMENTARY: Although there was no significant difference in outcome between individual and group play therapy, the author identified advantages of group play therapy. The group allows the children to identify with other sexually abused children, thus reducing their feeling of isolation. The group also acts as a pseudofamily and allows the child to experience parental and sibling relationships in which sexual abuse does not occur.

The relationship of the child to the abuser did appear to have some effect on the results of treatment. Victims of incest had higher average group scores than victims of extrafamilial abuse on both the self-concept and self-mastery instruments. While these increases did not reach a statistically significant level, the results do seem to imply that children involved in incest improve more in the areas of self-concept and self-mastery when compared to the victims of extrafamilial abuse.

SOURCE: Perez, C. (1987). A comparison of group play therapy and individual play therapy for sexually abused children. Doctoral dissertation, University of Northern Colorado. *Dissertation Abstracts International* 48(12A).

POSSIBLE *DSM-IV* DIAGNOSIS:

995.5   Sexual Abuse of Child

PLAY THERAPY WITH A SEVERELY NEGLECTED EMOTIONALLY ABUSED CHILD

AUTHOR: **Janet West**

FOCUS: *The use of play therapy to allow a child the freedom to regress and then emotionally mature.*

INTRODUCTION: Severe neglect and emotional abuse often result in acting-out behavior and impaired academic achievement. Child-centered play therapy provides a child with the opportunity to deal with her multiple therapeutic issues in the order of her preference.

CASE STUDY: Rosy, an underweight 6-year-old girl, had recently been placed in a children's home. She was manipulative, sought attention, and wanted to run her life by her rules. She spent a great deal of time wandering around aimlessly and showed very little academic achievement. Although long-term foster care appeared inevitable, it was decided she needed therapeutic intervention before a foster home would be appropriate.

Rosy was the fifth child of a mother in her late twenties. Two children were placed with grandparents and the other two suffered permanent developmental damage from severe neglect. Rosy's family moved several times as her father was frequently unemployed. Her mother was a prostitute. Her parents offered her some love, though it was expressed in inappropriate ways.

Several events immediately preceded Rosy's placement in the children's home. Her mother had killed a male client in their home and Rosy assisted in cleaning up the blood. The mother was jailed and Rosy moved in with a neighbor. Rosy's father was later hospitalized after she discovered him attempting suicide; she was then admitted into foster care. Three months after her placement, Rosy began play therapy.

INTERVENTION: The author identified her approach as child-centered play therapy and conceptualized the process of treatment with the use of Moustakas'[1] stages of play therapy. Because of Rosy's severe deprivation, food was added to the play therapy setting. The primary goal of each session was to provide a safe, therapeutic environment. Rosy was allowed to work at her own pace and to express whatever she desired (within appropriate limits). Thus material surfaced in the sessions as Rosy's needs dictated, not in a logical, adult-directed sequence.

Rosy was actively involved in play from the beginning of her first session. She easily picked up being in charge of the play and gave directions to her play therapist. A primary theme in Rosy's play was mother–baby relationships. In the first four sessions Rosy was an angry, bossy, unloving mother and directed the therapist to be the abused baby. Rosy, as the mother, threatened the baby with abandonment. So specific and detailed were many of the interchanges that the play therapist believed they were reenactments of actual incidents.

The fifth session proved pivotal in the parenting play. Rosy continued to insist on playing the mother, but chose to interact, in a much more positive manner, with a doll as the baby. Rosy soon decided she wanted to be the baby and demanded to be held, rocked, and fed by the play therapist. She snuggled into the arms of the therapist, fully trusting the care and nurturing of the therapist-mother.

From this point on Rosy continued to increase the developmental level of her play. She initiated play in which she was the little girl and the therapist was the mother. As trust in her therapist-mother continued to develop, she occasionally played the part of the baby again, as if to reassure herself that she was valued and accepted as a baby. Rosy used the play of the baby to reintegrate what it meant for her to be reparented. After she was able to enjoy being a baby, she had less need to take control in her everyday environment.

The therapist believed that the provision of food assisted in the strong relationship between her and this very deprived child. Not only did the real food meet the real need of a hungry child, but play food and play surrounding the issue of food continued to meet her emotional cravings as well. Rosy often pretended to feed herself and the therapist using mixtures of water, sand, and clay. The symbolism of

---

1. Clark Moustakas, *Children in Play Therapy* (Northvale, NJ: Jason Aronson Inc., 1973).

her being the provider of the food also gave insight into her need to care for herself after her perceived abandonment by both parents.

Jigsaw puzzles were also available for Rosy's use. The author indicated that Rosy selected increasingly more developmentally mature puzzles throughout the course of her treatment. The author believed that Rosy used the puzzles symbolically as a way to express her need to puzzle something out and integrate herself. These times of reintegration were additionally identified by her need to play the baby role again.

Other play themes included negative mother symbols of Dracula and a witch. A ghost contained many childhood illusions and fears. An old man, played by the therapist at Rosy's instruction, seemed to be the embodiment of her mother's clients.

COMMENTARY: During fifteen months of play therapy, Rosy was able to use the freedom of the self-directed child-centered play therapy to deal with her needs in her own way. It is exciting to see that a severely neglected and emotionally abused child is able to know what is best to deal with first, and even repeat dealing with, in order to get to a healthy place in life. In the presence of the play therapist, who knew how to facilitate therapy appropriately from the pseudomother role, Rosy used play therapy effectively.

SOURCE: West, J. (1983). Play therapy with Rosy. *British Journal of Social Work* 13:645–661.

POSSIBLE *DSM-IV* DIAGNOSES:

995.5   Neglect of Child
V61.20   Parent–Child Relational Problem

2

Aggression and Acting Out

Unlike the typical response to aggression and acting-out behavior by teachers, parents, and adults in authority positions, the objective in play therapy is not to stop the behavior but rather to understand the child and provide an acceptable avenue for the child to express unfulfilled feelings, wants, and needs. Many play therapists find it difficult to respond appropriately to acts of aggression because such acts in the playroom are often directed toward themselves. In such cases the therapist may react emotionally as though the act were a personal attack, thus shifting the focus to an issue of transference that must be worked through. As shown in the studies in this section, parents and therapists can successfully use play to help children effectively release aggressive feelings and in the process significantly improve their attitudes and behavior outside the playroom. Once the feelings and needs behind aggressive acts have been accepted and allowed to be expressed, children are able to go on to explore more positive behaviors.

PLAY THERAPY WITH AN AGGRESSIVE CHILD

AUTHORS: **John Allan and Keith Brown**

FOCUS: *Jungian play therapy is used as an approach to treat an aggressive third-grade boy.*

INTRODUCTION: Allan and Brown describe the framework for Jungian play therapy and the evolution of themes through three major stages: chaos, struggle, and resolution. Emphasis is placed on the importance of the human psyche as a self-regulating structure capable of self-healing. The Jungian therapist provides a safe and protected setting in which painful unconscious struggles and negative feelings can be externalized and projected onto the toys. The chaos of the first stage is transformed into themes of struggle between good and evil, with evil generally winning. As therapy approaches the resolution stage, good tends to take control and themes of construction and healing become common. Essential to Jungian play therapy are materials that allow the psyche to communicate through creative processes and symbolism. Consequently, the play therapy room should contain wet and dry sand tables, a sink for water play, a large dollhouse, and art materials.

CASE STUDY: Darren, an 8-year-old third grader, was referred to counseling because of his disruptive behavior in the classroom and aggression on the playground. Darren's father and mother had separated just prior to Darren's starting school. Darren's mother defended his behavior by protesting that he was being unfairly treated. After two assessment sessions, the school counselor saw Darren every day in play therapy the first week because of his severe problems both in and outside the classroom.

INTERVENTION: During the first three sessions, the therapist reflected Darren's actions and identified feelings evident in the play. Darren was apparently upset by such affective statements and would stop any comments he had been making for a period of time. Also during this time, Darren displayed aggression and destruction, and tested limits to which the therapist responded with redirection and limit-setting.

In the fourth session Darren was asked to draw a picture and tell a story about the picture. A depiction of "good guys" versus "bad guys" was portrayed and the therapist took this opportunity to provide some interpretation. During the same session, Darren created a sand tray scene and again the therapist provided an interpretation, this time drawing a connection between the feelings depicted in the sand tray scene and feelings Darren might possibly be experiencing in school. The struggles between the good guys and the bad guys continued to session thirteen, with interpretations generally kept within the context of Darren's play.

By the thirteenth session Darren was able to resolve the conflict between good and evil in a socially acceptable way by having good marginally defeat evil in a hockey game. During this session, Darren expressed some of his angry, confused, and hurt feelings related to his father's abandonment. In the final two sessions he chose to work in the sand tray. The theme of aggression was considerably neutralized and on the whole good feelings predominated over bad.

RESULTS: At the beginning of treatment Darren was considered the number one priority for counseling service in the school he attended. A year later he was coping and behaving in more positive ways at home and at school. His mother's only visits to school were for teacher interviews to discuss routine academic matters.

COMMENTARY: Allan and Brown found that a good relationship with a child, one that allows the child to release hurt and aggressive feelings through play, can positively improve behavior outside the play therapy room. In Jungian play therapy interpretive language serves as a catalyst that translates the unconscious material for the conscious ego. When a healthy connection is established between the child's conscious and unconscious, the child's psyche is able to grow and move toward self-actualization and a more fulfilling and socially acceptable way of being in the world. An interesting note in this study is the use of play therapy every day during the initial work of therapy as dictated by the severity of problem.

SOURCE: Allan, J., and Brown, K. (1993). Jungian play therapy in elementary schools. *Elementary School Guidance and Counseling* 28(1): 30–41.

POSSIBLE *DSM-IV* DIAGNOSES:

V71.02   Child or Adolescent Antisocial Behavior
312.9   Disruptive Behavior Disorder, NOS
313.81   Oppositional Defiant Disorder

PLAY THERAPY AND VIDEO FEEDBACK OF PLAY SESSIONS WITH OPPOSITIONAL DISORDERED CHILDREN

AUTHOR: **Patricia Beers**

FOCUS: *The effect of individual play therapy in conjunction with parent counseling and focused videotaped feedback of parent–child play sessions on parent–child interactions.*

INTRODUCTION: A research study was conducted to determine the effectiveness of two differing interventions for children exhibiting oppositional and disruptive behaviors. The treatment approaches selected included individual play therapy accompanied by parent counseling, and focused video feedback in which the parent(s) participated in videotaped play sessions with the child, followed by a feedback session between the parents and therapist. Statistically significant results were reported.

RESEARCH METHODS & DESIGN: Twenty intact families with at least one 4- to 9-year-old child diagnosed with Oppositional Disorder of Childhood (according to the *DSM-III*) were selected from a variety of area mental health agencies and clinics. The families were randomly placed into three groups: (1) traditional play therapy for the child and counseling with parents, (2) focused videotape feedback, and (3) control group.

The treatment goals were to improve parent–child interaction, described as increasing positive affect, decreasing both controlling and submissive behaviors, decreasing negative affect, changing physical and verbal interactions, and improving parental perception of the child. Also, the treatment sought to change the parental perceptions of their child's problems.

The Eyberg Child Behavior Inventory and the Interpersonal Behavior Constructs Scale were used to collect information about changes in behavior. Data were collected before treatment, in the middle of treatment (after eight weeks), at the end of treatment (after sixteen weeks), and at follow-up (four weeks after treatment ended, or at twenty weeks).

INTERVENTION: One group consisted of traditional play therapy for the child and individual counseling with each of the parents; each session lasted fifty minutes. The parent's sessions initially focused on the child and then seemed to focus on the intrapersonal issues of the parent.

The focused videotape feedback treatments consisted of one two-hour session weekly. The session began with three seven-minute sessions in the playroom, which were videotaped: first, the mother and child, next the father and child, and finally both parents and the child. The child then went to the waiting room and was watched by the receptionist. For the remainder of the session the parents had a conjoint session with the therapist that focused on a review of the videotaped activities in a therapeutic setting with attention directed to salient verbal and nonverbal behaviors in parent–child interactions. The control group received no treatment.

RESULTS: Generally speaking, after eight weeks significant improvement was seen in the children participating in play therapy with the parents participating in counseling, while the videotaped feedback groups showed no significant improvement until follow-up.

Nonacceptance behavior in parent–child interactions decreased significantly for the children in the play therapy group after eight weeks of treatment ($p<.05$). However, when nonacceptance was measured again at the follow-up, some of this positive change had been lost (score of 2.17 at eight weeks, 1.43 at twenty weeks). The videotaped feedback group actually had a statistically significant increase in nonacceptance behavior at both midtreatment and at follow-up (score of 1.95 at pretreatment, 3.58 at eight weeks, and 2.16 at follow-up). Thus the play therapy group had less nonacceptance behavior at follow-up than the videotaped group, even with the slight loss of their previous improvement.

The play therapy group increased at statistically significant levels in the amount of time a parent and child worked together (score of 1.8 to 5.1). There was little change in the videotaped feedback group (score of 3.7 to 4.2).

In the area of shared conversations the videotaped feedback group showed a significant increase. The play therapy group actually showed a slight decrease in the number of shared conversations between child and parent.

Each of the groups—play therapy, video feedback, and control—demonstrated a decrease in perceived problems and intensity of problems. The author hypothesized that the increased attention the parents were giving the children, in order to log their behavior, may have had a positive effect on both the parents and the children. Also, the contact between the parents and the researcher, who called regularly to get the weekly behavioral log information, may have become therapeutic in nature and thereby influenced all three groups.

COMMENTARY: This study revealed interesting information: the children who received play therapy showed the most dramatic positive changes after eight weeks. This may indicate that children with Oppositional Defiant Disorder respond well to the individual therapeutic contact. While these findings cannot be generalized to the entire population of children in play therapy, it may indicate that this possibility does exist. It appears unclear why the children in the videotaped treatment group did not show significant positive changes until follow-up. One conclusion may be that having only the parents working directly with the child may have caused the positive changes to occur more slowly. The combination of individual therapeutic intervention for both the child and the parent results in quicker relief for problematic child–parent interactions.

SOURCE: Beers, P. (1985). Focused videotape feedback psychotherapy as compared with traditional play therapy in treatment of the oppositional disorder of childhood. Doctoral dissertation, University of Illinois at Urbana-Champaign. *Dissertations Abstracts International* 46(04): B1330.

POSSIBLE *DSM-IV* DIAGNOSIS:

313.81   Oppositional Defiant Disorder

PLAY THERAPY AS AN INTERVENTION
FOR ACTING-OUT CHILDREN

AUTHOR: **Viola A. Brody**

FOCUS: *Developmental play therapy uses the dialogue of touch to impact behavior change in acting-out children.*

INTRODUCTION: The core of developmental play therapy is touch. Brody asserts that a child who experiences touch from a capable toucher will grow toward healthy maturity and will heal from earlier trauma and neglect. A disturbed child who experiences caring touch feels truly seen, validated, and acknowledged by another person, often for the first time.

CASE STUDY #1: Alan was one of eight 4-year-old boys in a developmental play group referred for severe acting out and unmanageable behavior. He was paired with a therapist who played with him each week through the medium of physical touch. The treatment period spanned twenty weeks. In the initial sessions Alan resisted the cradling. He displayed hyperactive and unfocused behavior, running about the room disturbing other pairs, unable to keep to his designated mat. The therapist set the limits of the session, explaining to Alan that he would be held for short periods of time each week. Alan was held loosely in an upright position so that he had room to push against the therapist, which he did in the beginning. Within a few sessions Alan had stopped running around and wanted to be with the therapist. He came to enjoy the touching contact with the therapist and was also aware that he was experiencing this as pleasing. He could communicate his awareness to the therapist and was able to provide much of the structure in their touching dialogue, directing the therapist and inventing games.

RESULTS: The goal of Developmental Play Therapy is not to solve problems or to change the child's behavior, but rather to build a relationship. Alan's behavior showed that he had accepted a core self and that he could relate to others. One year later the therapist accidentally ran into Alan during a visit to his classroom. The therapist was impressed by the quiet, comfortable, and confident way in which Alan was able to interact with him.

CASE STUDY #2:   Mira was a normal 4-year-old child whose mother wanted her to participate in the Developmental Play training program. Mira was described as being very difficult as a baby and now constantly fought with her older sister. The therapist observed her to be a very controlling child who constantly called attention to herself. During the initial sessions, Mira resisted everything the therapist did, screamed, threw her shoes, and disturbed others in the room. At the third session the therapist used redirection to provide Mira with an acceptable way of touching after she had spit at and bit the therapist. By the end of the third session Mira had invented a special game in which her leg would work only if the therapist kissed it ten times. By the sixth session Mira could not get enough touching, was very babyish, and enjoyed being sung to by the therapist. During the twelfth session, Mira shifted out of this attachment phase into the separation phase and began to treat the therapist less like a parent and more like a friend, asking the therapist how to do things and competing with her. Mira's treatment period ended with session sixteen.

RESULTS: When the therapist felt seen, heard, and acknowledged by Mira, she knew that Mira had shifted out of the attachment phase into the separation phase and was becoming more independent. Near the end of the treatment period Mira was able to compose a special poem that expressed her affection for and connection to the therapist.

COMMENTARY: Touch, if done sensitively and appropriately, enables the child to experience the therapist's physical presence as well as the child's own presence. A special dialogue develops between the therapist and child through touch, taking the child back to an earlier stage of development. The child is given the opportunity to regress to that earliest of touching experiences, that of being cradled and held like a baby. The child is then able to pick up and bring forward what is needed for healing.

SOURCE: Brody, V.A. (1992). The dialogue of touch: developmental play therapy. *International Journal of Play Therapy* 1:21–30.

POSSIBLE *DSM-IV* DIAGNOSES:

Case #1
314.01 Attention-Deficit/Hyperactivity Disorder, Predominantly Hyperactive-Impulsive Type
314.9   Attention-Deficit/Hyperactivity Disorder NOS

Case #2
313.89 Reactive Attachment Disorder of Infancy or Early Childhood

Both
V71.02 Child or Adolescent Antisocial Behavior
312.9   Disruptive Behavior Disorder NOS
313.81 Oppositional Defiant Disorder

A GROUP PLAY TECHNIQUE FOR REWARDING SOCIAL RESPONSIBILITY

AUTHORS: **Albert S. Carlin and Hubert E. Armstrong**

FOCUS: *Utilizing social learning theory in a play group to reduce hostility in four severely disturbed boys.*

INTRODUCTION: Carlin and Armstrong drew on social learning theory and operant techniques to devise a group treatment program with two main characteristics: (1) the encouragement of social responsibility, that is, teaching children that the behavior of other group members is partially their own responsibility; and (2) the token reinforcement of social participation in a natural setting.

CASE STUDY: Physical fighting and teasing among four boys on a children's day care unit had become sufficiently intense that it was interfering with treatment, not only for the boys concerned but also the rest of the children on the unit. Tony, age 7, was a minimally brain-damaged child who engaged in hyperactive, but not antisocial or destructive, behavior. John, age 9, was a schizophrenic child who engaged in ritualistic play and became enraged if other children did not carry out his directions. Paul, age 12, was a schizophrenic and minimally brain-damaged child who generally seemed completely puzzled by the world around him. He engaged in erratic aggressive behavior, impulsively lashing out at anyone within reach. Tom, age 7½, was explosive, hostile, and destructive. All four boys had difficulty interacting with peers and adults.

INTERVENTION: Four days a week, for five weeks, the boys were brought together in a group for a ninety-minute period of cooperative play. Carlin and Armstrong, together with the two nurses regularly assigned to the boys at this time, acted as therapists. The planned procedure was for the children to be involved in a situation structured so that cooperative play would be encouraged. For sequences of appropriate interaction involving at least three of the boys, token rewards would be placed in a common pool. Sequences of socially inappropriate behavior, such as spitting, hitting, kicking, or destroying a project, would result in a fine and tokens would be taken from the pool. Effort on the part of one or more children to solve group problems or to be extra helpful to the group would be rewarded by bonus tokens added to the pool. Fines or payments would be preceded by verbal evaluation of the behavior and announcement of rewarding or fining action. At the end of the session the tokens in the pool would be evenly divided among the children and they could cash them in for toys and sweets.

After several days of observation, during which the boys typically interacted by teasing and physically attacking one another, the plan was presented. It was mentioned that since the boys seemed to have difficulty getting along, the staff had decided to pay them to get along. The rest of the intervention was then outlined for the boys and they were reminded about the specifics each day before they began their group session.

The boys seemed enthusiastic about the plan and the first day produced a remarkable change in their behavior. Rather than provoking each other as usual, they worked together in harmony to build a spaceship out of blocks. When tokens were paid to the boys during the session, the amount and reason for payment were disclosed at the same time. When a fine was levied near the end of the session because of Tom's misbehavior, the group members were told it was their responsibility to stop Tom from throwing things at the adults. With the help of adult suggestions, the group was able to engage Tom in a constructive activity, which meant that the remainder of the earnings were preserved.

After several sessions it became obvious that the system of fines was not sufficient to halt all the disruptive behaviors. The group was just not able to cope with some members. Thus a "penalty box" was initiated, that is, an out-of-control child was physically placed in a penalty box by the adults. During this period the child could not receive rewards earned by the rest of the group, nor could his behavior in the box penalize the rest of the group.

Tony was discharged from the unit at this time, resulting in a group of three children. By this time John and Tom had become friendlier and begun to work together more, although Tom often had difficulty relinquishing control. They seemed to derive more satisfaction from their positive relationship than from the reward of including Paul in their play. At this point the fining procedure was eliminated and the boys were rewarded just on the basis of appropriate behaviors. All misbehavior was simply ignored. During the remaining sessions, a genuine warmth seemed to be developing among the three group members. There was also far less acting-out behavior during the sessions. The program was terminated on the discharge of a second group member.

COMMENTARY: Carlin and Armstrong stated that although their purpose was not to provide a sound methodological analysis of the principles attempted, these children, who were presumed to be "uncontrollable" as a result of brain damage and childhood schizophrenia, were found to be quite capable of inhibiting their aggressive acting-out behavior and working together in reasonable harmony. Although dramatic changes in aggressive behavior occurred almost immediately, a general reduction in aggression toward the rest of the ward was also reported by the staff. During the play sessions the children helped one another behave properly by the use of such techniques as distraction, avoidance, and reminders. Through the flexible use of operant and group techniques, Carlin and Armstrong were able to instill a sense of social responsibility. Disturbed children do not seem to lack the capacity to enjoy interpersonal relationships. Rather, they are more likely to lack the ability to experience interpersonal relationships that can supply a satisfying result. The token system provided an opportunity for these boys to experience positive social interaction.

SOURCE: Carlin, A. S., and Armstrong, H. E. (1968). Rewarding social responsibility in disturbed children: a group play technique. *Psychotherapy: Theory, Research and Practice* 5:169–174.

POSSIBLE *DSM-IV* DIAGNOSES:

295.90   Schizophrenia, Undifferentiated Type
314.01   Attention Deficit/Hyperactivity Disorder, Predominantly Hyperactive-Impulsive Type
312.34   Intermittent Explosive Disorder
V71.02   Child or Adolescent Antisocial Behavior
312.9   Disruptive Behavior Disorder NOS
313.81   Oppositional Defiant Disorder
312.8   Conduct Disorder

PLAY GROUP COUNSELING AS AN EFFECTIVE INTERVENTION FOR CHILDREN WITH BEHAVIOR PROBLEMS

AUTHOR: **Gary Lloyd Gaulden**

FOCUS: *Developmental play group counseling was explored as a potential intervention for reducing classroom disturbance behavior of second-grade students.*

INTRODUCTION: Developmental play group counseling was hypothesized to facilitate positive change in disadvantaged second-grade students who were exhibiting behavior problems in the classroom. The study was designed to measure change in self-concept, attitudes toward school, and classroom disturbance behavior of identified students who participated in developmental play group counseling, play group counseling, and a control group.

INTERVENTION: Subjects for the study were selected from a pool of fifty-six second graders from a Title I program who were rated by their teachers to be one or more standard deviations above the mean on the "classroom disturbance" factor of the Devereux Elementary School Behavior Rating Scale. Participation in the Title I program required that the students be economically and educationally deprived and functioning one to two years below grade level in reading and/or math. Students were randomly assigned in groups of four to developmental play group counseling and play group counseling. The remaining fifteen students were assigned to the control group. Students in the two experimental groups received treatment in two forty-five minute sessions per week for seven weeks for a total of fourteen sessions.

Developmental play group counseling combines the techniques of developmental group counseling and play group counseling. Developmental group counseling is a structured verbal approach in which the child can learn to verbally express and explore feelings by participating in a discussion triad as talker, listener, or observer. The discussion triad took place within the first fifteen to twenty minutes of a forty-five minute session and was followed by thirty to thirty-five minutes of play group counseling.

Play group counseling is an unstructured approach that uses play media to help the child experience self. The children are permitted to use the session as they wish. The therapist's primary emphasis is on relating to the here and now, interacting with each child by observing, listening, and reflecting content and feelings.

RESULTS: Children in the play group counseling approach made significant changes of one or more standard deviations in the reduction of "classroom disturbance" behavior and maintained that level of improvement eight weeks after the end of the study. There were no significant changes in measured self-concept or attitude toward school. The developmental play group counseling subjects and the control group did not achieve any significant change on measurement instruments.

COMMENTARY: Although the author had expected the combined approach of developmental play group counseling to be superior, the findings suggest that play group counseling alone was the more effective approach in dealing with classroom disturbance behavior of deprived second-grade students. In play group counseling children are free to use play materials as their natural language of expression. The author suggested that the discussion phase of the developmental play group counseling approach may have been facilitated by limiting to three the number of children in the group; however, all of the counselors involved in the research project concluded that the children in developmental play group counseling were much too young and immature to benefit from this approach.

SOURCE: Gaulden, G.L. (1975). Developmental-play group counseling with early primary grade students exhibiting behavioral problems. Doctoral dissertation, North Texas State University. *Dissertation Abstracts International* 36(05):A2628.

POSSIBLE *DSM-IV* **DIAGNOSIS:**

Insufficient information provided in the study.

BRIEF PLAY THERAPY FOR A PRESCHOOLER WITH SEVERE TEMPER TANTRUMS

AUTHOR: **David M. Levy**

FOCUS: *Using a form of brief play therapy with a 2-year-old girl who had severe temper tantrums.*

INTRODUCTION: Jane had reportedly been an "easy baby" until a nanny had begun toilet training her at 12 months. Jane did not take to toilet training easily, battling the nanny every time she was placed on the potty training chair. After a few months, however, bowel training was achieved, followed by bladder control at 25 months. It was believed that the temper tantrums and other behavioral problems were directly tied to the strict regime of toilet training by a highly disciplinarian nanny. The tantrums would last approximately two hours (if allowed to run their course) and consisted typically of Jane lying on the floor, kicking and screaming. Jane also showed little affection toward her parents or 4-year-old brother and displayed a generally negative and sulky attitude.

INTERVENTION: Jane was seen for a total of ten sessions. In her first session she would not come into the room without her mother. In fact, she clung to her mother's skirt and would not release it. The play therapist put several toys on the floor but Jane would not play with them. The therapist then took a play gun and shot several clay figures. When Jane was asked who else the therapist should shoot, she pointed at her mother and then at the play therapist. After the therapist shot both, Jane began to play, but when the therapist attempted to approach her she hid under a chair. The therapist attempted to give toys to her, but Jane shoved them aside. After several such attempts Jane again went to her mother and clung to her skirt. The therapist believed that the reluctance to play was due to Jane's negative attitude, not because of her fear of a stranger. He attempted to model destructive behavior in order to give Jane permission to release her own feelings.

The second session began much like the first. After several minutes, however, Jane's mother slipped out of the playroom and Jane accepted some clay from the therapist and began to form babies. Later she was able to initiate spontaneous play with other toys.

In the third session she again needed her mother present at the beginning of the session. Once her mother had slipped out, Jane again played with the clay, making babies, and frequently wanted her hands cleaned. The session ended with Jane playing easily and occasionally laughing. After this session Jane's parents reported she began to display "sudden and unusual affection." Additionally there was a reduction of the negative attitude, more positive compliance with parental requests, and freer play with other children.

In the next several sessions Jane made her clay babies sit on the potty chair. Some clay babies stood near the potty chair. Jane explained she had attempted to urinate at home like her older brother.

During the fifth play therapy session, Jane placed bits of clay in a bowl. When the therapist reflected that the clay represented bowel movements, Jane looked at the play therapist and smiled. After this session Jane began soiling at home, several times a day. Initially the therapist advised the mother to ignore the behavior. During the eighth session Jane displayed a marked increase in destructive play. This included pulling her clay babies apart, throwing the clay all over the room, tearing paper off the crayons, and so on. The next day Jane smeared herself with feces. At this point the therapist allowed the mother to intervene and Jane stopped soiling that same day. In the ninth session, one week after the cessation of soiling, Jane smeared clay and pretended to eat it. With her presenting behaviors successfully resolved, the tenth and final session was used for closure and termination.

COMMENTARY: The decision to select this form of brief therapy, general release play therapy, was based on the belief that the symptomatic behavior was the result of excessive demands or prohibitions made at too early a developmental age. In this approach the child is able to release anxieties through the use of therapeutic self-regression. Released from constricting emotions, the child is free to express self through the various play materials. This approach to play therapy would be applicable to many other children who have various maladaptive responses to general stressors during early child-hood. It should also be noted that the author stressed that release play therapy should be used only with children whose problematic behavior is not related to other family problems.

SOURCE: Levy, D. (1939). Release therapy in young children. *Child Study* 16(1):141–143.

POSSIBLE *DSM-IV* DIAGNOSES:

312.9   Disruptive Behavior Disorder NOS
300.00   Anxiety Disorder NOS
309.4   Adjustment Disorder with Mixed Disturbance of Emotions and Conduct

PLAY THERAPY FOR THE INSTITUTIONALIZED CHILD

AUTHOR: **Helen E. Miller**

FOCUS: *A mentally and physically normal 6-year-old girl who was display-ing behavioral problems related to abandonment and institutionalization was successfully treated with nondirective play therapy.*

INTRODUCTION: Deprived of their original family group, children in institutions feel rejection and have less opportunity to develop posi-tive relationships. Play therapy provides an opportunity for a relation-ship with an understanding, accepting adult. This case study exem-plifies the particular difficulties that face the institutionalized child and the positive impact of play therapy intervention.

CASE STUDY: Lucy was 4 years old when her father was killed in a mine accident and she came to live at Mooseheart Institution with her mother and three older brothers. After two years Lucy's mother remarried and left Mooseheart without the children. Two months later Lucy, who was now 6 years old, was referred for play therapy following uncontrollable outbursts after visits from her mother. She attended play therapy once a week for four months and then every day for a short period for a total of twenty-two contacts. Lucy had one therapist for the first five sessions and a different therapist for the remaining seventeen sessions.

During the sessions Lucy was allowed to direct the play. She did not interact directly with the first therapist, but primarily engaged in nurturing behavior with dolls. When abruptly changed to a new thera-pist at the sixth session, Lucy reacted by limiting her play to rolling a peg around on the floor. She resumed active play during the eighth session, shifting back and forth from nurturing to aggressive behav-ior. She remained nonverbal until the eighteenth session when two unique procedural changes occurred. Given the opportunity, Lucy chose to attend play therapy every day. In this same session another child whom Lucy knew happened to join the session. In this session Lucy began to talk to the therapist and affectionately hugged and kissed her, both firsts.

RESULTS: During the final four sessions, Lucy was verbally expressive and displayed affection for the therapist. She was able to use toys and materials that were of special significance to her. Lucy worked through her difficulties in accepting her new stepfather and his children. She was able to verbally request affection from her therapist. Lucy decided when it was time for her final session and announced that she might return when all the snow was off the ground. Reports from Lucy's teachers indicated that she was no longer uncontrollable after visits from her mother and was getting along better in school.

COMMENTARY: Although the author found it difficult to imagine that these play sessions held any significance for Lucy because of what was described as a "dearth of interplay between the therapist and child," the significance of the relationship was clearly demonstrated by the drastic behavior change when Lucy lost her first therapist. Lucy's second therapist often did not accurately reflect Lucy's actions and feelings during the play sessions. In fact, Lucy's first advances toward the therapist occurred only when she was in the presence of another child. However, if the therapist's recognition of what the child was trying to express was inadequate at times, the therapist's willingness to fulfill the role assigned by the child minimized these deficits. Play therapy provided an opportunity for the therapist to function as a therapeutic agent in the life of an institutionalized child by demonstrating that she could and would be able to meet the child's basic needs.

SOURCE: Miller, H. E. (1948). Play therapy for the institutionalized child. *Nervous Child* 7:311–317.

POSSIBLE *DSM-IV* DIAGNOSES:

309.3   Adjustment Disorder with Disturbance of Conduct
312.9   Disruptive Behavior Disorder NOS

PLAY THERAPY FOR BEHAVIOR PROBLEMS CENTERED AROUND ISSUES OF ANGER, FEAR, AND CONTROL

AUTHOR: **Mary Ann Par**

FOCUS: *Sand and water play were used by a child in play therapy to deal with numerous behavior problems that included aggressive tendencies, phobias about the dark and animals, noncompliance with authority figures, poor peer relations, and poor dietary habits.*

INTRODUCTION: Four-year-old James, the oldest of four siblings, came from an environment that did not facilitate the expression of emotions. His father was often unavailable to the family. His mother was considered overly strict and showed some compulsive tendencies. Both parents expected James to show far more control in his behavior than is generally expected from a child of comparable age. Expression of his feelings often involved noncompliant and controlling behaviors. His problems extended to the school setting where he had problems relating to authorities and peers. Play therapy was used to allow James to face his issues of anger, fear, and control and to free him to express his emotions in more acceptable ways.

INTERVENTION: Play therapy for James followed a child-centered approach in a playroom with typical toys and objects. James selected sand and water play as his primary play while in the playroom. During the beginning sessions he was apprehensive about entering the room and protested verbally and physically. Once inside, his play was serious, purposeful, and guarded. He initiated little contact with the therapist and played cautiously with the sand and water, careful not to mix the two. If the sand stuck to his body, he would compulsively wash every grain away before returning to play. The water used to wash with had to be warm because the use of cold water greatly disturbed him. His play centered primarily around the careful preparation of food. Such play was intentional and serious. Before leaving each session he was careful to clean up all of the sand even though he was not asked to do so.

The author specified two turning points during the course of therapy. The first involved James's expression of his repressed feelings about a new sibling in the family. Expressing these feelings allowed him in turn to exhibit the more nurturing qualities of a big brother. After building sand houses for two animal figures, James found a motorcycle man figure. The animals were terrorized by the figure until he buried the figure in the sand. After a short period of more play, James unburied the now happy motorcycle man. The animals and the motorcycle man played together in the following session. James expressed and laid to rest his aggressive feelings toward his new brother. He could then accept the new role as a caring older brother.

The second experience occurred when James was facing some obvious anxiety and fear due to a number of incidents occurring between his family and an aggressive neighbor. James entered the playroom, although he made it clear that he did not wish to do so. After violently throwing all the water and sand onto the floor, he assumed the role of a courteous bus driver as he carefully drove a busload of children through the sand–water obstacles to the safety of their homes. After dealing with his out-of-control emotions, James found he could provide a safe and nurturing environment for those he cared about. At the end of the session James seemed content with the mess he had made on the floor and made no attempt to clean it up. He seemed proud of the mark he had made on the room.

RESULTS: Toward the end of therapy James was less fearful of cold water and experimented with different temperatures of water by combining hot and cold. His play centered around less emotionally charged issues and more around typical childhood themes. The therapist remembered fondly James's use of sand to represent snow as he sang "Jingle Bells" in preparation for Christmas. The therapeutic experience was positive for James and he was reported to be better adjusted in dealing with his emotions and with those around him. He was more liked by himself and his peers.

COMMENTARY: Anticipating the possible reaction to the liberal use of sand and water play as demonstrated in this case, the author pointed out that the behaviors in the playroom with these mediums never "spilled over" into the classroom. James played with sand and water in acceptable and appropriate ways while in the school setting. The author also points out that if, with another child, such uses of sand and water threatened the structure and guidelines of the play setting, clearly defined limits about the use of the medium should be set.

SOURCE: Par, M. A. (1990). Sand and water play: a case study. *Association for Play Therapy Newsletter* 9(1):4–6.

POSSIBLE *DSM-IV* DIAGNOSES:

309.4   Adjustment Disorder with Mixed Disturbance of Emotions and Conduct
V71.02   Child or Adolescent Antisocial Behavior
312.9   Disruptive Behavior Disorder NOS

PSYCHOANALYTIC PLAY THERAPY WITH AN ACTING-OUT CHILD

AUTHOR: **Anneliese Ude-Pestel**

FOCUS: *Psychoanalytic play therapy using expressive art with a child demonstrating serious acting-out and self-injuring behavior.*

INTRODUCTION: Six-year-old Betty's parents requested therapy due to her severe acting-out behaviors. These behaviors included screaming, temper tantrums, beating her head against the floor, pulling out her hair, running around the house naked, and aggression toward her sibling. Psychoanalytic play therapy was employed, with Betty taking the lead in the play activities and Ude-Pestel interpreting the play and art expressions.

CASE STUDY: Betty lived with her parents, a 2-year-old brother, and a live-in babysitter. Following Betty's birth, the death of a relative caused severe depression in the mother, who reportedly sought comfort from Betty instead of providing her with appropriate nurturing. Severe constipation and persistent thumb sucking were reported in Betty's early development. A neurological examination revealed no abnormal conditions.

In addition to the behavioral history noted, Betty expressed her emotional pain in art creations in the home. Her parents brought approximately 1,500 pictures and paintings to the initial parent consultation. According to Ude-Pestel, Betty had a particular penchant for ghosts and skulls, which, Ude-Pestel hypothesized, Betty "had to paint, driven by her unconscious, in order to survive, lest she be flooded with these frightening pictures which are the mirror images of her inner fears."

INTERVENTION: Ude-Pestel provided a detailed description of the treatment process with Betty, including thirty-nine chapters and twenty-six color or black and white pictures of the artwork she drew during the process. The course of her treatment is exemplified in the first and last pictures displayed in the case study, "Crucified" and "Dancing Girl," respectively.

The play materials provided for Betty included a wide variety of toys in addition to art materials. Betty's established preference for expressing herself in art continued within the therapeutic process. In describing the play materials to Betty's parents, Ude-Pestel noted that children "aren't expected to do anything. Eveything you see in this room is simply an invitation. If a child wants to, he can play with these things, but he is not forced or influenced in any way."

During the initial phase of treatment, Betty engaged in nurturing activities with Ude-Pestel, including making milk and swinging together. These were accompanied by Betty's artwork involving ghosts, monsters, skeletons, and crocodiles. Child- and therapist-initiated storytelling was also a part of the initial stages of therapy, with fairy tales the focus. The drawings and stories were interpreted as Betty illustrating and processing her unconscious fears. As the therapeutic alliance was established, Betty was able to express her emotions more openly, and become verbally and behaviorally aggressive. She ordered the therapist around and during one session threw numerous toys at Ude-Pestel, requiring her to shield her face with a pillow. Betty grabbed the pillow, shoved it into the therapist's face and threw her whole body weight onto Ude-Pestel. This was followed by a calm, trancelike state.

Concurrent with the play therapy, Ude-Pestel also worked with Betty's parents and her teachers, both to obtain further background information and to provide therapeutic direction. As the treatment progressed, Betty's artwork reflected changes in her life: the drawings of ghosts and monsters were replaced by pictures of friends, animals, and ice-skating. The progress of treatment is described by Ude-Pestel in terms of a particular play item that had been used throughout the therapy process. A cardboard box had initially been a cradle for Betty (interpreted as the womb). It later became a pirate ship with a death banner. As the therapy approached termination, it became a playhouse with an open door. The behaviors for which Betty had been referred had ameliorated, and Ude-Pestel reported that a follow-up several years later revealed that Betty continued to function well.

COMMENTARY: Before Betty entered treatment for her difficulties, she was already expressing her emotional pain through expressive art and play, as well as the acting-out behaviors for which she was referred.

In the play and art therapy process Betty was allowed to continue expressing herself in her own way, rather than being compelled to pursue an adult therapeutic agenda. Although Ude-Pestel's interpretations may be open for discussion, Betty's emotional and behavioral history, and the healing change brought about in the play process, cannot be disputed. Allowing Betty to express herself and to heal on her terms through the play therapy process changed her life.

SOURCE: Ude-Pestel, A. (1977). *Betty: History and Art of a Child in Therapy.* Palo Alto, CA: Science and Behavior Books, Inc.

POSSIBLE *DSM-IV* DIAGNOSES:

312.8   Conduct Disorder
313.81   Oppositional Defiant Disorder
300.02   Generalized Anxiety Disorder

3

Attachment Difficulties

Attachment can be defined as a bond of affection that endures difficulties and is imperative for children's healthy development and adjustment. Emotionally needy children, especially those who have experienced severe neglect, often experience strong needs for affiliation, attachment, and acceptance. Children who experience poor mother–child attachment often become "hard-to-reach" children. The acting out of these needs in the playroom can cause the play therapist considerable difficulty because these children may have such a powerful need to be special to the play therapist. Maintaining a sense of objectivity and compassionate understanding is crucial at such times, particularly when limits may need to be set. The play therapist must be careful not to become overly responsive when the child insists on knowing that he or she is the most important person in the whole world to the therapist. Children who do not have a secure attachment bond have great difficulty accepting themselves and other people. The play therapist's acceptance of the child enables the child to accept self.

CHILD-CENTERED PLAY THERAPY FOR PROBLEMS ASSOCIATED WITH ATTACHMENT

AUTHOR: Lucy Colbert

FOCUS: *Long-term child-centered play therapy with an angry, defiant, destructive child who had experienced constant rejection from her parents.*

INTRODUCTION: Child-centered play therapy provides a situation in which the child can grow by playing out feelings of tension, frustration, insecurity, aggression, fear, bewilderment, and confusion in the presence of a warm and accepting person who displays genuine interest in and liking for the child as an individual. As described by Axline,[1] this play setting allows the child the opportunity to bring feelings out into the open and to face them, learn to control them, or abandon them.

CASE STUDY: Debra, a 9-year-old girl from an unstable and inconsistent home situation, had experienced constant rejection from her parents, who apparently favored her three younger siblings. She was described by her parents as impulsive, aggressive, destructive, quick-tempered, and cruel to animals and other children. Her teachers said she was restless, inattentive, quarrelsome, defiant, sullen, and often involved in stealing and lying. From the age of 4 on, Debra had exhibited behavior problems that culminated in a juvenile court hearing at which time she was made a ward of the court. After two years of foster care, Debra was eventually hospitalized for psychiatric care because of fighting, stubbornness, impulsiveness, setting fires, and sexual misbehavior with animals.

INTERVENTION: Debra's therapy took place in a playroom equipped with sand, running water, art materials, three games, and a variety of nurturing, aggressive, and constructive toys. Debra's treatment plan, as determined by her psychiatric team, included fifty-five-minute play

---

1. Virginia Axline, *Play Therapy* (New York: Ballantine Books, 1969).

therapy sessions twice a week. This schedule was rigidly maintained for seven months of treatment. Any need to reschedule was explained to Debra and she was reassured of the next meeting time.

Structuring limitations were decided upon before the play therapy began. However, no limits were presented to Debra until the need arose. If Debra refused to go to the playroom, the therapist stayed with her long enough to reassure her that the choice was hers and that the next session would be held as usual. Sessions were always held in the playroom and Debra was not allowed to stay longer than the time allotted. The session was terminated if Debra became bored and uninterested and left the room. The therapist straightened the room before and after each session. Debra was not allowed to remove any toys from the playroom, but could take drawings she had made. She was not allowed to attack the therapist, and if she became unduly destructive in any way this behavior was redirected using a four-step limit-setting sequence. The therapist: (1) recognized Debra's feelings or wishes, (2) clearly stated the limit, (3) provided alternatives through which the feeling or wish could be expressed, and (4) helped Debra bring out feelings of resentment that arose when the restriction was invoked.

During her seven months of therapy, Debra progressed through the four stages of the therapeutic process as identified by Moustakas (1953)[2]: (1) undifferentiated hostility and anxiety, (2) directed anger and hostility, (3) ambivalence, and (4) positive and negative feelings separate and consistent with reality. Debra's progress was observable in her changing behavior with the knock-down clown "Bozo," by her appearance, and in the way she played. In the beginning Debra beat up and threw Bozo around the room and shouted obscenities. This was followed by gluing curls to Bozo and calling him a "girl." In subsequent sessions Debra alternated between beating and hugging Bozo. During the last sessions Debra hugged Bozo and apologized when she bumped its nose. Debra came to the first ten sessions with her hair covering her face. By session fourteen she had combed her hair out of her eyes and was able to look directly at the therapist. During early sessions Debra would stop before completing a project,

2. Clark Moustakas, *Children in Play Therapy: A Key to Understanding Normal and Disturbed Emotions* (New York: McGraw-Hill, 1953).

game, or activity. For a period beginning around the ninth session Debra found it necessary to win at everything, often cheating and changing the rules in order to do so. She was unwilling to chance playing a game to its conclusion according to the rules until session forty-three.

At session twenty Debra was told of her parents' plan to have her return home. During the following twenty sessions Debra spent most her time working out feelings of ambivalence toward her mother and also toward the therapist. She was able to accept both her parents and the therapist only after the therapist clarified for Debra that she (the therapist) would be happy for Debra if she wanted to go home and that she wanted to spend time with Debra, but would do so only as long as Debra was in the hospital. After two successful home visits Debra was permanently reunited with her family.

COMMENTARY: Debra had entered play therapy as a negative, angry, defiant, and destructive little girl who had felt completely rejected. The accepting, safe environment of the play therapy relationship is freeing to children, enabling them to risk exploring more positive behaviors. With long-term and consistent intervention by Colbert through the medium of child-centered play therapy, Debra learned that it was all right to be angry, that it was safe to relate to another person, that she was liked for herself regardless of her actions, and that someone understood her pain.

SOURCE: Colbert, L. (1971). Debra finds herself. *Nursing Outlook* 19 (1):50–53.

POSSIBLE *DSM-IV* DIAGNOSES:

313.89   Reactive Attachment Disorder of Infancy or Early Childhood
V71.02   Child or Adolescent Antisocial Behavior
312.9   Disruptive Behavior Disorder NOS
312.81   Oppositional Defiant Disorder
312.8   Conduct Disorder

COGNITIVE, REFLECTIVE, AND PSYCHODYNAMIC PLAY THERAPY TECHNIQUES FOR PROMOTING THE ATTACHMENT PROCESS IN AN ADOPTED BOY

AUTHOR: **Ann Milston**

FOCUS: *Structured, behaviorally based play therapy within the framework of Kleinian theory with an emotionally disturbed 7-year-old boy who was experiencing attachment difficulties with his adoptive mother.*

INTRODUCTION: Milston utilized an eclectic series of techniques beginning with free reflective play while also focusing on transference and countertransference issues. Within the context of specific, identifiable themes, Milston introduced affirmation writing and meditation to assist in changing unconscious negative thoughts into positive self-statements. In addition, the child's mother, as primary caretaker, was brought into the play sessions for a period to help her learn to relate to her child in new and more positive ways through imaginative play. This case study illustrates the use of a combination of cognitive-type therapy, reflection, and psychodynamic techniques within the context of play therapy.

CASE STUDY: Adam was born to a 17-year-old girl who was hospitalized for depression shortly after Adam's birth. Adam had been in and out of foster care due to his mother's neglect and possible physical abuse and was adopted at age 2. His adoptive family included a mother who was described as bright, but rather tense and strict; a father who was described as easygoing; and an 11-year-old sister. At age 7 Adam was referred for outpatient treatment for being overly aggressive, lying, and stealing. His teachers described him as a bright but very unhappy child with no friends. He showed no signs of emotion or remorse and took little pleasure in life.

INTERVENTION: Treatment consisted of one-hour play therapy sessions each week for two years and then every other week for six months. In the initial phase of therapy Adam was living at home. He was then placed in a residential treatment center for children. During the last six months of therapy he was again living at home. In the initial phase of therapy Adam's behavior in the playroom was aggressive, lacking imagination, helpless, and rude. Early play included throwing things at and trying to frighten the therapist from the safety of a playhouse. Milston interpreted this as a reenactment of the birth mother's seemingly hostile rejection of Adam as an infant and Adam's need to test this new relationship with the therapist.

After a few weeks of free reflective play, Milston altered the play sessions. During the first fifteen minutes Milston was "the boss" and directed Adam in affirmation writing and meditation to help him change his unconscious negative life thoughts into positive statements about himself. During the rest of the session Adam was allowed self-direction. After six weeks Adam's mother joined some of the sessions. In one particularly memorable session, Adam was inside the sleeping bag and instructed his mother and Milston to hide. Holding a toy zebra, Adam then wriggled over to where they were hidden and told his mother to first find the zebra and then she would find him. Adam's mother was able to become involved in this play and, at the therapist's suggestion, was overjoyed to find a baby boy inside the sleeping bag. The symbolic rebirth from out of the sleeping bag into his mother's arms was reported to be a turning point for both mother and son.

RESULTS: Although Adam suffered several setbacks during therapy and was not able to control his aggressiveness consistently and sufficiently, upon termination with this therapist Adam was able to show remorse for inappropriate behavior and to show affection, enjoyed life, and had greater flexibility in relationships. His adoptive parents reported that Adam came out of his tantrums much more quickly and was more willing to accept responsibility for his actions.

COMMENTARY: Although the number of sessions in which this mother participated with her son was not clear, the inclusion of the mother as an integral part of the therapy seemed to be most beneficial for this child. At the end of their therapeutic relationship, Milston related that not all issues had been properly worked through, but that hopefully the emotional bond that had developed between mother and son would provide the foundation for further healing. The process of recovery for some very disturbed and damaged children may necessarily be long-term.

SOURCE: Milston, A. (1989). Establishing bonding: a case of rebirth? *British Journal of Occupational Therapy* 52(11):437–439.

POSSIBLE *DSM-IV* **DIAGNOSES:**

313.89   Reactive Attachment Disorder of Infancy or Early Childhood
V71.02   Child or Adolescent Antisocial Behavior
312.8   Conduct Disorder
300.4   Dysthymic Disorder

4

Autism

The little understood condition of autism seems to defy explanation of cause, and counseling procedures with autistic children have seldom been written about in counseling, psychology, or social work journals. Even fewer references can be found in the play therapy literature. Psychoanalytically oriented therapists have produced the only two case reports that were found on the application of play therapy procedures with autistic children. Both studies offer dramatic possibilities for making emotional contact with some autistic children. Lessons evident in these studies are that autistic children need to be in control of their play and their relationship with the therapist, and they feel safer in interacting with the therapist through toys, such as puppets. The technique described in this chapter of having a puppet verbalize for the therapist offers positive possibilities for the play therapist who experiences a wide variety of reluctant or withdrawn children.

PSYCHODYNAMIC PLAY THERAPY WITH A HIGH-FUNCTIONING AUTISTIC CHILD

AUTHOR: **Richard Bromfield**

FOCUS: *The reaffirmation of the relevance of traditional psychodynamic play therapy to the milder variants of the autistic syndrome.*

INTRODUCTION: Autistic children are often viewed as too limited in language and symbolic thought to benefit from therapy. However, higher-functioning autistic children seem capable of benefiting from traditional play therapy. These children appear autistic, yet display greater intellect and social interest than is typical of pervasive autism. This case history was presented to encourage the use of traditional play therapy with children who may seem suited solely for more highly structured and educative experiences.

CASE STUDY: Tim was born of an uncomplicated pregnancy and experienced no significant medical problems as an infant. Tim's mother described him as an unaffectionate infant, neither seeking nor appearing to enjoy her attention. Although early developmental milestones were met in a timely fashion, a general lack of responsiveness to others continued to increase. By age 3, other signs of autism had become evident, such as gross language deficits, inordinate need for sameness, aberrant eye contact, and delayed motor skills.

At age 6 Tim was referred to Bromfield for therapy at the point of transition from a therapeutic day program to a self-contained special education classroom in a public school. He had been treated by two previous therapists for approximately six months each. Both therapists described him as too autistic and unreachable to benefit from therapy. Tim's mother was described as well intentioned and overly involved with her only child. She had only recently begun to acknowledge the serious nature of her son's developmental delays. Tim's father was described as caring but strange, often sharing Tim's idiosyncratic view of the world.

INTERVENTION: Bromfield met with Tim in twice-weekly play therapy sessions during the first year of treatment. The first few sessions lasted only about fifteen minutes each as Tim became unduly anxious. Early sessions involved solitary play with a racetrack gameboard, joylessly pursuing laps around the track, stopping only to spit occasionally or to smell the game materials. Although Tim rejected Bromfield's rare overtures to join in his activity, he would watch the therapist closely whenever Bromfield turned away.

The first instance of verbal interaction involved Bromfield's use of a puppet. Bromfield had commented that Tim was smelling the game. Direct verbal interaction proved to be too invasive. However, when the puppet copied Tim's frequent action of smelling the race-track, Tim responded to the puppet by saying "You smell stuff" and the puppet verbally agreed. Several weeks later Tim recalled this play with the puppet, which provided an opportunity for Bromfield to explain how the puppet smelled in order to learn more about the world. Tim confessed that he also "smells the things that happen to him." He was able to use the puppet during a later session to direct anger at Bromfield, indicating that he was capable of processing and integrating the therapeutic experience, however slowly.

Tim's use of the play therapy sessions progressed as he moved from reclusive play in the corner of the office to the use of mailboxes and telephones to receive letters and calls. By doing so he provided himself modes of communication allowing for varied degrees of inti-macy. Throughout play therapy, puppets also served as vehicles for Tim's communication. Different puppets were attributed specific characteristics, such as the angry wolf, the hungry pig, and the baby cow. The therapist was also assigned a puppet through which Brom-field was expected to communicate. A predominant theme during the play therapy sessions was Tim's wish to be liked by the therapist. Tim would work hard to obtain gifts and extra time, and the thera-pist's failure to provide gratification resulted in tremendous frustra-tion, anger, and intensification of autistic behaviors.

After a year of play therapy Tim showed increased comfort and more direct communication with Bromfield. Tim's parents and teach-ers observed positive growth outside of therapy. He also showed en-hanced capacity to express himself, to tolerate frustration and anxi-ety, and to manage closeness with peers and school staff. An extensive neurodevelopmental assessment conducted at age 7 showed consid-erable positive change in Tim's intellectual functioning as compared with an assessment done two years earlier.

COMMENTARY: Play therapy permitted Tim to experience play in which he could securely be in control. The therapist's responsiveness to Tim's need to control the relationship helped Tim feel less vulnerable and thereby more willing to risk greater investment in the therapist. Through nonverbal and spoken validations of his autistic life experience by way of the puppets, Tim experienced himself and the therapist more directly.

This case history tends to reaffirm the use of traditional forms of play therapy as being helpful in treating milder forms of childhood autism. Therapy that addresses the child's inner world and relationships can complement broader educational and behavioral programs. Bromfield admits that play therapy with a high-functioning autistic child can be a labored experience, but rewarding for both the child and the therapist. Nonintrusively seeking meaning in the child's behaviors and unusual verbalizations conveys an interest in the child's communication. Bromfield warns that preconceived notions of what constitutes valuable fantasy or play will blind the therapist to what is there and workable.

SOURCE: Bromfield, R. (1989). Psychodynamic play therapy with a high-functioning autistic child. *Psychoanalytic Psychology* 4:439–453.

POSSIBLE *DSM-IV* DIAGNOSES:

299.00   Autistic Disorder
300.00   Anxiety Disorder NOS

TREATING AUTISM WITH PSYCHOANALYTIC PLAY THERAPY

AUTHOR: **Monica Lanyado**

FOCUS: *Psychoanalytic play therapy with a child with autism involves patience by the therapist in the process of waiting for the child's cues.*

INTRODUCTION: Lanyado describes a child's new experience of awareness of separateness and subsequent positive development through the formation of symbols.

CASE STUDY: Five-year-old Enid was described as an autistic child, hovering between fleeting awareness of people and events around her and total withdrawal. A psychologist had found her to be untestable and possibly mentally subnormal. Enid's parents experienced severe marital problems during the mother's pregnancy and the first year of Enid's life and divorced when she was 2 years old. The mother then literally lost herself in her child. Mother and child retreated into their own private world until the mother experienced some recovery from the trauma of the divorce and realized the need for help for Enid and herself.

INTERVENTION: For a variety of reasons Enid was seen only once a month. During the same interval Enid's mother was seen by another psychoanalyst. For the first four sessions Enid was absorbed in obsessional sand play. At the fifth session a dramatic change occurred. Enid arrived for therapy carrying a doll. She stood directly in front of the therapist and stared into her eyes as if to say, "Here I am." Enid initiated communication by showing the therapist that the doll's batteries were missing. She then began to stare at the sand tray, but seemed unable to move away from the therapist. The therapist responded to this dilemma, verbally recognizing that Enid wanted the therapist to go with her to the sand tray. As in previous sessions, Enid absorbed herself in the sand play, occasionally asking about her mother. Only at this point was the therapist able to interpret the symbolic meaning in Enid's attempts at communication. For Enid, being separated from her mother was like having a piece of her body missing, just like the doll whose battery was missing. Enid responded to this interpretation with a nod and a grin; she had experienced a need to communicate and she had been heard. Over time, Enid became more able to tolerate her separateness from her mother. She first used primitive sign language and then more complex verbal and playful communication with others. She continued toward normal development at a steady, although much delayed, pace.

COMMENTARY: The disturbed attachment between Enid and her mother interrupted normal development and did not allow Enid to see herself as separate from her mother. This attachment manifested itself in autistic behaviors. Through play therapy Enid was able to express her separation anxiety symbolically and to be understood. Psychoanalytic play therapy's emphasis on symbolism and interpretation supported Enid in developing a symbolic language and the ability to communicate with others.

SOURCE: Lanyado, M. (1987). Asymbolic and symbolic play: developmental perspectives in the treatment of disturbed children. *Journal of Child Psychotherapy* 13(2):33–44.

POSSIBLE *DSM-IV* DIAGNOSES:

299.00   Autistic Disorder
315.31   Expressive Language Disorder
313.89   Reactive Attachment Disorder of Infancy or Early Childhood
V61.20   Parent–Child Relational Problem
309.21   Separation Anxiety Disorder

5

Burn Victims

Pediatric burn patients present a multifaceted challenge to child care personnel who must help them cope with emotional issues of trauma, separation, loss of control, isolation, disfigurement, and chronic pain. Prolonged hospitalization is accompanied by an array of emotional reactions: anxiety, fear, anger, depression, aggression, disorientation, and withdrawal. These reactions can be exacerbated by the never-ending process of dressing changes, which can be an especially anxiety-provoking time for child burn victims.

Modifications in play materials may be necessary for children who require a sterile environment. If a sand tray is being used, glass beads or paper punch holes can be substituted for the sand as these can be sterilized. It is important that child burn victims be provided an opportunity to develop a feeling of control. The manipulation of toys and the creation of play scenarios serve this purpose. It is not necessary for these children to experience actual control of their environment; the important dimension is that they feel they are in control, which will then enable them to begin the process of dealing with the trauma of their experience.

MULTIMODAL TREATMENT OF A BURNED CHILD

AUTHORS: **Lilly Schubert Walker and Mark Healy**

FOCUS: *Multimodal treatment of an 8-year-old girl with severe burns, including medication, relaxation exercises, and behavior therapy for the treatment of trauma and pain, and play therapy and storytelling for emotional adjustment.*

INTRODUCTION: The case study presented is that of 8-year-old Amy, who was hospitalized with second- and third-degree burns covering 80 percent of her body. In addition to the medical treatment for pain, relaxation, imagery, and behavior therapy were designed to help Amy adjust to the hospitalization. Play therapy and storytelling were used to assist Amy in gaining "understanding of herself, her emotions, and her motivations."

CASE STUDY: Walker and Healy described Amy as a "controlled" child who did not readily express emotions. Her parents described her as normal, active, and self-confident. She was additionally reported to be very sensitive to others' disapproval and nonacceptance, and felt very guilty following any misbehavior. The burn injuries were a result of an accident in which her nightgown caught fire from a gas heater. Following her hospitalization, Amy was delirious, and her chances of survival uncertain. Her hospital behavior was "whiny, easily irritated, and ingratiating." As the burn treatment continued, Amy developed fears of the medical procedures, resisted the hospital staff with combative behavior, and refused to eat or to participate in physical therapy.

INTERVENTION: The first intervention focused on Amy's difficulty with the medical procedures, primarily the dressing changes. The chosen intervention was relaxation training, emotive imagery, and a behavior therapy program. The reward for cooperative behavior was "time spent in play." (See below.)

The refusal to eat, a common issue for pediatric burn victims, was also dealt with by a behavioral intervention. Amy was able to maintain an adequate daily caloric intake, but the results of the psychotherapeutic intervention were inconsistent.

Storytelling, using Gardner's[1] Mutual Storytelling technique, was also employed to help Amy in her adjustment. The specific treatment goal was to assist her with self-concept and body-image issues. The storytelling intervention consisted of Amy reading stories to the playroom director and a therapist later reviewing them, and Amy occasionally composing her own stories with similar themes.

The play therapy interventions included artwork, games, and so on. The authors suggested that some of the play materials promoted catharsis (e.g., play dough and artwork), some were mediums to deal with control issues (e.g., board games), and some facilitated the goals of physical therapy (e.g., coloring and embroidery).

Parent counseling was also included in Amy's treatment. This included both training in behavior management and designed play activities involving Amy's mother.

COMMENTARY: Walker and Healy suggested that psychotherapy needs to be indirect and nonthreatening for pediatric burn patients. The primary interventions that meet those criteria in this case are the modalities of storytelling and play therapy. The authors noted that "play therapy provided a useful mode to help this child discuss some of her concerns." This certainly appeared to be the case. It is interesting to note the relationship between the behavioral interventions and play therapy. The "reward" for Amy's cooperative behavior was time to play, often in the hospital playroom. It might be assumed that Amy cooperated with the medical procedures in order to have the opportunity to process her emotions surrounding the situation in the play experience. Although various therapeutic interventions were employed with Amy, it appears that the play therapy interventions were crucial elements in her adjustment to the challenging medical circumstance.

SOURCE: Walker, L. J. S., and Healy, M. (1980). Psychological treatment of a burned child. *Journal of Pediatric Psychology* 5(4):395–404.

POSSIBLE *DSM-IV* DIAGNOSES:

293.89   Anxiety Disorder Due to a General Medical Condition
309.81   Posttraumatic Stress Disorder

---

1. Richard Gardner, *Storytelling in Psychotherapy with Children* (Northvale, NJ: Jason Aronson Inc., 1993).

DEVELOPMENT OF A PREOPERATIVE
PLAY PROGRAM FOR BURNED CHILDREN

AUTHOR: **Debra L. Walls**

FOCUS: *The development of a play therapy program using preoperative techniques for burned children based on a survey of pediatric play programs in the United States.*

INTRODUCTION: A review of the literature did not reveal the existence of a standard preoperative play program for burned children. A survey was conducted to research the existence and development of such programs for children hospitalized for burn treatment. The focus was on programs that included preoperative play for their patients and on determining the procedures, materials, and staff involved in the programs. The author's objective was to develop a model program.

RESEARCH METHODS & DESIGN: The development of the program consisted of five phases: (1) a literature search of the topic, (2) compiling and analyzing data obtained from a questionnaire and follow-up telephone interviews, (3) development of a preoperative play program for burned children, (4) evaluation of a developed program by a panel of experts, and (5) field testing of the program with five burned children.

INTERVENTION: A nineteen-item questionnaire was distributed to 239 pediatric play therapy programs in the United States to determine the number of programs that used preoperative play, procedures and materials used, and the medical events for which pediatric patients are prepared. Follow-up telephone interviews were conducted with those agencies that included preoperative play for burned children. Using the information gathered from the questionnaire and telephone interviews, a program was developed to teach these children about their burn care and treatment, including tanking, debridement, donor sites, skin grafts, and jobsts. The program was then sent to a panel of experts for review, including persons in the fields of medicine, burn care and treatment, therapeutic recreation, and special education.

RESULTS: Of the 239 questionnaires sent out, 145 (62 percent) were returned, with fifty-eight (40 percent) indicating the existence of a preoperative play program for burned children. A follow-up telephone interview was conducted with these fifty-eight, of which eighteen (31 percent) responded. Based on the findings and a review of the literature, a curriculum was developed. The program was evaluated by a panel of four experts and accordingly revised and field tested with five children admitted to the North Carolina Jaycees Burn Center in Chapel Hill, North Carolina. A qualitative evaluation following each preoperative preparation session was completed with positive results.

COMMENTARY: Walls concluded that the programs surveyed in the study were inconsistent and disorganized, and that the developed program for burned children was a relevant and potentially valuable teaching tool. Although there are common issues for children experiencing hospitalization (see Chapter 13), burned children face unique challenges that make a program tailored for their needs essential. Walls concluded her research with recommendations that the program be expanded to adolescents, and that development of further tactile and visual play materials would be beneficial to accommodate children with other disabilities or from varied cultural backgrounds.

SOURCE: Walls, D. L. (1981). *The development of a pre-operative play program for burned children.* Unpublished doctoral dissertation, Virginia Polytechnic Institute and State University.

POSSIBLE *DSM-IV* DIAGNOSES:

293.89   Anxiety Disorder Due to a General Medical Condition
309.81   Posttraumatic Stress Disorder

6

Chronic Illness

Chronically ill children often experience high levels of pain, stress, and anxiety that can prevent their natural coping behaviors from being utilized. Episodes of severe asthma attacks, for example, may be so frightening and stressful as to debilitate the child. The natural calming effect of play can help the child to relax and experience natural recovery. Chronically ill children often feel helpless, and in play therapy can experience being in control of their play and in charge of the outcome, thus returning to a state of feeling in control. Play reduces the world of reality to a child's dimension in which the child is the master and the person who determines direction. Families of chronically ill children face a myriad of concurrent challenges that affect the entire family system. In such cases filial therapy has been shown to be an effective intervention of choice. Adaptations in play materials or expectations of play may be necessary when working with the chronically ill child who may be immobilized or whose physical activity has been significantly restricted due to the illness. These children may not be able to fully act out the range of their emotions in typical kinds of play activities, for example, being physically aggressive to express anger.

PLAY THERAPY WITH AN ASTHMATIC CHILD

AUTHOR: **Joanne Bentley**

FOCUS: *Play therapy was used to treat a boy with severe asthma and eczema, with the aim of reducing the number and severity of asthma attacks while he was in a residential treatment program.*

INTRODUCTION: Bentley presented the case of John, a 9-year-old boy who had been placed in a residential treatment center for severe, persistent asthma and eczema. John was referred for psychotherapeutic treatment after being in the treatment center for five months. His skin condition had worsened, and he was wheezing almost daily. Unlike the other children at the center, John had to remain on corticosteroid medication. The staff was also concerned about his social relations as John constantly complained about his treatment by the other children. They discovered, however, that John was provoking attacks upon himself and was a primary scapegoat at the center. Therapy was conducted for a period of fourteen months.

CASE STUDY: Before being placed in the center, John had been hospitalized several times for severe asthma attacks. During the most recent episode, a tracheotomy had been performed, which assisted respiration for two days. John was reported to have had a skin rash since the age of 1 month and daily sneezing from 8 months. At age 2 he was diagnosed with severe asthma and eczema. By the time of admission to the residential program, John was having severe attacks almost every week.

There was no information about John's biological parents or the conditions under which he lived prior to his adoption at 8 months other than that John had lived in at least two foster homes. Bentley reported that the parents had a genuine affection for John and there was no evidence of pathology in either parent.

INTERVENTION: Before treatment began, John met with the therapist for an initial diagnostic impression. Bentley remarked on this because John was initially on guard when the therapy began, viewing the therapist as a person who asked many questions. During the first stage of treatment John set up scenarios with toy soldiers in which both sides were destroyed. He also played competitive games with the therapist in which he would become belligerent when losing and depressed when winning, often stopping the game or trying to lose. Bentley interpreted this as anger related to wanting things and feeling guilt about wanting. She believed that a major therapeutic task was to help John accept and find appropriate ways to gratify his wishes.

As the treatment progressed, the therapist took a more active role, responding to John's destruction with the modeling of healing and nurturing. John would create clay dinosaurs and destroy them; the therapist would repair the dinosaurs and feed them. John initially resented the therapist as interfering, but eventually began to identify with her role. Interestingly, if the therapist had to change the appointment time or if John felt cheated out of another activity by coming to therapy, he reverted to smashing animals and preventing their repair.

In the final phase of therapy John became more focused on the theme of food. He moved from making dinosaurs to making food with the clay and began to be less depressed about winning games. He also "fed" himself and the therapist. Bentley posited that John was beginning to communicate in a new way at this point, and that he was processing the issue of having needs and wants and the appropriateness of having those met. John began to accept both real food and play food from the therapist. An important incident that occurred outside of therapy pointed to John's progress with his initiation of a fight with one of his tormentors at the treatment center, "the first time he [residential counselor] had seen John stick up for himself."

John's parents removed him from the treatment facility before therapy was completed. Although Bentley believed that the termination was premature, she reported that John had no serious asthma attacks after returning home.

COMMENTARY: The effects of play therapy in the processing of intrapsychic issues have a corresponding benefit on the physiological condition of chronically ill children. The frequency and severity of John's asthma attacks was substantially ameliorated through the play therapy process. Bentley suggested that John was able to process some of his internalized anger related to his infant deprivation through the play therapy. His aggressive and passive-aggressive behaviors, related to the fear of having needs and wanting them to be met, emerged in the play, were accepted by the therapist, and were resolved to some degree. The experimentation that John was allowed to act out in the latter stages of treatment led to his learning new behaviors that translated outside of the playroom.

SOURCE: Bentley, J. (1975). Psychotherapeutic treatment of a boy with eczema and asthma. *The Journal of Asthma Research* 12(4):207–214.

POSSIBLE *DSM-IV* DIAGNOSES:

313.81   Oppositional Defiant Disorder
V61.9   Relational Problem Related to a Mental Disorder or General Medical Condition

FILIAL THERAPY WITH PARENTS OF CHRONICALLY ILL CHILDREN

AUTHORS: **Hilda Glazer-Waldman, Judith Zimmerman, Garry Landreth, and Douglas Norton**

FOCUS: *The use of filial therapy as an intervention with families of chronically ill children.*

INTRODUCTION: Families of chronically ill children face a myriad of concurrent challenges that affect the entire family system. Most interventions offered to these families involve the provision of education and support, which has proved to be beneficial. This study addressed an alternative approach, which focused on providing parents with skills to help bring about changes in the family environment disrupted by the chronic illness of a child. These skills were taught in a filial therapy training program.

Filial therapy is described by the authors to be a "client-centered family skills training program." Essentially, parents are trained in child-centered play therapy techniques to develop skills in reflecting feelings, communicating acceptance, and setting appropriate limits. The emphasis is upon building and enhancing the parent–child relationship. The parent is to become the therapeutic agent for the child.

RESEARCH METHODS & DESIGN: A one-group pretest–posttest research design was employed. The filial training group consisted of six volunteer parents whose children were patients at two local hospitals. The group completing pretests and posttests consisted of five women between the ages of 29 and 36. The children ranged in age from 4 to 8 years and had diagnoses including muscular dystrophy, cerebral palsy, asthma, and a severe feeding disorder.

The following instrumentation was used to assess the effectiveness of the filial therapy intervention. Spielberger's State–Trait Anxiety Inventory (STAI) was used to assess the parents' perception of their current level of anxiety. The Child Anxiety Scale (CAS) was used to measure the child's perception of the current level of anxiety. The Porter Parental Acceptance Scale (PPAS) was used to measure parents' self-reports of feelings of acceptance and actions taken in relationship to their child.

INTERVENTION: The filial therapy training format consisted of ten two-hour weekly sessions. A presession was held before the training began, during which the general procedure was explained, pretests were administered, and informed consent was obtained. As noted above, the parents were trained in basic child-centered play therapy skills, and were required to have regularly scheduled play sessions with their children. The training format followed the outline developed by Garry Landreth[1] for a ten-session filial therapy group. Following the last session, the instruments were again administered. All sessions were videotaped.

RESULTS: Although there was no statistical significance on the measurement instruments, qualitative reports indicated significant change in the parents and the children. Several mitigating circumstances affecting the parents were postulated by the authors to have affected the measurement outcomes. On the qualitative level the parents were observed (by the group leaders and a third observer) to have learned the child-centered play therapy techniques taught during the ten sessions. The parents additionally reported positive changes in themselves and their children when compared with the descriptions of their children given at the beginning of the training. The parents all recommended the training to other parents.

COMMENTARY: Although the number of subjects in this study was limited (significant statistical results are difficult with small samples), positive change was reported by all participants. All participating parents "reported significant changes in their relationships with their children." The authors suggested that these qualitative changes are the significant results of this study. The challenges faced by children with chronic illnesses are positively impacted by this unique form of play therapy.

---

1. Garry L. Landreth, *Play Therapy: The Art of the Relationship* (Muncie, IN: Accelerated Development Press).

SOURCE: Glazer-Waldman, H. R., Zimmerman, J. E., Landreth, G. L., and Norton, D. (1992). Filial therapy: an intervention for parents of children with chronic illness. *International Journal of Play Therapy* 1:31–42.

POSSIBLE *DSM-IV* **DIAGNOSIS:**

Insufficient information provided in the study.

7

Deaf and Physically Challenged Children

Children who are physically challenged are often reacted to in terms of what is physically observable, with the resulting effect that they may feel incomplete, unworthy, or unacceptable. The problems and challenges these children face are of only secondary concern to the play therapist. What is important is that these children are persons in their own right and as such they experience the same feelings and reactions as all other children. Their condition does not make them any less of a person, just as a child who experiences reading difficulties, speech difficulties, academic problems, poor peer relationships, overwhelming anxiety, or some other difficulty is not thought to be less of a person. All children need understanding, acceptance, feelings of adequacy, and a sense of personal worth. A child's physical condition does not change these needs. It is understandable that these children may be slow to trust the play therapist because of the rejection they may have experienced from other significant adults in their lives.

The play therapist will need to be sensitive to the fact that some challenges these children have faced may have resulted in their approaching the world differently, as in the case of deaf children. Studies show that during the preoperational stage, ages 2 to 7, these children display less mature play patterns, exhibit very little make-believe play, and engage in less symbolic solitary play. Such information is essential for the play therapist to adequately understand the play of these children. Likewise the play therapist may need to make significant adjustments to accommodate the physically challenged child—for example, they may have to tape a paintbrush to the hand of a cerebral-palsied child.

SAND PLAY WITH HYPERKINETIC, EPILEPTIC CHILDREN

AUTHORS: **Itsuo Kawai, Hayao Kawai, and Hiroshi Naniwa**

FOCUS: *The effects of sand play therapy on the restless behavior of epileptic children.*

INTRODUCTION: The authors explored the use of sand play therapy with psychomotor epileptic children with hyperkinetic or restless behavior disorders in which medication had little to no effect.

CASE STUDY: Eleven children ages 5 to 14 were seen for sand play therapy once a week for a total of thirty to 150 sessions. Anticonvulsant and psychotropic medicines did not seem to affect the behavior disorders in eight of the cases. Although the three other children developed seizures during the sand tray sessions, the restless behavior did not decrease with the introduction of medication.

INTERVENTION: The authors report the use of Kalff's[1] style of sand play. Over the course of the sessions three primary characteristic features of children with epilepsy were noted: irrelevant or irrational content, a stormy or rigidly ordered world, and persistent battles. An example of irrelevant or irrational content would be the child having a witch and a monster jump out of a volcano, or baseball bats and airplanes laid out together in a line. Another child displayed stormy and rigidly ordered worlds, violent throwing of sand, and splashing of water "floods," which contrasted with ordered lines of miniatures such as animals, cavalry, and vehicles. The authors note that battles are often displayed by neurotic children, and that epileptic children never tire of repeating them. One therapist indicated that catharsis had occurred upon seeing a town reappear where there had been destruction after a fierce battle, only to have the destruction begin again.

---

1. Dora Kalff, *Sandplay*, 2nd ed. (Santa Monica, CA: Sigo, 1980).

RESULTS: The behavior of five of the eleven children improved remarkably. At a five-year follow-up, these five had no recurrence of restless behavior. Four other children became less restless, their school adjustment was above average, and they displayed only occasional violence with their families. The final two children showed no improvement during their sand play therapy and participation in this study was terminated.

Six children experienced seizures during sand play therapy. Three of these children improved psychologically, two showed less restless activity, and one remained unaffected by the sessions and continued to have seizures.

COMMENTARY: The results of this study serve as encouragement for further psychotherapy with children who are epileptic. Although little information is given by the authors on the sand play sessions, the three major characteristics identified in the sand play could reveal some of the inner thoughts of the child with epilepsy and behavior disorders, such as the ongoing struggle of living a life that can be out of control and chaotic and certainly, for a child, filled with irrational content.

SOURCE: Kawai, I., Kawai, H., and Naniwa, H. (1980). Effects of play therapy on hyperkinetic children with psychomotor epilepsy. *Folia Psychiatrica et Neurologica Japonica* 34(3):400–401.

POSSIBLE *DSM-IV* DIAGNOSES:

312.9   Disruptive Behavior Disorder NOS
293.9   Mental Disorder NOS Due to a General Medical Condition

PLAY THERAPY WITH PRESCHOOL DEAF CHILDREN

AUTHOR: **Viola Jackson Oualline**

FOCUS: *The use of short-term child-centered play therapy with preschool deaf children having behavioral disturbance.*

INTRODUCTION: Since deaf children rely on nonverbal means of communication, play therapy as a nonverbal intervention should be expected to yield positive results. The investigation involved the effects of short-term child-centered play therapy with preschool deaf children exhibiting some level of behavioral difficulty.

RESEARCH METHODS & DESIGN: The children who participated in this investigation had impaired hearing and had been referred for therapy to classes for the deaf. The children selected for the study were those (1) whose hearing impairment had existed prior to language acquisition; (2) who had a hearing loss of 70 decibels or more; (3) who had an IQ of 80 or above; (4) who were between 4 and 6 years of age; and (5) who were described by a hearing therapist as having behavioral problems. Twenty-four children met the selection criteria and were paired according to age and gender. They were then assigned randomly to a treatment or control group.

Pre- and posttests administered included the Vineland Social Maturity Scale, the Child Behavior Rating Scale, and the Behavior Problem Checklist. Parents and hearing therapists completed questionnaires concerning the children before and after the intervention.

INTERVENTION: Children assigned to the treatment group received fifty minutes of individual play therapy per week for ten weeks with a trained play therapist. The therapeutic approach was described as nondirective, following Axline's[1] eight basic principles. The play materials used were standardized, and included toys recommended by Axline and Ginott.[2] Children assigned to the control

---

1. Virginia Axline, *Play Therapy* (New York: Ballantine Books, 1969).
2. Haim Ginott, *Group Psychotherapy with Children: The Theory and Practice of Play Therapy* (New York: McGraw-Hill, 1961).

group were given thirty minutes of free individual play with an untrained volunteer.

RESULTS: Statistical analysis of the scores on the Vineland indicated a significant increase in mature behavior patterns for the children who had experienced the play therapy intervention. The scores on the other instruments did not show significance, although Oualline suggested that the instruments may not be adequate measures for children with severe hearing impairment. On the qualitative level, data from questionnaires revealed that all the parents and teachers of seven of the children in the treatment group reported positive behavioral change in the children at the completion of the play therapy intervention.

COMMENTARY: Oualline noted that the true "language" of the deaf child is nonverbal communication. This fact would appear to indicate that play therapy would be a very appropriate and beneficial intervention for the deaf child requiring counseling. The child born deaf does not have the ability to inquire orally about the curious world in which he/she lives, which may result in frustration and anger or withdrawal and apathy. Oualline asserted that the need for all children to experience self-acceptance is unfulfilled for the deaf child because of these dynamics. Play therapy can be a means to reach these children and to provide them with an opportunity to "communicate" in a way that was previously impossible.

SOURCE: Oualline, V. J. (1975). *Behavioral outcomes of short-term nondirective play therapy with preschool deaf children.* Unpublished doctoral dissertation, North Texas State University, Denton, TX.

POSSIBLE *DSM-IV* DIAGNOSES:

309.30   Adjustment Disorder with Disturbance of Conduct
309.40   Adjustment Disorder with Mixed Disturbance of Emotions and Conduct
313.81   Oppositional Defiant Disorder

TREATING A DEAF CHILD WITH PLAY THERAPY

AUTHOR: **Elizabeth Urban**

FOCUS: *Play therapy as treatment for a 10-year-old child experiencing profound deafness and adjustment difficulties at home and school.*

INTRODUCTION: The case study presented is that of 10-year-old Virginia, a profoundly deaf girl. Urban described her approach to treatment as "psychodynamic play therapy." She discussed the treatment process and her psychoanalytic interpretation of various play therapy themes. The treatment process spanned two school years.

CASE STUDY: Virginia had considerable difficulty communicating; she could not speak discernibly except for a few words, and although having been taught sign language, did not have a command of it. Virginia was referred for therapy as a result of reported incidences of stealing at home and at school. There was also concern over Virginia's excessive clumsiness, lack of language development and understanding, and her generally depressed presentation. Her teacher was also concerned about her being out of control in the classroom, characterized by stubbornness. Virginia was noticeably unpopular in school, drew unfavorable attention to herself, and was criticized by the boys.

Virginia wore thick glasses to correct her vision, and had a squinting problem that was apparently "outside her conscious control." She had curly blond hair and a pretty face. Virginia used hearing aids, and seemed to have a varying degree of sensitivity to sound. The cause of her profound deafness was not known, and was presumed to have been present since birth.

INTERVENTION: Urban discussed the case in two parts because of the separation of treatment phases dictated by the school schedule. The first phase ran from the spring term until the summer holiday, and the second the entire next academic year. She noted a pronounced qualitative difference between the two periods, with the first marked by an "intensity and spiritedness" that was absent during the second phase.

The first session was marked by awkwardness, and little communication between Virginia and the therapist, which Virginia viewed as rejection. Virginia drew an unflattering picture of a person, which was interpreted as her self-perception. By the fourth session a pattern of play developed that continued for the remainder of the term. In this pattern Virginia "acted out" her rejection of the therapist with heightened anticipation and intense fun. She selected a variety of toys, but "never played with them" beyond setting up a classroom and later a medical room. The play included a "harsh teacher–pupil relationship" and later a "cruel doctor–patient relationship." By the end of the term Virginia had become more accepting of the therapist and more in touch with feelings of attachment. Virginia's parents reported that she had changed very positively in terms of attitude and was more relaxed, less stressed, and more interested in social activities. There were also no further reports of stealing at home or school after therapy began.

The second phase of treatment, which began as the school year recommenced in the fall, was marked by increased emotional and physical contact between Virginia and the therapist. Virginia's play became a series of pretend telephone conversations between "friends." When the treatment process began, Virginia equated being deaf with a total inability to communicate to an "audience" that was highly critical and persecutory. At the end of the treatment process Virginia experienced not only the positive gains noted above, but also markedly improved self-esteem and significant improvement in her signing skills.

COMMENTARY: Play therapy has been demonstrated to be effective in dealing with issues of self-control and mastery. The opportunity for a child to "communicate" in her own language is an empowering experience, especially for the child with communication deficits in other areas. Virginia experienced obvious benefit from the play experience, despite Urban's summary comment that "therapy failed to address directly what feelings Virginia had about being deaf." It would appear that although she may not have addressed these concerns, many issues and emotions were processed in the play experience. Virginia seemed to be more impacted by the play therapy relationship than by psychoanalytic concerns. Urban admitted that although she included interpretive comments as part of the treatment process, Virginia "was not interested in what I was saying." The multiple issues of power and control that characterize children who are frustrated by their inability to hear and be heard were addressed in the process of play. Urban concluded her case study by stressing how important it was for Virginia to be the "initiator" in the therapeutic process, a role that was a key element in Virginia's positive response to treatment.

SOURCE: Urban, E. (1990). The eye of the beholder: work with a ten-year-old. *Journal of Child Psychotherapy* 16(2):63–81.

POSSIBLE *DSM-IV* DIAGNOSES:

312.8   Conduct Disorder
300.4   Dysthymic Disorder

8

Dissociation and Schizophrenia

According to Gil, "Dissociation is understood as a process of separating, segregating, and isolating chunks of information, perceptions, memories, motivations, and affects. Dissociation serves as a defense against severe stress, allowing the individual to protect against the original trauma but leaving a predisposition to react to subsequent stress or familiar stimuli as if they were a reoccurrence of the trauma."[1] Multiple Personality Disorder is the most severe of the dissociative disorders, and it is important to note that although the age of onset is almost invariably childhood, it does not typically come to attention until much later. Reports in the literature support the conclusion that there is a significant correlation between ongoing or severe childhood sexual or physical abuse and dissociated states. Due to the secretive nature of posttraumatic play, direct observation by therapists of posttraumatic play is most likely to occur only in a play therapy experience and then only after therapeutic condi-

---

1. E. Gil. *The Healing Power of Play: Working with Abused Children* (New York: Guilford, 1991), p. 22.

tions of acceptance and great safety are felt by the child. Play therapy seems to offer the most promise for effecting change and trauma resolution for traumatized children. There have also been promising reports in the literature describing the use of play therapy with child alters of adults with multiple personality disorders.

JUNGIAN PLAY THERAPY WITH A SCHIZOPHRENIC BOY

AUTHOR: **John Allan & Sarah Lawton-Speert**

FOCUS: *The use of Jungian play therapy with a profoundly sexually abused boy diagnosed as schizophrenic.*

INTRODUCTION: The case study presented is that of a boy named Kim, referred for treatment by his adoptive parents. Kim's history included severe neglect and sexual abuse; it was noted that he had been diagnosed with Schizophrenic Disorder, Disorganized Type. Jungian play therapy was utilized, and the play therapy was conducted by a graduate student under the supervision of Dr. Allan.

CASE STUDY: Kim was 4½ years old at the start of treatment, and had been diagnosed as schizophrenic. His behavior at the time of referral was characterized by incoherent and disorganized speech, a wide range of affect, loose associations and bizarre and illogical language. Kim thought that toy snakes were real and would bite him. Much of his play was sexual in nature, including frequent masturbation, indiscriminate urination, touching adults' genitals, and attempted sex acts with other children. He also suffered from sleep disturbances, including night terrors.

   Kim and his older brother were initially raised by their mother, who exhibited several abusive parenting patterns: severe neglect, abandonment for up to three days, physical abuse of the older boy, and sexual abuse of Kim. Kim was removed from his mother's care at the age of 4 months (for a four-month period), and then permanently at the age of 10 months. He remained in foster care settings until 23 months of age when he went to live with his adoptive parents. Kim was adopted together with his older brother.

INTERVENTION: The 18-month treatment process consisted of three stages: initial, middle, and termination. The initial stage of therapy was marked by terror and rage. Kim refused to enter the playroom, and would kick, scream, and run away. After being carried into the playroom, he would spit, swear, throw toys and water, and attempt to hurt the therapist. Kim would occasionally have to be restrained. By the seventh session, his anger having gradually diminished, he would respond to limits and engage in some nurturing play.

Seductive and erotic play emerged following the seventh session, and continued for the next three months. Kim took off his clothes and attempted to engage the therapist in sexual activity. When the therapist set a limit on this, Kim became angry and began to stimulate himself with the play materials. He also frequently washed himself with sand, soap, and water during this stage, and urinated in a tub. After sixteen sessions, Kim moved to some intense infantile play, including sucking on a bottle and being fed and diapered by the therapist. This evolved into Kim's providing these nurturing behaviors for himself. Following this, Kim moved to tender play toward the therapist, with occasional conflicted moves into aggressive and sexualized play. He processed emerging feelings of attachment with the therapist and the conflict he felt, in comparison, toward his adoptive mother.

After a year of play therapy, much of the play activity centered around themes of domestic animals, cars, and houses. Kim included the therapist less frequently in his play. Toy animals that had been attacking became pets. Sexual themes disappeared. Doll play involved typical family scenes.

Toward the end of the treatment (eighteen months), Kim's behavior was no longer characterized by unpredictable outbursts. His behavior improved significantly at school, he did not act out sexually inappropriately, and he was a play leader with other children. His parents reported that he was responsive and affectionate, and he was integrated into a regular kindergarten class.

COMMENTARY: This case study demonstrates the Jungian position that the psyche knows how to heal itself, and that children will go where they need to go. It should be pointed out that careful supervision and consultation were an integral part of the effectiveness of the play therapy intervention in this case. The profound nature of Kim's situation and diagnosis was certainly not outside the effective sphere of the play therapy intervention. The integration and development that occurs for the severely abused and fragmented child in play therapy is testimony to the resilience of children and the effectiveness of play therapy.

SOURCE: Allan, J., and Lawton-Speert, S. (1993). Play psychotherapy of a profoundly incest abused boy: a Jungian approach. *International Journal of Play Therapy* 2(1):33–48.

POSSIBLE *DSM-IV* DIAGNOSES:

295.10 Schizophrenia, Disorganized Type
V61.21 Sexual Abuse of Child
312.80 Conduct Disorder
313.81 Oppositional Defiant Disorder

PLAY THERAPY WITH A DISSOCIATIVE CHILD

AUTHOR: **Jane Gorman**

FOCUS: *Child-centered play therapy with a dissociative 10-year-old boy.*

INTRODUCTION: Steve was referred for psychotherapeutic intervention by his school. He exhibited bizarre and problematic behavior in the classroom and dissociative behavior in the playroom. A child-centered play therapy approach was utilized.

CASE STUDY: Steve was 10 years old and in the fourth grade when referred for psychotherapeutic services. Although he spoke in complete sentences and had a large vocabulary, he was difficult to understand. Steve's teacher reported that he was not able to write, but was able to read. In the classroom he was easily distracted, sought attention, disrupted the class, continued talking, and wandered out into the halls.

Evaluations indicated that Steve had average intelligence, speech difficulties, impulsive behavior, impaired attention and concentration, fine motor difficulties, perceptual problems, poor peer relationships, and severe emotional problems. Speech therapy and special academic placement were recommended in addition to mental health services.

INTERVENTION: The treatment process included twenty weeks of twice-weekly play therapy sessions. Initially Steve used the play times to talk fast and throughout the session. He began to play for brief periods, and by the fifth session was engaged in play for the entire session. Despite the wide variety of play materials available, Steve seldom used the toys, preferring instead to use empty boxes, water, window shades, and other miscellaneous objects.

In the play therapy sessions Steve immediately began referring to "Thomas," to whom Steve attributed much of his activity. There were sessions in which Steve would use "Thomas," "Thomas and me," or "I" interchangeably. This changed markedly in the fifteenth session, in which Steve locked the punching bag in the closet and began increasingly to use "I"; in the next ten sessions he no longer attributed his actions to Thomas. Although in the last four sessions prior to termination Steve referred to "John," he was able to claim many parts of his own behavior.

Steve's behavior in the playroom was characterized by his constant separation of affect from various situations, particularly by the use of loose associations. Gorman notes that loose associations served to allow expression of emotional content without clearly connecting it to a specific or appropriate context. Steve would use Thomas to accomplish this, to tell sadistic fantasies or explain playroom behavior that was aggressive, destructive, regressive, or messy. He would also use Thomas to extend his solitary activity into shared experiences in fantasy, thus addressing his feelings of aloneness and poor peer relationships.

The play therapy intervention was based on three goals: reduction of anxiety through the release of repressed impulses, opportunities for ego development, and enhancement of self-esteem. Steve's expression of impulses was described in his selection and use of play materials, many of which could be destroyed or used aggressively. Ego development occurred for Steve as he mastered the environment of the playroom. Gorman suggested that as Steve developed his mastery over objects he was able to imagine that he was the master of his life predicament as well. As Steve experienced the acceptance and regard of the therapist in the play process, his self-esteem grew.

Steve exhibited positive progress in the play therapy process. He moved from verbally expressing aggressive fantasies to acting them out in the play. Increased mastery of particular motor skills was evident, as well as an improved ability to communicate effectively. Steve's verbal behavior became more related to the content of his play. Articulation improved, and he was able to seek and acknowledge feedback on his communication. Steve progressed from "Thomas tells me what I can do and what I can't do" to claiming his own behavior. Although Gorman recommended continued therapeutic intervention, Steve's progress at the point of termination was clearly evident.

COMMENTARY: Steve's dissociative behavior in the play served the purpose of giving expression to the deficits in his emotional integration. This process was facilitated by the environment and process of play therapy. The freedom to express himself in an accepting and caring environment combined with the structure of the playroom and the relationship enabled Steve to address anxiety-producing and frightening issues. The safety of the play therapy process allows the child with dissociative behaviors to get past the hypervigilance of protecting self in order to explore self.

SOURCE: Gorman, J. N. (1972). Dissociation and play therapy: a case study. *JPN and Mental Health Services* 10(2):23–21.

POSSIBLE *DSM-IV* DIAGNOSES:

300.14   Dissociative Identity Disorder
295.10   Schizophrenia, Disorganized Type
314.01   Attention-Deficit/Hyperactivity Disorder, Combined Type
313.81   Oppositional Defiant Disorder
315.2   Disorder of Written Expression
315.39   Phonological Disorder

PLAY THERAPY WITH A REGRESSED SCHIZOPHRENIC ADOLESCENT GIRL

AUTHOR: **Bernadine Irwin**

FOCUS: *The use of play therapy with a schizophrenic girl hospitalized for decompensation and regressive behavior.*

INTRODUCTION: Jane (name given by reviewer) was a 16-year-old female who had been hospitalized with the diagnosis of Schizophrenia, Chronic Undifferentiated Type. The author's experience as a nurse in various psychiatric facilities led her to conclude that regressed patients were often ignored because of their inability to respond to traditional treatment methods. A brief play therapy program was developed with specific treatment objectives, using a child-centered approach.

CASE STUDY: The adolescent female presented in this case had been hospitalized following eight months of progressive decompensation. A social worker assigned to Jane's case described her home situation as "intolerable." She was unable to attend school, where she had been making high grades, and regressed to the point of necessitating hospitalization.

Jane was unable to control urine and feces, and was mute except for frequent repetitions of the word "yellow," particularly when anxious. She remained in bed throughout the day, except when taken to meals. There was no indication of affect, and she would stare without any expression. The social worker noted that during her two weeks in the hospital prior to the play therapy intervention, there was no eye contact given to any person.

INTERVENTION: Six sessions of child-centered play therapy were included in the treatment process. Prior to the beginning of treatment, seven behavioral objectives were established in order to assess progress: making occasional eye contact with others, leaving bed voluntarily and interacting, controlling urine and feces, occasionally making a facial expression, taking voluntary showers, wearing pressed clothes, and answering when spoken to.

The therapist had to help Jane to her feet and lead her to the playroom for the first session. She did not engage in any play during this session, choosing instead to stand and stare at the dollhouse while wringing her hands. In the last ten minutes of the session Jane sat down and repeated "yellow" over and over. Following the session, she returned to her bed. Before the second session the therapist found Jane at her bed getting help in dressing from a staff member. Although her appearance had not changed, the staff reported she was no longer incontinent. Jane willingly followed the therapist into the playroom and played with colors (especially yellow), the xylophone (the yellow key), and a ball. When the therapist summoned Jane for the third session, she was sitting in a corner of the room staring at the floor. The staff reported that she was voluntarily leaving her room and taking regular showers. The play routine was the same as the previous session, except that Jane made clear eye contact with the therapist at the end of the session and asked: "May I go now?"

Prior to the fourth session, Jane was found sitting in the day room reading a book. The staff reported that she had asked for the book, and that she was taking more interest in observing ward activities. She did not stay in her room except at night. When the therapist greeted her, she responded and stated that things were going "pretty good." The play session again was similar to the previous one. At the beginning of the fifth session Jane was again found reading in the day room. The staff reported that she had been overheard reading aloud around other patients. The play began with Jane coloring. When the therapist told her that the next session would be the last, she began striking the yellow key on the xylophone very hard. The therapist reflected her anger, to which Jane made eye contact, smiled, and continued her play.

Two months after completion of the play therapy, the therapist made a return visit to Jane, who was pleased to see her. Jane told the therapist that she had begun to attend school. She had achieved six out of seven of the treatment objectives, the exception being not wearing pressed clothes.

COMMENTARY: Play therapy has been demonstrated to be a safe and effective alternative in the treatment of severely impaired mental health clients. Although regressed and schizophrenic patients are often unresponsive to traditional forms of treatment, the freedom of the play therapy process and the safety of the play therapy relationship are effective in reaching these challenging individuals. The adolescent female in this study demonstrates both the efficacy and utility of play therapy with the schizophrenic population and with adolescents. Play reaches through and beyond many of the defenses of mental illness. The profound effects of the short-term play therapy are especially noteworthy.

SOURCE: Irwin, B. L. (1971). Play therapy for a regressed schizophrenic patient. *JPN and Mental Health Services* 9:30–32.

POSSIBLE *DSM-IV* DIAGNOSIS:

295.90   Schizophrenia, Undifferentiated Type

GROUP PLAY THERAPY WITH PSYCHOTIC ADOLESCENT GIRLS

AUTHORS: **Dorian Rose, Catherine Butler, and Florence Eaton**

FOCUS: *The use of group play therapy with seven adolescent girls hospitalized for psychotic behavior.*

INTRODUCTION: Group play therapy was used with seven adolescent females, ranging in age from 16 to 20, who had been hospitalized for some type of schizophrenic disorder. All of the group participants exhibited schizophrenic features and had manifested disturbances of psychotic proportions for some time prior to the intervention. A nondirective therapeutic play therapy approach was employed with the group, which met intensively for ten months.

CASE STUDY: The seven female group members were selected because they had substantial difficulty in expressing themselves verbally, were not optimally improving in their treatment, and all had shown an interest in the play materials provided. Four of the participants had been specifically diagnosed as schizophrenic, and the remaining three as "mentally defective," having an "inadequate personality," and suffering from "convulsive disorder with no organic deterioration." These conditions were considered chronic.

    The histories of the group participants were markedly similar. The majority had been psychiatrically referred prior to the hospitalization, were mentally ill for longer than one year, had experienced failure academically, and had no identified causes for the mental illness. Additionally, several of the following "neurotic traits" had been apparent during childhood: enuresis during puberty, aggression and discipline problems, play difficulties, and sibling rivalry. At the time the group was formed three participants had been assaultive and three had attempted self-injury.

INTERVENTION: For the first three months of the play therapy group, sessions were held five times a week for one hour; for the remaining seven months, sessions were held three times a week. One of the females discontinued therapy during the fourth month and another during the seventh month because they were unavailable due to a change in their home placement. The sessions were held in a special room equipped with toys and games, including dart guns, dollhouses, finger paints, playing cards, checkers, and other games. The authors pointed out that the group members had a high degree of freedom in terms of attendance and choice of activities. Due to the "destructive potentialities" of the group, two therapists were always present, with one taking a more active role than the other. Both therapists assumed the role of facilitator, and were careful not to initiate any activity.

The first two months of therapy involved gunplay and war games of various kinds. The following four months were dominated by arts and crafts, and the last four months involved primarily game activity.

As the group progressed, there was a measurable decrease in assaultiveness, destructiveness, temper tantrums, and self-injury. The group members engaged in increased verbalization, group games supplanted individual activities, and they began to gather in one area in the group play therapy room.

A two-year follow-up evaluation of the group members indicated that four of the patients had "strikingly improved" over any previous level of adjustment. Five of the six patients who had returned to the community had accepted outpatient treatment, and four of the patients were employed and were at least partially self-supporting. The authors noted that the behavior patterns that appeared to be most affected by the group play therapy process had been those involving hostility and aggression.

COMMENTARY: The social isolation prevalent in schizophrenic disorders and hospitalization can be effectively addressed in the process of group play therapy. The authors appropriately concluded that the use of play "provided a vehicle for modifying the inadequate and inappropriate social behavior" of the adolescent females in the group. Clearly, a verbally based group intervention would not have impacted this challenging group as meaningfully or effectively as the group play therapy. The participants were able to acquire a greater sense of belongingness, self-esteem, and self-control in the process of the group play. Group play therapy is effective, even with a population as challenging and unpredictable as that described in this case study.

SOURCE: Rose, D .M., Butler, C., and Eaton, F. L. (1954). Play group therapy with psychotic adolescent girls. *International Journal of Psychotherapy* 4:303–311.

POSSIBLE *DSM-IV* DIAGNOSES:

295.90   Schizophrenia, Undifferentiated Type
298.9   Psychotic Disorder NOS

9

Emotionally Disturbed Children

The behaviors of emotionally disturbed children do not differ significantly from those of well-adjusted children. What is different is the degree, frequency, and intensity of those behaviors. Emotionally disturbed children experience intense feelings of confusion, ambivalence, loss, lack of control, detachment, and poor relationships. Children cannot learn to cope or make adequate adjustments when their emotional energy is focused on defending a limited view of self. Individual and group play therapy provide for these children a safe environment, including a safe, consistent, and predictable adult—an environment in which they can play out the confusion and intensity of feelings they experience. The feelings of emotionally disturbed children are often inaccessible at a verbal level. Play is the concrete expression of children; it is their way of coping with their world. The cases in this section demonstrate the healing potential of the play therapy relationship with children who experience personal detachment and a broad range of emotional, social, and learning difficulties.

DEVELOPMENTAL PLAY GROUP COUNSELING WITH EMOTIONALLY DISTURBED CHILDREN

AUTHOR: Jim Gumaer

FOCUS: *The use of developmental play with a group of emotionally disturbed children in an elementary school setting.*

INTRODUCTION: Gumaer presented the development and implementation of a developmental play group with a group of emotionally disturbed children in an elementary school class of disturbed children. Gumaer was approached by the class teacher who sought a nonbehavioral intervention for the benefit of the eight students. The program designed was to "help children who are experiencing personal detachment and other emotional, social, or learning difficulties overcome these problems through the development of positive, loving interactions and attachments with important adults, who then serve as models for the children in learning how to relate to others."

RESEARCH METHODS & DESIGN: The self-contained classroom of emotionally disturbed children consisted of four boys and four girls. The children were 8 to 9 years old and possessed IQ scores in the normal range. Mean behavior scores were equal to or higher than the mean scores of atypical children in residential treatment centers.

The eight children were divided into two groups for the developmental play group intervention and met once a week for twelve weeks in forty-five-minute sessions. Standardized play activities were developed for the two groups. Prior to the implementation of treatment, the children were administered the Piers-Harris Self-Concept Scale.

INTERVENTION: The plans followed in each group were specific as to objectives, description of activities, and recommended counselor responses. Within these specific plans the facilitators focused on three primary concepts of nonverbal communication that were considered key to developmental play: touching, spacing, and using facial language.

Specific activities for the twelve sessions were outlined and included having the child draw an animal and then move and act like the animal, followed by discussion of how it felt; having the child close his or her eyes and then take the hand of the child on each side ("holding the paw of the animal on each side"); having the children pair up and trace the partner's body on large paper; and expressing feelings by pantomime.

RESULTS: One week after completion of the sessions, the self-concept scale was readministered. One child failed to complete the instrument properly, but the remaining seven showed an overall score increase of 44 points, a mean increase of 6.3 points per child.

On the qualitative level the classroom teacher reported that the learning that had occurred in the group sessions generalized to the classroom. The children were more appropriate in behaviors with their peers and interactions with the teacher, and discipline problems diminished. There was an increase in displays of "warmth and caring" in the classroom, and the general environment was reported to be more relaxed.

COMMENTARY: The opportunity to develop relationship skills in a nonthreatening and accepting environment such as a developmental play group proved beneficial for this group of emotionally disturbed children. Gumaer's presentation exhibited the successful adaptation of an approach to individual play therapy to a group setting. The issues of loss, detachment, and disruption that characterize emotionally disturbed children are positively impacted by a group play experience. Developmental play groups may be one positive way for school counselors to provide relief for children and teachers.

SOURCE: Gumaer, J. (1984). Developmental play in small group counseling with disturbed children. *The School Counselor* 31 (5):445–453.

POSSIBLE *DSM-IV* DIAGNOSIS:

Insufficient information provided in the study.

PLAY THERAPY TREATMENT OF EMOTIONAL DISTURBANCE AND TRICHOTILLOMANIA IN A CHILD WITH MILD MICROCEPHALY

AUTHOR: **John A. Perry**

FOCUS: *A qualitative case study of a boy with emotional disturbance, trichotillomania, and mild microcephaly using play therapy and family therapy.*

INTRODUCTION: Perry presented the case of Tim, a 9-year-old with a long history of emotional and physical problems. The microcephaly, considered a minor case, appeared to be a precipitating factor in considerable emotional difficulties, the most overt being the issue of trichotillomania. Perry provided considerable detail in his discussion of Tim's case, including case history and psychological theory. The treatment essentially amounted to a multimodal and multidisciplinary approach. Individual play therapy was a prominent aspect of the treatment plan. The study covered a treatment period of three and one-half years.

CASE STUDY: Tim was referred for treatment by a local government clinic. He was the first of two children of a couple who had been separated for nine months prior to the commencement of therapy. The microcephaly, diagnosed by a pediatric neurologist, was reportedly minimal (below the second percentile on a standard head-circumference chart). Tim had several specific learning disabilities, including disorders of spoken and written language.

Tim's mother reported numerous emotional and behavioral concerns. She described Tim as impulsive, aggressive, and destructive; he threw temper tantrums, had difficulty socializing with peers and adults, engaged in stealing and lying, and pulled out his hair (Tim presented in an initial evaluation with a small patch of hair beginning to grow on the crown of his head). He had also had difficulties with enuresis, poor attention span, and low self-esteem. Prior to the treatment described in this case study, multiple medications had been prescribed, including Benadryl, Ritalin, Cylert, Melaril, Dilantin, and megavitamins. These had varying degrees of success.

INTERVENTION: The "ecological systems" approach taken by Perry in the treatment of Tim initially incorporated a child-centered approach to weekly play therapy sessions and weekly family therapy. Perry described the playroom and the therapeutic process as unstructured, with the intent of allowing Tim to feel freedom from pressure to act in any certain way, and to project his own issues in any manner he chose. Tim initially engaged in doll play, during which he processed issues of anger toward his father. Detailed discussions emerged in the doll play regarding the rejection and loss that Tim was feeling. Tim channeled considerable aggression and frustration through various media, including pounding on clay.

Tim developed a positive therapeutic relationship with Perry, and soon began to look forward to the play therapy sessions. As Tim learned to verbalize feelings, his acting-out behaviors diminished outside the playroom.

COMMENTARY: Perry posited that there was a direct relationship between "losses and threatened losses" and Tim's hair-pulling behaviors. The hair-pulling, as well as the other difficulties noted above, diminished as Tim was able to process issues in the play therapy and as relationships at home began to stabilize. Perry appropriately noted that "individual insight-oriented directed therapy requires specific ego strengths of the patient that Tim did not have." The projective and developmentally appropriate nature of play therapy provided Tim with an environment in which to address concerns that had previously been treated from a noneffective medical approach. The positive results noted prevented the imminent hospitalization that was the next consideration for Tim's case.

SOURCE: Perry, J. A. (1988). *Reduction of trichotillomania in a microcephalic child: an ecological systems approach.* Unpublished doctoral dissertation, Union Graduate School, Cincinnati, OH.

POSSIBLE *DSM-IV* DIAGNOSES:

312.8   Conduct Disorder
313.81   Oppositional Defiant Disorder
312.39   Trichotillomania
307.6   Enuresis
314.9   Attention-Deficit/Hyperactivity Disorder NOS

GROUP PLAY THERAPY WITH EMOTIONALLY DISTURBED CHILDREN

AUTHOR: **Mortimer Schiffer**

FOCUS: *Group play therapy with emotionally disturbed children as part of a guidance program in a public elementary school.*

INTRODUCTION: Group play therapy has been demonstrated to be an effective intervention for children experiencing various difficulties. A group play therapy project for emotionally disturbed children in an elementary school setting was presented. The treatment was offered in a challenging environment, as the school was located in a slum area surrounded by industrial developments. There was a high incidence of delinquency and children were often left unsupervised due to the difficult financial situations of the neighborhood families. The public school reflected the neighborhood, with children bringing to the classroom the effects of family discord and neighborhood tensions. Group play therapy was offered to emotionally disturbed children for whom no additional services were available.

CASE STUDY: Several play therapy groups were organized, with eight groups meeting regularly at one point. Most groups were homogeneous in terms of age and gender. Schiffer described three children in one group that had been meeting for two years at the writing of the case study. Alfred, 8 years old and in the third grade, was reported to be shy, nervous, and unhappy. His behavior vacillated considerably from amenable and compliant to provocative and abusive. The school counselor's attempts to incorporate Alfred's parents in counseling proved unsuccessful as they were described as rigid and unsympathetic. Jack, aged 9 and also in the third grade, was a frequent truant. His father reacted with severe physical abuse, and his mother "babied" him, which the father resented intensely. Significant marital discord was reported. Jack's teacher reported that he demanded an unusual amount of attention from her and solicited overt expressions of affection. He acted out in the classroom for attention, and also attacked other children without provocation. Jack's parents also refused all offers of help and denied the existence of a problem. William was 7 years old when referred by his second-grade teacher. He was reported to have poor peer relationships and frequent temper tantrums, was restless and hyperactive, and required an inordinate amount of attention. The parents of all three boys, while unwilling to be involved in the intervention process, gave consent for participation in the play group.

INTERVENTION: A room set apart in the school building for the use of the play groups was equipped with tables, chairs, workbenches, and a sink. The play materials provided included doll families, doll furniture, paints, easels, sand, clay, paper, toys, and games. The play groups were led by teachers, supervised by a psychologist and social worker, and with Schiffer's consultation. Supervision meetings facilitated by Schiffer were held weekly. The play therapy groups met for an hour once a week.

Schiffer described the play groups as "neither programmed nor structured; motivation stemmed from the needs of the children." The leader was permissive, accepting, and neutral. Overt aggression was permitted within acceptable limits. Schiffer noted that "identification and transference phenomena were dramatically revealed in the children's play behavior."

RESULTS: All three boys exhibited improved behavior in the classroom. Alfred's teacher reported that he related better to her and to his classmates, and that he seemed happier in general. Jack also showed improvement, with decreased truancy, more security in his relationship with his teacher, and less inclination to monopolize the teacher's attention. He was also reported to be friendlier. William too exhibited improvement in his school adjustment; he was more responsive to his teacher, more amenable and compliant, and participated more in classroom activities.

COMMENTARY: Group play therapy has been demonstrated to be effective in assisting children in developing interpersonal and intrapersonal skills as well as facilitating the processing of emotional issues. Schiffer appropriately encouraged the incorporation of play therapy groups into the elementary school setting; although he did not promote its effects as a panacea, he did suggest that the therapeutic benefits are clear. He posited that the emotional deprivation experienced by children exhibiting some level of emotional disturbance may be addressed in the "positive surrogate identification" involved in the group play therapy process. Alfred, Jack, and William experienced this positive dynamic. Children in any treatment setting would experience the same.

SOURCE: Schiffer, M. (1957). A therapeutic play group in a public school. *Mental Hygiene* 41:185–193.

POSSIBLE *DSM-IV* DIAGNOSES:

312.9   Disruptive Behavior Disorder NOS
309.4   Adjustment Disorder with Mixed Disturbance of Emotions and Conduct
995.5   Neglect of Child

10

Enuresis and Encopresis Problems

Toilet training may be one of the most difficult tasks of childhood and may easily be one of the most trying and stressful experiences for parents with young children. Fortunately most children progress through this developmental task quite rapidly. However, some children relapse. Enuresis or wetting is common in preschool-age and early school-age children; some estimates claim that 15 to 20 percent of 5-year-olds experience nocturnal enuresis. Encopresis is usually defined as voluntary or involuntary fecal incontinence that results in soiled clothes and usually occurs more often in boys than girls. Enuresis and encopresis problems may not occur in the presence of other children, but are usually known by other children by the smell and because such information readily passes from one child to another as interesting information. Consequently, the resulting peer difficulties may have drastic consequences on a child's self-esteem, and other psychological problems secondary to the wetting or soiling problem may develop. Play therapy provides children with a safe place to act out the accompanying frustration, anger, and helplessness and restore a sense of personhood.

PLAY AND DRAMA THERAPY FOR ENURESIS
AND ACTING-OUT BEHAVIORS

AUTHOR: **Caroline Burton**

FOCUS: *Using hide-and-seek and peekaboo games within play therapy to treat a boy with enuresis, social withdrawal, and acting-out behaviors.*

INTRODUCTION: Burton presented the case of Tommy, a 7-year-old boy who was referred by his school and local child welfare. The presenting problems included enuresis, disruptive behavior, social withdrawal, and conflict with his foster mother. As background for the case study presented, various theoretical models of hide-and-seek play were discussed along with developmental considerations for peekaboo games. It was hypothesized that these games, typical of most children's play in early development, address many of the emotional and attachment issues of children in crisis.

CASE STUDY: Tommy had a long history of emotional difficulties. A psychological report described him as "very regressed," stating that the "intrusion of primitive thinking was interfering with his learning and social interaction." Tommy's play was described as infantile and fragmentary, absent of themes or sequencing. His foster mother reported considerable noncompliance and oppositional behavior. Tommy's history included early neglect and abuse as well as four previous foster placements. He had been diagnosed as having "psychogenic mental retardation" as well as an organic learning disability. Tommy was referred for therapy while a new foster placement was sought for him.

INTERVENTION: Tommy's foster mother brought him to his first play session. In the office Tommy was able to play only with clay, which involved hitting it and throwing it against the wall, with accompanying sounds of "kaka" and "peepee." The therapist attempted to lead Tommy into less regressive play, to which Tommy responded by banging his head against the wall. The second session began much like the first, with Tommy attempting to remain out of sight of the therapist, which she first identified as withdrawal; she then redefined it as "hiding" and commenced a game of peekaboo. Burton reported that Tommy was quickly engaged and spent the next year and a half in therapy playing progressively more advanced forms of hide-and-seek and peekaboo.

By the fourth month of treatment Tommy began introducing more fantasy and drama into his hide-and-seek games. He created elaborate stories and scenes and invented all of the roles in these stories. Throughout this phase he was essentially nonverbal. By the sixth and seventh months, Tommy was playing out specific and "traditional" roles and themes in the play. These included interactional games of burglar and victim, and doctor and patient, as well as other games involving aggression, rescue, and self-defense in which he played both sides of the issue. After the seventh month Tommy began to use the puppet theater and his final sessions included large dance dramas. Themes that developed dealt with feelings of abandonment and fear of parental loss. Tommy also expressed fear that his acting-out behaviors might cause his new foster parents to reject and abandon him.

RESULTS: In addition to the many positive strides in the play therapy, Tommy's social worker, foster mother, and teacher noted many important changes. He reportedly had improved impulse control, increased ability to delay gratification, and the ability to behave appropriately within stimulating settings in which he had been previously out of control. Tommy also exhibited improved peer interactions, had a more positive affect, and experienced improved cognitive skills. Surprisingly, although the enuresis was a primary presenting issue, the outcome of this concern was not addressed in the case presentation. The assumption is that there was substantial amelioration of this problem.

COMMENTARY: Play therapy has been effective with children experiencing issues of rejection and abandonment. The presenting concern of enuresis was not identified as a physiological issue, and was likely a somatic side effect of the multiple emotional issues. Within play therapy Tommy was given the experience of playing games in which he set up the rules. Burton noted the importance of Tommy being "in control of the interaction" and feeling "understood." She further suggested that the symbolic nature of the play could be viewed in terms of object constancy and as reflecting Tommy's developing progress toward a sense of personal identity. The opportunity for self-expression led to the benefit of self-validation. Although Burton suggested that Tommy did not have the opportunity to process important issues as he did not remain in therapy long enough, the therapeutic benefit of his play therapy experience is clear.

SOURCE: Burton, C. (1986). Peekaboo to "All the all the outs in free" hide-and-seek as a creative structure in drama therapy. *The Arts in Psychotherapy* 13(2):129–136.

POSSIBLE *DSM-IV* DIAGNOSES:

307.6   Enuresis
313.81 Oppositional Defiant Disorder
313.89 Reactive Attachment Disorder of Infancy or Early Childhood
319.0   Mental Retardation, Severity Unspecified
V61.20 Parent–Child Relational Problem

COGNITIVE-BEHAVIORAL PLAY THERAPY IN THE TREATMENT OF ENCOPRESIS

AUTHORS: **Susan Knell and Douglas Moore**

FOCUS: *Use of cognitive-behavioral play therapy with primary encopresis and language deficits.*

INTRODUCTION: Knell and Moore presented the case of a 5-year-old male triplet with primary nonretentive encopresis as well as a language disorder. The treatment included a structured, focused cognitive-behavioral play therapy program in combination with a behavioral management program implemented by the parents.

CASE STUDY: The child was reported to be the quietest and most passive of a set of male triplets. He reportedly did not want to be like his brothers, and became angry when adults could not tell them apart. Psychoeducational testing noted an average intellectual range, but indicated evidence of developmental expressive and articulation language disorders. The child's parents reported that he soiled several times daily, and would remain in soiled clothing unless changed by an adult. He had been toilet trained for urination at the age of 3, but resisted all attempts at training to use the toilet for bowel movements. He denied any phobia about the toilet, but stated that he did not want to learn to use the toilet like his brothers.

INTERVENTION: Baseline data were collected for twelve days prior to any treatment intervention. During this time the parents recorded the number of soiling incidents, as operationally defined by the authors. The therapist then employed cognitive-behavior play therapy with the child and worked with the parents in the behavioral management of the child's encopresis. According to the authors, cognitive-behavioral play therapy differs from other behavioral treatments of encopresis in that it helps the child incorporate "positive self-statements and more adaptive coping skills." Additionally, this approach incorporates cognitive interventions that reportedly directly address the "child's distortions and misperceptions about the presenting problem."

The child initially engaged in play that exhibited the themes of his toileting struggle and competition with his brothers. The cognitive-behavioral intervention was developed following the emerging theme of a stuffed bear being repeatedly "flushed away." The following treatment situation was given as an example of the developed intervention: "The therapist acknowledged the repetition of this theme (identification of irrational belief), gradually had the bear sit on the toilet (shaping) without getting flushed down (exposure, response prevention), and stated that the bear would not get flushed away (changing an irrational belief)." This led to the child's beginning to "compete" with the bear, expressing a desire to "beat the bear" in the acquiring of stars in a contingency management program similar to the one being established with the parents.

The behavioral management program implemented by the parents began simultaneously with the play therapy. The program consisted of a sticker program in which the child was reinforced for appropriate toilet use and not soiling his pants.

Positive results were reported. The child was soiling during the baseline period approximately 77 percent of the time. After the twelfth session the child spontaneously and regularly used the toilet for bowel movements. Following the fourteenth session, appropriate toileting without soiling accidents was reported. Follow-up at eight and forty-five months noted a continuation of this pattern.

COMMENTARY: Knell and Moore suggested several benefits of the cognitive-behavioral play therapy intervention in their discussion of this case. They proposed that the soiling behavior provided the child with a way to be different and gave him identity. Play therapy in turn provided the opportunity for cognitive self-perceptions and self-statements to be addressed; the cognitive-behavioral elements of the play therapy provided the child with the opportunity to address his anger and "modify the cognitive distortions associated with it." Additionally, the authors suggested that the child's language deficits made aspects of the play therapy, such as "symbolic modeling," more useful to him than a more verbal approach to treatment. Certainly it appears that this child benefited from the opportunity to express his behaviors and emotions in the play modality, and he was the primary choreographer of the behavioral intervention designed. The concurrent work with the parents appeared to facilitate the translation of learned experiences in the play to the soil-ing situation at home. The significant positive results attest to the child's taking control of his issues, both in the play and at home.

SOURCE: Knell, S. M., and Moore, D. J. (1990). Cognitive-behavioral play therapy in the treatment of encopresis. *Journal of Clinical Child Psychology* 19(1):55–60.

POSSIBLE *DSM-IV* DIAGNOSES:

307.7   Encopresis
315.31   Expressive Language Disorder
315.39   Phonological Disorder

PSYCHODYNAMIC PLAY THERAPY
WITH AN ENCOPRETIC CHILD

AUTHORS: **Samuel Warson, Marilyn Caldwell, Alice Warinner, A'Lelia Kirk, and Reynold Jensen**

FOCUS: *Use of psychodynamic play therapy with a young girl with primary encopresis since infancy.*

INTRODUCTION: M.J., a 6-year-old girl who had exhibited encopresis since infancy, was referred for psychotherapy following several unsuccessful medical interventions. She was described as having "psychogenic" encopresis, including the comorbid symptoms of temper tantrums, fears, and excessive thumb sucking. Psychodynamic play therapy was chosen as the treatment modality.

CASE STUDY: M.J. was the second of three children in an upper-middle-class family. Her parents were described as highly intellectual, compulsive, and exhibiting very little warmth. The mother was reported to be emotionally disturbed and preoccupied with feelings of failure as a parent. Both parents were reported to be disgusted with M.J.'s condition, and the father was described as angry at her for not responding to the various treatment applications attempted. He was also angry at the physicians for their lack of success in treating her.

M.J. was described by her mother as a happy infant until the age of 2, when her brother was hospitalized. She was frequently cared for by neighbors and babysitters at this time. The family also had to sell their house and move, as the father had transferred to a new job and was available only on weekends for three months prior to the move. M.J. received scant attention during this period, and changed from a contented child to a whiny and demanding one. Between the ages of 2 and 3, M.J. was reported to purposefully restrain her bowel movements. The encopretic behavior began at this time. She exhibited indifference to the problem, refusing to "cooperate with the mother who spent a lot of time keeping her clean." Interventions by the family pediatrician were unsuccessful.

INTERVENTION: M.J. was seen in a nondirective and interpretive form of play therapy for forty-two sessions over fourteen months. During the initial play therapy sessions, she moved restlessly from one play activity to the next, and called the toys "dirty, black, nasty brown, or broken." If she touched any of these "condemned" toys, she immediately ran to the sink to wash her hands. She seemed afraid of finger paint and clay, and apparently soiled frequently during the play sessions.

M.J.'s play progressed to smearing the finger paints while she verbally attacked her siblings. Although initially this caused considerable anxiety, she progressed in this play through one session where she spent the hour aggressively pushing the "brother" doll through a mound of brown finger paint. M.J. gradually moved to expressing hostility toward her mother though doll play, with mother dolls being described as angry and punishing. She eventually began engaging in nurturing activities with the dolls, and introduced play in which the dolls had bowel movements using clay and finger paints. During the final sessions, M.J. began to use the paints and clay in a constructive manner, and expressed the desire to terminate therapy since she was no longer soiling.

The mother was also seen separately in therapy. In follow-up visits, two and twelve months after termination, M.J. continued to be symptom free, and was described by her mother as a "changed" child. M.J. and her mother exhibited increased confidence and positive affect.

COMMENTARY: The authors suggested that both M.J. and her mother benefited from the acceptance and support of psychotherapy and the removal of the stigma of an inadequate mother and a nonconforming child. They offer the psychodynamic interpretation that the "emotional disturbances in mother and child were similar (resentment and hostility, fears of rejection and abandonment)." Play therapy offered M.J. the opportunity to process anger and hostility in the safety of the playroom, instead of through the encopresis. The tactile play with the clay and finger paints gave expression to intrapsychic needs that previously had no outlet for expression. In addition to addressing relationship concerns in the play, the encopretic child has the opportunity to process the self-esteem and control issues inherent to this childhood challenge.

SOURCE: Warson, S., Caldwell, M., Warinner, A., Kirk, A., and Jensen, R. (1954). The dynamics of encopresis. *American Journal of Orthopsychiatry* 24:402–415.

POSSIBLE *DSM-IV* DIAGNOSES:

787.6   Encopresis with Constipation and Overflow Incontinence
V61.20   Parent–Child Relational Problem
313.81   Oppositional Defiant Disorder

11

Fear and Anxiety

A commonly expressed concern of parents and teachers is how to cope with children's anxieties and fears. Anxiety over separation from parents is frequently identified in initial referral sessions and in parent training groups. Play therapy provides an accepting and nonthreatening environment in which children are able to express their fears and anxieties through the safety of symbolic play. What cannot be talked out can be played out in a manner that allows the child to move at his own pace as his level of comfort dictates. In the process of playing out frightening experiences, children experience being in control of the frightening experience because they are in control of the play and can thus determine the outcome. This chapter illustrates the effectiveness of play procedures in alleviating school phobia, anxiety attacks, self-injuring hair pulling, and fear of pain. The demonstrated effectiveness of play therapy leads us to recommend the use of this approach in hospital settings where children often experience severe stress brought on by a strange and threatening environment over which they have no control.

EXTREME ANXIETY IN A PRIMARY-GRADE CHILD

AUTHOR: **Eugene D. Alexander**

FOCUS: *Play therapy in an elementary school setting with a highly anxious, withdrawn child who would shake his hands as though they were foreign objects.*

INTRODUCTION: The emotional healing power of the play therapy relationship is demonstrated in this case of Chucky, an extremely anxious, seemingly detached child, whose elementary school teacher described him as having a faraway look in his eyes and who would sometimes not respond when spoken to. At other times he would respond in irrelevant, unrelated sentences. She reported times when Chucky would cling desperately to her. This case report is unique in that the play therapy took place in an elementary school building. The play therapist utilized any available quiet place and the toys and materials were carried in a suitcase. The approach to play therapy was child-centered, with an emphasis on the importance of the relationship and a willingness to trust the child.

CASE STUDY: Chucky began his once-a-week play therapy experience by standing in the corner of the room shaking his hands in the air. He briefly examined the toys and then spent most of the remainder of the session rooted to one spot in the room checking out the therapist with sidelong glances. In succeeding sessions Chucky began to talk a little about things that raised his anxiety—walls of the building, storms, big animals, time—but he played very little, seeming to prefer just to sit and stare at the clock or the therapist's watch and call out the time. Slowly he began to verbalize his anxieties that the walls would fall in, that the next minute would not come, or that a big snake would come in and eat him. Chucky was then able to hold the therapist's hand and look at his watch. This physical contact seemed to provide the security Chucky needed to become actively and expressively involved with the toys. Chucky became aggressive and destructive with the toys, even struck the therapist, and limits had to be set.

An interesting development was Chucky's loss of interest in the toys and his complete focus on making physical contact with the therapist, seeming to need to touch all parts of his body and to sit on his lap. In later sessions Chucky verbally expressed anger toward his father. Alexander reported that much of Chucky's anxiety seemed to be related to his father's attempt to control and mold him. Chucky's attitude toward his father changed gradually, and his conversation during play therapy indicated he was having more of a mutual sharing relationship with his father. Alexander reported that Chucky developed new confidence in himself and was able to accept the love that his father had for him.

COMMENTARY: This case amply demonstrates the power of the play therapy relationship and the value of allowing the child to choose the communication medium he or she feels comfortable with at the moment. As is often the case, Chucky needed to be accepted on his own terms when he said nothing and did nothing. That kind of total acceptance is freeing to children and facilitates their movement toward expressing and exploring those parts of their lives they may find frightening. This case study suggests the importance of being patient and understanding with the child in play therapy.

SOURCE: Alexander, E. (1964). School-centered play therapy program. *Personnel and Guidance Journal* 43:256–261.

POSSIBLE *DSM-IV* DIAGNOSES:

300.02 Generalized Anxiety Disorder
300.14 Dissociative Identity Disorder
V61.20 Parent–Child Relational Problem

PLAY THERAPY WITH A CHILD
WHO HAD PULLED OUT ALL OF HER HAIR

AUTHORS: **Karen Barlow, Garry Landreth, and JoAnna Strother**

FOCUS: *Play therapy with a 4-year-old child who reacted to being "dethroned" by a younger sibling, fear of separation from her mother, and overcontrolling caregivers by pulling out all of her hair and eating it.*

INTRODUCTION: The authors suggest a parallel between early emotional development in the family and emotional growth in play therapy. Nancy lived with her mother, father, and sister, aged 4 months. Her mother was overprotective of the 4-month-old infant and seldom had any time for Nancy. In addition, the mother suffered from an illness that resulted in frequent hospitalization for periods of several days. It seemed likely that Nancy's fear was associated with her perception of the lack of anything permanent in her life. In addition, Nancy's mother and grandmother were overcontrolling and placed limits on almost all of her behavior. Nancy reacted by rebelling. In the once-a-week sessions in the playroom, the therapist took a child-centered nondirecting approach.

CASE STUDY: In the first session Nancy tentatively explored the room. By the middle of the second session she was playing with the sand and water. In the third session she shoved two baby dolls into the stove and took their place in the baby bed while she sucked on a bottle. Baby play continued as the primary act in the next three sessions. Nancy further released her emotions by crumbling play dough and walking in it, and spilling paint. In the fifth session she had an angry outburst, threw the baby dolls out of their bed, got into their bed, sucked on the bottle, and then climbed into the therapist's lap with the baby bottle and wanted to be rocked. In this fifth week the therapist noticed wisps of fine baby hair covering Nancy's head. Baby play became a thing of the past after the fifth session.

In the seventh session the therapist noted that Nancy's head was covered with short blond hair. Painting, cutting up play dough, sticking her hands into the paint, and using lots of glue and paper became the primary play activities. During a role-play episode in the seventh session, Nancy indicated her awareness of her hair-pulling habit by saying, "When Mother says 'No,' you suck your thumb and pull your hair and eat it." Nancy's therapy was terminated after eight sessions.

COMMENTARY: The play therapy experience provided Nancy with a way in which to organize her experiences, express her feelings, and explore relationships. The authors concluded that the atmosphere created by the play therapist was the single most important factor of the therapeutic procedure and enabled Nancy to feel a freedom to express herself that she had never felt before. Nancy's play with babies, bottles, and baby bed provided her a unique experience through which she experimented and began to resolve her inner conflict. As in this case, sometimes important actual events in children's lives fail to enter either into their play or into their associations. Nancy never pulled out her hair in the playroom or acted out this procedure. She did refer verbally to the behavior once. The regrowth of Nancy's hair is dramatic evidence of the effectiveness of play therapy.

SOURCE: Barlow, K., Landreth, G., and Strother, J. (1985). Child-centered play therapy: Nancy from baldness to curls. *The School Counselor* 34(1):347–356.

POSSIBLE *DSM-IV* DIAGNOSIS:

312.39   Trichotillomania

USE OF STRUCTURED PLAY TO DISCOVER THE CAUSE OF THE FEAR OF BEING KIDNAPPED

AUTHOR: **Jacob Conn**

FOCUS: *The use of structured play therapy to assist a child in coming to terms with the cause of her fears.*

INTRODUCTION: A structured play situation has been found useful in the intervention of many children's problems, such as somatic complaints, sibling rivalry, car sickness, tics, and parental neglect. The case study provided as an example of this intervention is a child who was afraid of being kidnapped. The procedure outlined allows the parent to provide information regarding the child's problem, thereby reducing the parent's tension and overconcern. It also provides the clinician an opportunity to ascertain what, if any, role the parent may play in the child's presenting problem.

CASE STUDY: For approximately two years 9-year-old Harriet had been afraid of the dark. She believed there might be kidnappers in the dark, and consequently could not tolerate bedtime unless her father lay down with her until she fell asleep. After hearing about the kidnapping and killing of three children, she was unable to sleep without someone near, and even then often cried in her sleep. Harriet told her father she was afraid the kidnappers would take her younger sister away.

INTERVENTION: Harriet's mother was interviewed first to obtain Harriet's and the family's background information. After it was discovered that financial problems were causing the mother severe anxiety, she was referred for her own therapy. During testing Harriet was found to have a reading problem and was referred to a special remedial class. It was also learned that Harriet never went into a dark room alone, was afraid of strangers, and cried easily.

   In the playroom Harriet was allowed to explore the various toys. The therapist gave no formal information regarding what was to happen in the playroom or what her mother had said about her problem. Harriet was put at ease and shown acceptance. After a few minutes she was asked to come and sit next to the dollhouse. The therapist proceeded to illustrate Harriet's problem by using dolls and doll furniture. Allowing children to speak through dolls enables them to present their view of a problem and their role in it.

In the first session, Harriet said she was afraid of the dark and hid under her covers. She also volunteered that she was afraid a kidnapper might come and take her younger sister, but then confided that it was only the doll who said that, and it wasn't really true. The second session began with the therapist again selecting the specific toys for the specific scenario and asking Harriet to summarize what they had learned. Harriet responded that the two dolls had been kidnapped, and it was all in the big girl's thoughts. The therapist then added another doll and had Harriet speak for each doll. In this way Harriet was able to share that she hated her little sister because she "got everything" and was "a lot of trouble" and she wished she could get rid of her. The therapist added a male adult doll as the kidnapper and asked Harriet several questions. During this interchange Harriet admitted she felt she had lost her father's love to her little sister, and she wanted a kidnapper to come and take her sister away. The therapist did not stay within the fantasy of the play situation, but had Harriet identify the bigger girl doll as herself and state she had made up the fear of the dark and the kidnapper in her own mind.

At the beginning of the third session the therapist asked Harriet what she wanted to play. Harriet responded that she wanted to play what they had done before. Again, through the use of the dolls and the therapist's carefully worded questions, Harriet was able to realize she had thought about the fear of the dark and the kidnappers so long that she had made herself scared. She also acknowledged that she wasn't thinking those thoughts anymore and was able to go to bed without being afraid of either the dark or kidnappers. Her mother reported after the third session that there had been marked improvement. Harriet could now enter dark rooms and turn on the lights and go to bed without crying or needing her father to stay with her. Her mother also noted that Harriet was able to interact with strangers more easily.

In the fourth and subsequent sessions Harriet and the therapist continued to work through her feelings of having to share her father with her sister. Harriet continued to acknowledge how she had made up the stories and had ended up frightening herself. The seventh and eighth sessions were two months apart, with the ninth and final session five months later. "At the ninth session the child was asked: How are you? A: All right. Q: Are you scared any? A: No. Q: Why? A: I learned there was nothing in the dark to be afraid of. Q: Who was scaring you? A: It was myself" (Conn 1941, p. 749).

Harriet's mother continued to report improvement. Harriet was playing with children her age rather than dominating younger children, and she was doing better in reading. The mother's own therapy was helping her reduce her anxiety attacks, resulting in less stress in the home. It appeared the intervention in this family brought about lasting and positive results.

COMMENTARY: This form of structured play intervention places the emphasis on the child's ability to express feelings and sort out the cause of the problem. It provides for reorientation and then synthesis of the child's experiences. All this occurs with the setting up of specific play scenarios, consistent with the child's reality, by a caring, accepting, and insightful therapist. The vehicle of play with the dolls provides enough emotional distance for the child to allow this to occur. As this case shows, the child is the one who reveals the root cause of the fears and is skillfully guided to further self-realization.

SOURCE: Conn, J. (1941). The treatment of fearful children. *American Journal of Orthopsychiatry* 11:744–751.

POSSIBLE *DSM-IV* DIAGNOSES:

300.02 Generalized Anxiety Disorder (Overanxious Disorder of Childhood)
309.24 Adjustment Disorder with Anxiety
V61.20 Parent–Child Relational Problem
V61.08 Sibling Relational Problem
315.00 Reading Disorder

HOME PLAY THERAPY AND TOILET TRAINING

AUTHOR: **Natalie Rogers Fuchs**

FOCUS: *The use of play therapy at home by a mother to alleviate a child's fear of pain during bowel movements.*

INTRODUCTION: Despite efforts by her parents and pediatricians, 1½-year-old Janet would not allow herself to have a bowel movement because she was afraid of possible pain. Through the use of play therapy at home, provided by her mother, Janet was able to overcome this fear.

CASE STUDY: Janet was constipated as an infant and occasionally experienced pain during elimination. Some rectal fissures that probably also caused pain were discovered on two or three other occasions while she was still an infant. Now 1½ years old, Janet cried during diaper changes and avoided the new potty chair. As medical exams found no physical reason for the current problem, the mother sought a psychological solution.

Janet's mother was instructed to provide play therapy for her daughter in the home. The mother-therapist introduced specific toys for these sessions: dolls, furniture, a potty chair, toilet paper, and brown clay. In the initial session Janet surprised her mother-therapist by attempting to sit on the toy toilet. She did so playfully and without any expression of fear. Janet then moved on to dollhouse play, which continued for several sessions. The mother-therapist then added brown plasticine to the selection of toys, and play for the next few sessions focused on Janet's making brown cakes for her parents. She made more and more cakes but did not overtly communicate any connection between the cakes and fecal material. Next, Janet put diapers on the doll and instructed the doll to say repeatedly, with increasing emotion, "B.m. hurt you." The mother-therapist continued to reflect Janet's feelings: "The baby thinks the b.m.'s hurt too much."

Janet next relabeled the cakes as b.m.'s and began putting them in the play toilet and around the dollhouse. She asked her mother to eat one, her mother-therapist responded that it would give her a tummyache but that she would pretend to eat it. Janet was delighted with this response and continued to be preoccupied with the idea of b.m.'s in her mother's tummy.

RESULTS: Janet stopped displaying negative behaviors or emotions about her bowel movements and returned to being a pleasant child. She began using her potty chair without any further problems. Two years later, at the age of 3½, she still had no problems with bowel movements. Her development continued to be normal and typical. These special playtimes were used to assist Janet through two additional stressors during these two years: the emergency departure of her mother to the hospital for an appendectomy and the arrival of a baby sister.

The mother-therapist indicated that she also noted changes in herself. She stated that she experienced increased patience with Janet and a willingness to listen to her. As the mother's ability to accept Janet's feelings grew, she found it easier to express her own attitudes to her daughter. The mother-therapist believed that accepting her daughter's feelings without judging them was the key to the successful outcome of the play therapy at home.

COMMENTARY: Janet clearly played out the fears of her situation through the use of the brown plasticine. Assisted by her mother's acceptance of her feelings, Janet mastered her anxiety and put herself back on a normal developmental track.

The mother-therapist and author of this case, Natalie Rogers Fuchs, is the daughter of Carl Rogers. Her father recommended that she read Virginia Axline's *Play Therapy*[1] to build on her previous experience with children in therapeutic settings. This may well have been one of the first forms of filial therapy as later developed by Bernard Guerney.[2] As professional play therapists, we must remember to utilize the power of an effective parent–child relationship. With proper training parents are able to be competent and effective therapeutic agents in their own home and with their own children.

---

1. Virginia Axline, *Play Therapy* (Boston: Houghton Mifflin, 1947).
2. Bernard Guerney, "Filial Therapy: Description and Rationale," *Journal of Consulting Psychology*, 28, 1964, pp. 304–360.

SOURCE: Fuchs, N. R. (1957). Play therapy at home. *Merrill-Palmer Quarterly* 3:89–95.

POSSIBLE *DSM-IV* DIAGNOSIS:

300.29   Specific Phobia, Situational Type

BRIEF PLAY THERAPY FOR STAMMERING

AUTHOR: **David M. Levy**

FOCUS: *Using a form of brief play therapy with a 2-year-old boy who began stammering after being hit and scratched by another child in day care.*

INTRODUCTION: Continuing problems often result after a child has had a specific traumatizing experience. In this case Paul was attacked by a child and responded with high anxiety. Initially that anxiety was manifested by withdrawal, but additional reactions of stammering and a general fearful demeanor also developed.

CASE STUDY: Paul, a 26-month-old child, had developed speech rapidly and had a larger than typical vocabulary without any history of speech problems. Within the span of a week, another child had hit and scratched Paul on two occasions. This was reportedly the first time he had experienced this kind of behavior. He did not hit back and appeared to respond to the initial incident with indifference. After the second incident, however, Paul began stammering and developed a generally fearful demeanor. He was referred to play therapy approximately one week after his stammering began.

INTERVENTION: Paul's stammering was considered to be the result of anxiety due to the two attacks. To provide Paul with the opportunity to release his anxiety, the attacks would be reenacted through the use of toys within the play therapy milieu. This reenactment would be repeated until Paul was able to discharge his anxiety by being aggressive. This was accomplished in four play therapy sessions.

Paul's first session was typical. He explored the room, touching and naming toys. Clay, often used in this form of brief therapy, was introduced, and Paul manipulated it in a tentative manner. The second session began with spontaneous, child-directed play. Paul then asked the play therapist to break off some clay and initiated interactive play, using the clay, with the therapist. Once this interaction had been established, the play therapist asked Paul what the boy at school did to him. Paul responded by making a slapping movement at both cheeks. The play therapist picked up two dolls, labeling one as Paul and the other as the other boy. Reenacting the slapping incident, the therapist asked, "Then what does Paul do?" Paul moved to hit the doll, stopped mid-move, and asked to leave the room. After being redirected to other play, Paul was able to remain in the playroom until the end of the session.

During initial spontaneous play in the third session, Paul exhibited short displays of aggression. After about thirty minutes the play therapist again introduced the slapping incident through the doll play. This time Paul hit the doll out of the therapist's hands and onto the floor, then stomped on it. He immediately asked for his nanny (who brought him to play therapy), but made no attempt to leave the playroom. Paul was then able to engage in other play, some of it aggressive, including aggression toward the play therapist.

Following this session, Paul's mother reported a cessation of the stammering and fearful attitude. Follow-up one and two years after play therapy indicated Paul had no recurring problems with stammering. His parents and school personnel reported normal, healthy development.

COMMENTARY: Paul's ability to deal so rapidly with the anxiety may have been due in part to the quick referral for play therapy after the onset of his stuttering. The decision to select this form of brief therapy, release or abreactive play therapy, was based on awareness of the connection between the attacks by the other child and Paul's maladaptive response.

During Paul's second and third sessions his anxiety disruptions were clear. The play therapist using this approach must be able to identify the appropriate time to introduce the abreactive play. The child must be able to tolerate a certain amount of anxiety. Paul displayed this ability by being able to remain in the playroom and engage in other play. It should also be noted that acting out the anxiety reactions in play enabled Paul to discharge the anxiety through aggressive play.

This approach to play therapy would be applicable to many children who have various maladaptive responses to a specific, disturbing experience.

SOURCE: Levy, D. (1939). Release therapy in young children. *Child Study* 16(1):141–143.

POSSIBLE *DSM-IV* **DIAGNOSIS:**

307.0   Stuttering

BRIEF PLAY THERAPY:
PINOCCHIO AND SCHOOL PHOBIA

AUTHOR: **Theodore J. Machler**

FOCUS: *Brief treatment of school phobia through the use of hand puppets playing out the Pinocchio theme.*

INTRODUCTION: Puppetry is used to assist a child in expressing feelings and to work through problems in a nonthreatening manner. The use of the Pinocchio theme is highlighted in therapy with a 10-year-old girl who exhibited school phobia. The Pinocchio story was selected by the therapist because it deals with a young boy who has difficulty with school and shows how, despite his troubles and irresponsible behavior, he ends up better than he began.

CASE STUDY: Nora had begun describing seeing "little brown men" during hallucinations that coincided with her fear of going to school. When initially referred to a community guidance center, she was able to tolerate going to school only one day a week. Nora completed a course of brief therapy, consisting of five consecutive sessions.

INTERVENTION: In the first session Nora was reluctant to engage in play. After reassurance from the therapist, Nora spent the majority of the session playing with the dollhouse, acting out scenes of the mother and baby in the house while Nora and her father sat outside and talked.

In the second session Nora continued to maneuver the dolls around in the dollhouse, then decided to put on a puppet show for the dolls. For the remainder of the session Nora and the therapist acted out scenes of rescue using maiden, beast, and hero puppets. During this puppet play Nora totally ignored the Pinocchio puppets.

In the third session Nora continued to act out scenes similar to those in the previous session and then added the Pinocchio puppets. Her dramatic puppet play centered around Pinocchio's missing school even though warned of trouble by Jiminy Cricket. Nora insisted that a good fairy would rescue Pinocchio and would only tentatively consider that Pinocchio would return to school.

Pinocchio play permeated the entire fourth session. Nora manipulated the Pinocchio puppet while the therapist played the parts of the other characters. There was extensive dialogue, with Pinocchio admitting that he liked school and wanted to learn, but that he had his reasons for not wanting to go to school. Gepetto and the good fairy repeatedly told Pinocchio that they loved him and tried to talk him into going to school. Pinocchio would answer only that he had his reasons and would just pretend to be sick and stay home. Nora had Pinocchio request that the good fairy give him a magic wand so he could get nice things for Gepetto.

During the final session Nora initiated talking with the therapist, expressing her excitement over what she was learning in school. Nora and the therapist discussed the fact that her parents loved her and how she felt about that. She admitted the little brown men had not been real and asked the therapist to reassure her parents that they would not return. Nora appeared pleased about the changes that occurred.

COMMENTARY: Nora was able to communicate, through the use of puppets and the Pinocchio story theme, the dynamics of her school phobia. Using this form of dramatic play she was able to work through her feelings regarding her parents and free herself to enjoy school. This case highlights the facilitative use of a familiar and common child's story as a metaphor for children to work out their own very real problems.

SOURCE: Machler, T. J. (1965). Pinocchio in the treatment of school phobia. *Bulletin of the Menninger Clinic* 29(4):212–219.

POSSIBLE *DSM-IV* DIAGNOSES:

300.23   Social Phobia
300.29   Specific Phobia, Situational Type

FOCUSED PLAY TO RESOLVE SEPARATION ANXIETY

AUTHORS: **Mary Ellen Milos and Steven Reiss**

FOCUS: *The effective use of separation-relevant play to reduce separation anxiety in young children.*

INTRODUCTION: Play has long been understood from the child development view as a way children develop mastery. A basic assumption of play therapy is that play can reduce anxiety associated with many psychological problems. This study explored the effectiveness of nondirected and directed play with young children experiencing separation anxiety as they played with toys directly related to the anxiety producing experience.

RESEARCH METHODS & DESIGN: The Hall inventory was used by teachers to rate the level of difficulty children had in separating from their parents. The thirty-two boys and thirty-two girls, 2 to 6 years of age, were randomly assigned to one of four groups: free play, directed play, modeling, and the control group. Pre- and postmeasures of speech disturbance were also taken to assess the child's anxiety level. The speech disturbance measure was used to identify the level of speech disturbance evident in each child's response to six anxiety-relevant and four nonanxiety-relevant questions.

INTERVENTION: Each of the three treatment groups was presented with the same toys: a dollhouse, furniture, and flexible dolls arranged to look like the nursery school. The children in the control group were provided with several wooden puzzles, blocks, crayons, and coloring books. The children in all four groups received three individual, ten-minute play sessions with two to three days between sessions. All sessions for the children in the treatment groups were conducted by the same adult female. This adult was unaware of the purposes of the study but was given specific instructions to use with each type of group. Children in the free play group were told they could play with any of the dolls and toys they wanted. The directed play group was shown the dollhouse and teacher's desk and so on that served to identify the dollhouse specifically with the nursery school. The children were also instructed to identify the dolls as teacher, child, and mommy. A scenario was then described, such as "Mommy brings the child to school and then. . . ." In the modeling group the adult controlled the behavior of the children by playing out make-believe scenes of parents bringing children to school, focusing on separation scenes, feelings of fear and anger, and then the possible positive feelings of the child. The control group children were simply allowed to use the toys and materials in any way they liked.

RESULTS: The opportunity for children to play with anxiety-relevant toys in the presence of a nonjudgmental adult resulted in a dramatic reduction of anxiety. There was no significant difference in the results between the three treatment groups.

The results appeared to be tied to factors about the play itself. As might be expected, there was more separation-relevant play in the directed play sessions than by children in the free play sessions, but there was no significant difference in the reduction of anxiety in the respective children. Apparently the most important factor was the quality of separation-relevant play. Higher quality of play was directly related to lower anxiety levels in the children. High and low quality of play, however, was not found to be tied to whether the children were in the free play or directed play sessions. This indicates it is the individual child's level of emotional involvement in the play and not the setting in which this play occurs that influences the quality of play.

The authors acknowledge that while this study was not meant to be a clinical-outcome study comparing types of play therapy, the point is made that the free play was an analog of child-centered play therapy, the directed play an analog of structured play therapy, and the modeling reflected modeling procedures used by many play therapists.

COMMENTARY: This study again supports the basic belief of play therapists: that children are able to work out their problems through play given an accepting atmosphere in which they sense the freedom to explore their feelings. The specifically selected toys focused the children's work on a specific issue, much like structured play therapy. It is quite possible these children may have worked on other issues if given the wide variety of communicative possibilities of a fully equipped play therapy room and in a trained play therapist.

SOURCE: Milos, M. E., and Reiss, S. (1982). Effects of three play conditions on separation anxiety in young children. *Journal of Counseling and Consulting Psychology* 50(3):389–395.

POSSIBLE *DSM-IV* DIAGNOSES:

309.21   Separation Anxiety Disorder
309.24   Adjustment Disorder with Anxiety

A BEHAVIORAL APPROACH USING PLAY THERAPY TO CHANGE THE INTERACTION PATTERN BETWEEN MOTHER AND DAUGHTER

AUTHOR: **James Straughan**

FOCUS: *The desensitization of a child's anxiety through involving the child's mother in the play therapy sessions and the teaching of play therapy techniques.*

INTRODUCTION: An 8-year-old girl had developed a negative interaction pattern with her mother. The mother would react to her daughter with anxiety and tension and respond by placing additional demands on her. The daughter would respond with her own increased anxiety and tension. This dysfunctional interaction style carried over to school, where the girl reportedly had few friends and frequently told exaggerated stories and lied. A behavioral approach involving the mother in the play therapy sessions provided counterconditioning, modeling, and direct teaching.

CASE STUDY: The child was referred for therapy because of constant lying at school and at home. At school the girl had very few friends. Her mother stated that she was too hard on her daughter and realized, recently, that her daughter seemed sad. Using play with dolls as part of the assessment at intake, the author identified that the girl was not emotionally disturbed, but rather that she had learned to inhibit the free, spontaneous emotional expression typical of an 8-year-old because of interactions with her mother. The child did, however, relax and play boisterously in the playroom during the diagnostic session.

INTERVENTION: The child and her mother were each assigned a therapist. The child's therapist was instructed to adapt himself to her play and to help her stay happy and relaxed in the playroom. The child was informed that her mother would observe the sessions and join them in the playroom for a portion of the sessions. The purpose of having the mother in the playroom was to provide counterconditioning for both child and mother.

The mother received instruction about play therapy from her own therapist. It was explained as a way for children to find out what bothered them. The role of the therapist was to guess at the meaning of the child's play and discuss it without requiring the child to participate, but expecting to see a recognition reflex if the guess was correct. During the observation time of each session, the mother and her therapist would discuss various other aspects of play therapy, including limits, allowing the child to lead and be responsible for the content of the play, keeping the rules simple and honestly explaining the rationale for the rules.

Five sessions were held. The mother and mother's therapist joined in the first session after the child and her therapist were settled in the playroom. The mother did not interact with the therapists or her daughter but observed how the therapists interacted with her daughter. The mother's presence did not appear to affect the child's free and enthusiastic play. In the second session the child was subdued in her play during her mother's lengthier stay in the room, even though the mother only observed. During the third session the child's play became so exuberant that limits were needed. The importance of limits was discussed with the mother.

The mother stayed in the playroom for most of the fourth session. The child briefly seemed affected by her presence, but soon returned to her typical exuberance in the playroom. The mother was allowed to make the majority of responses to her daughter, who became frustrated when her mother attempted to get her to perform better. The play therapist then took the lead in interacting with the child until she again became relaxed and happy. In the fifth session the mother spent the majority of the time in the playroom and was encouraged to participate directly in her daughter's play.

Prior to the fifth session the child's behavior was reported to be greatly improved. She was interacting with other children at school and her behavioral problems had ceased. Her mother also reported being happy with her daughter's changes at home. Based on this information the fifth session became the final session.

The positive gains were still being maintained at an eight-month follow-up contact. The mother indicated her daughter had made several friends at school and remained more relaxed. She realized she had been too controlling once she saw how free her daughter was in the playroom. From a behavioral perspective the author suggested that the child's new behaviors provided the stimulus for the mother to be more relaxed with the child. Other changes in the mother occurred from imitation learning and direct teaching. This child benefited from being the only focus of the therapist as well as the mother during the play therapy sessions.

COMMENTARY: The assessment of this child's problem identified a specific, negative interaction style between the mother and her daughter. The intervention selected focused on breaking that cycle and replacing the negative stimulus with a positive one. Both the mother and child benefited from the play therapy. The child was provided with a permissive atmosphere in which to play freely, which she did not have at home. Her mother was able to watch the play therapist model appropriate interactions and learn the dynamics of play therapy, which helped free her daughter to express emotions more age-appropriately. Parents sometimes need the kind of training that play therapists can provide.

SOURCE: Straughan, J. (1964). Treatment with child and mother in the playroom. *Behavior Research and Therapy* 2:37–41.

POSSIBLE *DSM-IV* DIAGNOSIS:

V61.20   Parent–Child Relational Problem

THE 'SQUIGGLE' DRAWING USED TO OVERCOME ANXIETY IN A NEW CLIENT

AUTHOR: **Robert Ziegler**

FOCUS: *Using the Squiggle drawing technique in both assessment and intervention.*

INTRODUCTION: The Squiggle drawing technique is used to make contact with a child, develop rapport, and help a highly anxious child explore identified concerns using the safe distancing of metaphors in drawings. The Squiggle drawing provides the therapist with insight into the extent of a problem, the level of attached affect, how the child organizes internal anxieties, and whether the child is constricted or blocked. It can also be used during the course of treatment as a way to clarify and refocus—or if necessary reestablish—contact and therapeutic alliance. The Squiggle drawing technique is also recommended for crisis intervention and brief counseling.

The Squiggle technique is a back-and-forth drawing game. The only items needed are paper and colored markers or crayons. First the therapist draws a squiggle (a line of any shape) on a piece of paper. The child then makes a drawing out of the squiggle, identifies it, and tells a story about it (What is it? What has happened? What will happen?). The child then draws a squiggle and the therapist makes a drawing from it, also identifying it and telling a story about it. The back-and-forth flow develops a therapeutic relationship and allows the therapist to clarify the metaphor the child presents and allows the child to add more details, as described in the following case.

CASE STUDY: Margot, an adopted 9-year-old, was experiencing rejection by her adoptive family and threats of being sent to a foster home. She had increasing problems with family rules, and her adoptive mother's threats and harshness only added to Margot's anxiety.

INTERVENTION: From the first squiggle drawn by the therapist to establish contact in the initial session, Margot drew a shoe and said it was going to the store to buy things; she was unable to add any more details, however. From Margot's squiggle the therapist drew a key. Before he could begin to talk about his drawing, Margot indicated it was a giraffe, but again could not offer any more details. The therapist then went on to show his concern about her shoe by suggesting the key was to a car so the shoe could get to the store.

Margot next turned the therapist's squiggle into a lady with an apron who was baking cakes for a party. She was uncertain about who could go to the party. To show his concern for her and to communicate that he understood how tenuous she felt her position in her family was, he turned her next squiggle into a sad girl. He then told of a girl who was sad because she did not know if she was invited to the party. To his surprise, Margot turned his next squiggle into a giraffe. She reported that the giraffe was running through a forest and being chased by people. When the therapist commented on the giraffe's large tail, she quickly took a marker and cut off the tail. Margot was saying, within the metaphor, "At my house, if you don't like something you cut it off." When asked what would happen next to the giraffe, she simply said, "DEAD." With this, Margot was finished with the squiggle game. She had shared as much as she was able in this session about her view of her situation. Indeed, during the time this therapist saw Margot, she was placed in a foster home.

COMMENTARY: The Squiggle technique can be used for many purposes at many different stages of intervention. Ziegler uses it to facilitate a connection with children who are too anxious to play, for assessment, and for refocusing during ongoing intervention. The Squiggle, like play, allows the child to remain within the metaphor and express what may otherwise be inexpressible.

SOURCE: Ziegler, R. (1976). Winnicott's squiggle game: its diagnostic and therapeutic usefulness. *Art Psychotherapy* 3:177–185.

POSSIBLE *DSM-IV* DIAGNOSES:

313.81   Oppositional Defiant Disorder
312.8   Conduct Disorder

12

Grief

Contrary to what many adults think, very young children do experience grief. Even infants have been shown to experience sadness. The experience of grief is not dependent on a person's mental facility or ability to understand, but rather on the person's capacity to feel and ability to experience. Thus all children can be assumed to grieve and should be dealt with accordingly, that is, through their most natural medium of expression and communication, play. Separation from an object of love can be considered loss for very young children—and can precipitate the experience of grief, which should be considered a process rather than a specific emotion and can be expressed in a variety of ways, often undetected by the significant adults in their lives since children do not express grief in the same way as adults. Children do not generally experience acute pain in lengthy periods, but rather in short bursts, almost as though their attention span for pain is short. They deal with their feelings through play, often in a kind of symbolic distancing that allows them to feel safe in the midst of acting out the experience.

SANDPLAY THERAPY WITH A GRIEVING CHILD

AUTHOR: **Lois Carey**

FOCUS: *Sandplay therapy as treatment for a 9-year-old child grieving over the loss of a parent.*

INTRODUCTION: Jack was referred to therapy for multiple symptoms surrounding his response to the death of his father. The discussion of the process of sandplay with Jack included detailed descriptions and several photographs of individual sand trays created during therapy. Jack displayed several themes in his sandplay that were indicative of his emotional problems.

CASE STUDY: Jack experienced two primary losses ("double abandonment") before entering treatment: the sudden death of his father the previous year and the ensuing full-time employment of his mother. Jack was referred by the school psychologist, who reported evidence of enuresis, encopresis, pica, and a general deterioration in affect and behavior. Jack was in a class for neurologically impaired children, and had been making continual progress until his father's death and his mother's return to work.

The psychologist was also concerned that Jack might have been sexually molested. This was not found to be true, but it was discovered that Jack had been viewing pornographic movies with his older brothers (Jack was the youngest of four boys).

INTERVENTION: In the first sandplay session Jack entered the room with wide eyes and a sense of wonder as he viewed the substantial display of sandplay miniatures. After receiving minimal instructions, Jack created a sand picture in the dry sand tray. Carey noted that the initial selection of dry (versus wet) sand is typical of children with learning disabilities as well as those with enuresis and encopresis. Jack's speech was difficult to follow, as he spoke in a monotone with little affect, and he became angry when asked to repeat a word or phrase. Several themes emerged in the first tray, including a struggle for autonomy, depression, and "magical thinking" (including the belief that he had caused his father's death and might undo it as well).

One of the themes addressed in the early sessions was Jack's fantasy that if he used the bathroom, he might have a heart attack. Jack told Carey that on the night his father died, his father had gone to the bathroom, and that was why he had died. Jack began to cry during this exchange, and said that if he (Jack) was not so "stupid," his father would not have died. The encopretic episodes stopped almost immediately following this session.

Jack constructed multiple trays that were chaotic representations of his own chaotic world included burying and unburying objects (representative of loss, buried rage, and protection of self). Eventually the sand tray themes were organized as Jack attempted to make sense of his life. He eventually began using the wet sand, which Carey suggested indicated his willingness to move to deeper psychological issues. Shortly after this move, Jack's mother reported that he had become increasingly outspoken and displayed some temper outbursts ("positive growth"). His nightmares had apparently stopped, he no longer requested a night light, and no recurrences of enuresis were reported. The pica had not continued past the second session. Carey reported that during the six months of treatment, Jack achieved "significant relief from his presenting symptoms, made a better ego adaptation, and was far less depressed."

COMMENTARY: Sandplay therapy provided Jack with the opportunity to illustrate and process issues of low self-esteem, abandonment and lack of control over his father's death and mother's return to work, resolution of grief issues, and confrontation of guilt and rage. The many issues that grieving children present are effectively addressed in the projective nature of play therapy approaches. Integration of losses and relationship issues can be processed symbolically through the safety of play, which Carey demonstrated through Jack's case. Sandplay has been shown to be an effective modality with many issues, including grief, and has been used with all age groups.

SOURCE: Carey, L. (1990). Sandplay therapy with a troubled child. *The Arts in Psychotherapy* 17(3):197–209.

POSSIBLE *DSM-IV* DIAGNOSES:

V62.82 Bereavement
307.6   Enuresis
307.7   Encopresis
307.52 Pica
309.4   Adjustment Disorder with Mixed Disturbance of Emotions
         and Conduct

PUPPETS IN THE TREATMENT OF TRAUMATIC GRIEF

AUTHOR: **Stephanie R. Carter**

FOCUS: *The use of puppets in nondirective play therapy grief with a 10-year-old child experiencing traumatic grief.*

INTRODUCTION: Steven had witnessed his father's murder two years before entering treatment. His behavior at school and home had deteriorated following the event, and he was referred for therapy by his teacher. In the nondirective treatment approach, Steven selected puppets to process his previously denied traumatic grief.

CASE STUDY: Before witnessing the murder of his father, Steven was described as a "normal boy" who functioned well academically, socially, and behaviorally. Afterward, the child became aggressive, frequently hit teachers and other children, used profanity, and destroyed property. His mother reported similar behaviors at home. Steven's academic progress virtually stopped at the time of the trauma, and within two years he was placed in a class for emotionally disturbed children. He would not talk about his father, the murder, or his feelings.

INTERVENTION: Carter described her rationale for employing nondirective play therapy, and suggested that "Steven freely chose puppets in a neutral play atmosphere that was unstructured and nondirective and began to break through his defenses of traumatic anxiety, to understand his feelings, and finally to experience the full range of grief and its accompanying anger." Steven began weekly therapy as a 10-year-old fifth grader, and continued the one-hour sessions for two years. An important issue that Carter noted was that during these two years three additional people close to Steven also died, which he processed in the play.

The treatment process began with Steven covering his head with a towel and turning his back on the therapist. He informed the therapist that talking about his father made him angry and that he would refuse to talk about anything related to his father. By the third session Steven had chosen the puppets to focus on, and continued to use them throughout treatment. Eventually the father puppet was shot, and Steven staged the funeral and burial. The following sessions included the puppets engaged in numerous fights, and the themes of violence, his father's death, and the little boy puppet narrowly escaping death. During session eight there appeared to be a break-through, as Steven grieved for the father puppet, dropped the boy puppet, and cried out: "My daddy died . . . oh no, my daddy died. Don't let him die. What am I going to do? My daddy died."

Following this session, positive changes began to occur outside the playroom. Steven's teacher reported academic improvement. His social skills improved and his anger was expressed more appropri-ately. The teacher also reported that Steven was much more "joyful," and his mother reported fewer incidents of misbehavior at home. By the termination of treatment Steven was in junior high school, and was being taken out of the special academic program and returned to the mainstream population. In addition to the reduction in act-ing-out behaviors, Steven talked about his future, visualized himself as successful, and displayed personal confidence.

COMMENTARY: Play therapy is effective for children dealing with trau-matic grief since it gives them the opportunity to have control over the issues, to proceed at their own pace, and to experience the safety of projection and communicating in the language of play. In sum-marizing Steven's puppet play, Carter says: "He used [the puppets] to test reality, to express his needs symbolically, and to relieve the pressure of his traumatic anxiety." The play clearly provided Steven with a safe outlet in which to express and ultimately experience his grief and anger. Grieving children need the safety of play therapy to process their pain.

SOURCE: Carter, S. R. (1987). Use of puppets to treat traumatic grief: a case study. *Elementary School Guidance & Counseling* 21(3):210–215.

POSSIBLE *DSM-IV* DIAGNOSES:

V62.82   Bereavement
312.8   Conduct Disorder
313.81   Oppositional Defiant Disorder

GROUP PLAY THERAPY WITH BEREAVED CHILDREN

AUTHOR: **Donna Casey Tait and Jo-Lynn Depta**

FOCUS: *The use of group play therapy with children experiencing emotional and behavioral difficulties following the death of a parent.*

INTRODUCTION: The planning of a bereavement group and the rationale for using a group play therapy approach to treating this population is explored. Cofacilitators were used for the group, which consisted of ten children who had experienced the loss of a close family member. In addition to a discussion of the group process and summary of the sessions, guidelines for bereavement group facilitators and discussion questions are provided.

CASE STUDY: The ten children ranged in age from 7 to 11 years. The family deaths had occurred eighteen months to three years before the group therapy. Two of the children had observed the death of a parent following a prolonged illness, while the remaining eight had had no warning of the death of their relative. Nine of the ten experienced the death of a parent.

    The children were described as experiencing nightmares, anger outbursts, academic and social difficulties, withdrawal, hypervigilance, abandonment, and depression. Their families described them as having difficulty expressing anger and being withdrawn and depressed. Additionally, most of the surviving parents had considerable difficulty talking objectively about the death.

INTERVENTION: The treatment consisted of eight sessions. Each session focus, together with corresponding play activities, was planned before the group began therapy. Some of the play activities included were drawing, clay work, charade games, family sculpting, storytelling, and puppet play. Most of the sessions began with fifteen minutes of free play prior to the structured activities.

    The facilitation of normalization and the benefit of peer support in group therapy became quickly evident in session two, when one of the children (Justin) fashioned a train out of clay—the train that hit his mother and sister and killed them. He started to cry, and in addition to the reflection and support of one of the group facilitators, Justin was supported and comforted by the other children. Session seven included a symbolic activity developed to assist the children in letting go by asking them to write a message to the deceased family member. The message was placed inside a helium balloon with an attached string, and the balloons were released outdoors as a group. Session eight consisted of a formal goodbye, and included a "graduation party" with pizza, certificates, and picture taking. Pre- and postassessments were given to the parents and a posttest questionnaire was given to the children. Positive results were reported.

COMMENTARY: Group therapy provides participants with a safe place to share difficult issues; it breaks the sense of isolation, normalizes the recovery process, and provides peer support. The combination of group work and play therapy procedures provided these grieving children with the opportunity to process their sense of being in an out-of-control situation. They were able to bring some sense of empowerment and control to their lives, which were marked by the opposite feelings. The authors acknowledge that group play therapy with grieving children is a recent innovation and that limited guidelines are available. At the same time the potential benefits for this challenging population are limitless.

SOURCE: Tait, D. C., and Depta, J. (1994). Play therapy group for bereaved children. In *Helping Bereaved Children: A Handbook for Practitioners*, ed. N. B. Webb, pp. 169–185. New York: Guilford.

POSSIBLE *DSM-IV* DIAGNOSIS:

V62.82   Bereavement

CHILD-CENTERED PLAY THERAPY
WITH A GRIEVING CHILD

AUTHOR: **Jane LeVieux**

FOCUS: The use of child-centered play therapy with a 5-year-old girl grieving over the death of her father following terminal illness.

INTRODUCTION: Celeste was referred for treatment six months after the death of her father. She was described as being uncooperative, defiant, and depressed. Child-centered play therapy was the chosen treatment modality.

CASE STUDY: Celeste was the oldest of three children. Her mother explained that the father's illness (cancer) involved multiple short hospitalizations and rounds of chemotherapy. From December through February of the year he died, the majority of the father's time was spent in the hospital. The children saw little of him in the weeks prior to his death because the father did not want them to see him in such pain. He died at the hospital. Memorial services were held, which the children attended.

Her mother reported that Celeste was moody and irritable since her father's death. There were also increased incidents of uncooperative and defiant behaviors, which were not previously evident. Celeste presented as periodically depressed, and had become increasingly impatient with her younger siblings. Over the following summer Celeste's preschool teacher had given birth to a new child, which precipitated crying and concern by Celeste about the upcoming school year. Her mother then decided to request treatment.

INTERVENTION: The treatment process began with a family intake session in which LeVieux gathered background information and introduced Celeste and the rest of the family to the playroom. The initial session with Celeste was typical of the entire treatment process, which was child centered and thus led by Celeste. The treatment plan included providing Celeste with "opportunities for her to express feelings, either verbally or symbolically through her play." The objective was to help Celeste to integrate her father's death into her own life, and to process the grief and anger issues through play, which in turn would lead to a reduction in aggressive and noncompliant behaviors in the home.

Given the lead in the play therapy process, Celeste began to talk about her father, play with the toys, and do artwork. Celeste repeatedly buried items in the sand and drew pictures of her sadness, and of her father. In one session she drew a picture of her father with big hands and verbalized that she remembered how safe she felt with him, especially when they held hands. By session seven Celeste's mother reported that she was able to talk more easily with Celeste about her father. LeVieux was still seeing Celeste in treatment at the writing of the case study, and noted considerable progress in her integration of her father's death and the processing of grief and anger issues. LeVieux noted the importance of working with the surviving parent, as well as the importance of allowing the child simply to play (to be a child) as opposed to focusing constantly on the presenting grief issue.

COMMENTARY: Play therapy is effective in assisting grieving children to process the out-of-control issues of loss and anger in a safe and empowering environment. Celeste was able to address previously unprocessed grief concerns, and to begin to make sense of a situation, life without her father, that was frightening and produced powerlessness. The therapeutic approach of child-centered play therapy provided Celeste with an opportunity to manage what seemed unmanageable. As LeVieux summarized: "Perhaps during those moments of play where freedom is granted and creativity abounds, Celeste feels safe and comfortable."

SOURCE: LeVieux, J. (1994). Terminal illness and death of father: case of Celeste, age 5½. In *Helping Bereaved Children: A Handbook for Practitioners*, ed. N. B. Webb, pp. 81–95. New York: Guilford.

POSSIBLE *DSM-IV* DIAGNOSES:

V62.82   Bereavement
313.81   Oppositional Defiant Disorder
309.4   Adjustment Disorder with Mixed Disturbance of Emotions
              and Conduct

13

Hospitalization

Hospitalization can be a frightening experience for children. They are suddenly uprooted from what is familiar (home, parents, siblings, school, peers) and predictable and placed in an environment that is neither familiar nor predictable. In addition, children no longer have personal freedom, privacy, or control. They are suddenly thrust into a new, strange, and bewildering environment in which they are poked at, looked at, made to swallow weird substances, and subjected to mysterious machines and procedures. Is it any wonder that these experiences may contribute to severe stress in children that may be manifested in behavioral changes? Behavioral changes that occur as a result of hospitalization may persist well beyond the time of discharge from the hospital if there is no systematic intervention. Play therapy provides children with an opportunity to experience a familiar activity and thus reconnect with life outside the hospital. Through play, children can construct their lives to be the way they want them to be, and in that process experience being in control. The most important factor in this process, however, is the establishment of a consistent relationship with a play therapist who is understanding, accepting, and completely trustworthy.

THERAPEUTIC PLAY WITH A HOSPITALIZED 5-YEAR-OLD BOY

AUTHOR: **Leota Thoman Acord**

FOCUS: *A 5-year-old hospitalized boy utilizes a therapeutic play experience to reveal and process fears of injections and intrusive medical procedures.*

INTRODUCTION: Jason was hospitalized as a result of injuries from an automobile accident that necessitated a body cast. Therapeutic play sessions in the hospital were followed by play sessions at home after discharge. Jason used the sessions to identify and process his fears related to the treatment procedures, particularly injections, intravenous infusions, and catheterization.

CASE STUDY: Jason was described as energetic and verbal prior to his hospitalization. The second of two children with two working parents, Jason was cared for at home by a hired caretaker when he was not attending kindergarten. Both his parents visited the hospital daily during his hospitalization.

Hospitalization was precipitated by Jason's being struck by an automobile while crossing the street in front of his house. He was rushed to an emergency room, where he was treated for a fractured left femur, ruptured spleen, and minor contusions of his arms and forehead. After surgery he was placed in traction in a surgical ward. He received intravenous infusion and a catheter for urine drainage. He also received injections for pain. After seven days Jason was transferred to an orthopedic unit for three and a half weeks, where he was maintained in traction, then released with a full body cast, which was removed two months following his discharge.

INTERVENTION: Six play sessions were facilitated, four in the hospital and two in Jason's home. The play materials included toys representative of the hospital setting and of the home.

In the first session Jason began to address the issue of the injections with some ambivalence. He picked up his stuffed bear and pointed to a syringe, telling the stuffed animal: "This is a special kind of needle; it doesn't hurt." He later stated: "I like shots. I don't like the way they feel." In the second play session he gave the bear an injection and screamed "Ouch!" At the end of the session he announced: "I hate shots." Jason became increasingly aggressive in administering injections to the bear and other doll figures.

Upon returning home from the hospital Jason began to play out his anger toward the hospital staff who had given him the injections. Consistent with other hospital research findings regarding ventilation of anger toward adult male figures, Jason expressed considerable hostile play behavior toward the male doctor doll. After playing out these issues with various doll figures, Jason moved toward giving injections to the child doll in traction. He was able to verbalize his own feelings of helplessness: "What if you were as little as one of these dolls and got a shot this big? Would you like that?"

COMMENTARY: Through the play therapy intervention Jason was given an opportunity to express his fears within the safety of projective play. He was able to make some degree of sense out of a frightening situation that did not make sense. Acord's case study highlights the need for children who are traumatized by intrusive hospital procedures to identify and process emotions within the protective boundaries of a play therapy medium.

SOURCE: Acord, L. T. (1980). One five-year-old boy's use of play. *Maternal Child Nursing Journal* 9:29–35.

POSSIBLE *DSM-IV* DIAGNOSES:

293.89   Anxiety Disorder Due to a General Medical Condition
309.81   Posttraumatic Stress Disorder

TREATING HOSPITAL FEAR REACTIONS
WITH PLAY THERAPY

AUTHOR: **Pauline H. Barton**

FOCUS: *Play therapy as treatment for a 5-year-old child exhibiting an inability to trust and significant fear regarding open heart surgery.*

INTRODUCTION: Kathy was hospitalized twice for open heart surgery. The second hospitalization included a play therapy experience, using the child-centered approach of Clark Moustakas.[1] Situational hospital doll play was employed to help Kathy express her feelings of fear and anxiety.

CASE STUDY: Kathy was an intellectually superior child and her home environment stimulated this aspect of her development. During a previous hospitalization for heart catheterization, Kathy had demonstrated high levels of distrust and hostility, yelling at hospital staff, calling them names, and accusing them of lying about medical procedures. Before her second admission for surgery, the hospital staff arranged for play therapy utilizing situational hospital doll play as a means to assist Kathy in dealing with her fears about the surgery and her distrust of staff.

INTERVENTION: *Presurgery*—The first play therapy sessions were held in a "play hospital," an exact replica of a two-bed hospital ward with all the appropriate and expected equipment. Dolls were dressed to represent patients, nurses, doctors, and parents. After a cursory examination of the room, Kathy picked up the hypodermic syringe and needle and asked how to attach the two. She then gave the girl doll an injection. After being shown how to fill the syringe with water, Kathy shot the fluid into the air. Consistent with children who are extremely anxious, Kathy's expression remained stony and impassive.

The therapist was then called from the play/hospital room for a

---

1. Clark Moustakas, *Children in Play Therapy* (Northvale, NJ: Jason Aronson Inc., 1973).

few minutes. She remained in the hall where she could observe Kathy without being seen. Kathy quickly picked up the mother doll and gave her repeated injections. Although Kathy's body posture remained rigid and tense, she displayed a wider range of emotions during this play, including joy, intense concentration, and considerable anger. When the therapist returned to the playroom, Kathy left the play with the mother doll, but continued to play with the syringe.

To assist in developing Kathy's trust of the hospital staff, the therapist took her on a tour of the recovery room, where she met the nursing staff who would provide her care following surgery. In addition, the therapist and the nurses walked Kathy through the complete surgical procedure, from preparation through recovery.

During the next play therapy session, Kathy's mother was present. The therapist suggested they get the doll hospital and play out what would happen when someone has surgery. Initially Kathy wanted the mother doll to undergo surgery, but then changed to the girl doll, which she identified as herself. Kathy included the therapist in the play as her assistant, and was able to play through the entire procedure. This included Kathy bandaging the girl doll and pushing a large needle into the doll's chest to represent the stitches. Despite Kathy's mother's request to be a part of the play, Kathy chose not to include her.

Postsurgery—The recovery nurses reported that Kathy was one of the best-behaved children they had worked with in postoperative care. She was cooperative and did not appear frightened of any of the procedures; her doll play reflected the change the staff had seen in Kathy. The doll play was focused on routine daily events, including bath time, bedmaking, stitch removal, injections, and playing. She identified one doll as "Kathy," and often talked through the doll: "Kathy, you have to have a shot now. It will hurt just a little, but not very long. Now, now, it's all over, you have just three shots more today." Kathy's play appeared self-comforting and reassuring. It was also relaxed and cheerful.

Follow-up Hospital Visits—Kathy continued to be cheerful, and happy to see the hospital staff. One visit took place primarily because Kathy begged her mother to let her visit her hospital friends. Kathy's family reported she was taking greater responsibility in her own care, including remembering to take her own medications and following guidelines regarding exercise and avoiding overexertion. Kathy was also seen as being more mature and considerate, having greater ability to concentrate on tasks, and more attached to her mother.

COMMENTARY: Play therapy is a proven and effective procedure for helping children release anxiety and develop a sense of mastery and self-control in a hospital environment. Kathy was able to process some feelings toward her mother in the first play session (her repeated injections of the mother doll), including anger toward her for allowing Kathy to be placed in a frightening and painful situation. Kathy also developed trust in the staff (talking with the doll about the number of shots to be given), believing, as she had been told, that there would be only four shots that day in the recovery room. The directed play experience allowed Kathy not only to express a variety of feelings, but also to clarify her perceptions of the medical procedures, her mother, and herself. As in this case with Kathy, many children are able to apply this new sense of self in hospital situations to other areas of their lives.

SOURCE: Barton, P. H. (1962). Play as a tool of nursing. *Nursing Outlook* 10:162–164.

POSSIBLE *DSM-IV* DIAGNOSES:

293.89   Anxiety Disorder Due to a General Medical Condition
309.81   Posttraumatic Stress Disorder

BRIEF PUPPET THERAPY FOR CHILDREN FACING CARDIAC CATHETERIZATION

AUTHOR: **Sylvia Cassell**

FOCUS: *Investigation of the effect of brief puppet therapy on the emotional responses of children hospitalized for cardiac catheterization.*

INTRODUCTION: Previous research has shown that children can express emotions more easily through a "third person" (such as a puppet or doll) than they can directly. The research hypotheses were that children who received puppet therapy would be (1) rated by the cardiologist as less disturbed, (2) rated as showing less emotional disturbance on the hospital ward following the catheterization, and (3) more willing to return to the hospital for further treatment.

RESEARCH METHODS & DESIGN: The subjects for this study included forty children, ages 3 through 11, admitted to a children's hospital for cardiac catheterization. Twenty children were randomly assigned to each of the experimental and control groups.

The play materials consisted of a miniature mock-up of the catheterization facilities, including puppets representing a doctor, nurse, boy, girl, mother, and father. Miniature hospital equipment was also used. The children in the experimental group were given two sessions of puppet therapy, one before and the other after the catheterization. The children in the control group received routine hospital services.

Three measures of the children's emotional responses were employed with both groups: parental questionnaires, ward observations, and catheterization observations.

INTERVENTION: During the puppet therapy sessions, the child and the therapist acted out the catheterization procedure. In the initial phase of the first session, the therapist played the role of the cardiologist, explaining as many of the medical procedures as possible. Play included giving injections, changing into hospital gowns, and placement on the examining table. Following this initial enactment of the hospital procedure, the patient–doctor roles were reversed, and the child played the medical role(s). After the puppet play the child was encouraged to discuss aspects of the role plays and to use any of the puppets in a free manner.

RESULTS: Children participating in puppet therapy showed less emotional disturbance during the cardiac catheterization and expressed greater willingness to return to the hospital for further treatment. These results were attributed to two assumptions: (1) that understanding of the staff's empathy reduced the child's need to communicate his/her feelings, and (2) that the puppet therapy offered a combination of mastery, acceptance of professional empathy, and release of emotions.

COMMENTARY: The healing power demonstrated in two sessions of play therapy is amazing. By projecting fear and anxiety related to hospitalization onto the puppets, children are able to make sense of a situation that seems out of control. When given the opportunity to process emotional issues and release anxiety through the play, children can build some level of mastery and control over an experience that is otherwise unmanageable, leading to the development of emotional coping mechanisms.

SOURCE: Cassell, S. (1965). Effect of brief puppet therapy upon the emotional responses of children undergoing cardiac catheterization. *Journal of Consulting Psychology* 29(1):1–8.

POSSIBLE *DSM-IV* DIAGNOSES:

293.89   Anxiety Disorder Due to a General Medical Condition
309.24   Adjustment Disorder with Anxiety

THE EFFECTS OF PLAY THERAPY ON HOSPITALIZED CHILDREN

AUTHOR: **Stephanie Clatworthy**

FOCUS: *Play therapy was demonstrated to be an effective treatment of hospital-induced anxiety with children.*

INTRODUCTION: The effectiveness of play therapy in the treatment of children experiencing hospital-induced anxiety was investigated in this study. The stabilization or reduction of anxiety levels in hospitalized children has been determined to be associated with a greater degree of cooperation with medical staff and treatment procedures. The effect of therapeutic play on hospitalized children was investigated at two large hospitals over the course of several years, focusing on levels of anxiety.

RESEARCH METHODS & DESIGN: The subjects involved in this study were a total of 114 children in three phases. Phases I and II were conducted in the general pediatric unit of a private hospital in a large metropolitan area, and consisted of twenty-three and twenty-six children, respectively. Phase III was conducted in a large university hospital, and consisted of sixty-five children. All children between the ages of 5 and 12 years were considered candidates for the study. The length of the anticipated hospital stay (2 to 4 days) and number of previous hospitalizations (no more than three) were controlled in the first two phases. Parental reports of previous "good" mental health and normal intelligence were required for all participants.

The total study was conducted over a four-year period and consisted of fifty-five children in the treatment group and fifty-nine in the control group. All groups were homogeneous in relation to family size, economic status, previous hospitalizations, experience with separation, and preparation for this specific hospitalization. The mean age for children in the study was 7.4 years for the experimental group and 8.53 years for the control group.

Upon admission and during the last or seventh day of hospitalization, the children were given the Missouri Children's Picture Series

(MCPS) to assess levels of anxiety. This test instrument consisted of 238 cards with line drawings depicting children in daily activities.

INTERVENTION: The experimental group received daily individual play therapy conducted by a nurse play therapist. Play materials considered conducive to hospital and family role play were provided, including fantasy play through dolls, puppets, and storytelling; art with paints and crayons; and aggressive play with punching bags, clay, cars, and balls. The play was directed primarily by the child, with the therapist providing reflection and some interpretation of feelings.

RESULTS: The children's current level of anxiety was measured with the MCPS during the first twenty-four hours of hospitalization and again at discharge and/or the seventh day. In Phase I of the study (children who were hospitalized for four days), the children in the experimental group exhibited a significantly lower level of anxiety at the conclusion of the intervention. The statistical analysis indicated that the intervention did not decrease the anxiety of the children in the experimental group, but rather prevented them from developing as much anxiety as the children in the control group. In Phase II of the study (children who were hospitalized for two days), similar results were attained. For children experiencing longer hospitalizations (Phase III), the same significant, positive results were reported. Children in the experimental group continued to exhibit less anxiety as measured by the MCPS.

COMMENTARY: This research demonstrated significant differences in the anxiety levels of hospitalized children who received regular play therapy, regardless of setting, age, gender, or diagnosis. In general, the play therapy appeared to act as a deterrent to anxiety in children, in an environment in which anxiety routinely manifests. The authors suggested that play therapy should be routinely included in the treatment program for pediatric patients. Children who experience less anxiety during the hospitalized experience are more amenable to medical treatment and more cooperative with family and hospital staff. The positive effects of play therapy with hospitalized children appears experientially clear—this study offers empirical evidence in support.

SOURCE: Clatworthy, S. (1981). Therapeutic play: effects on hospitalized children. *Journal of Association for Care of Children's Health* 9(4): 108–113.

POSSIBLE *DSM-IV* DIAGNOSES:

293.89   Anxiety Disorder Due to a General Medical Condition
309.24   Adjustment Disorder with Anxiety

HELPING YOUNG CHILDREN MASTER INTRUSIVE PROCEDURES THROUGH PLAY

AUTHORS: **Mary-Lou Ellerton, Suzanne Caty, and Judith Ritchie**

FOCUS: *Analysis of play interviews with chronically ill 2- to 6-year-old hospitalized children revealed that nine of the ten children were able to use clinical equipment to express their concerns about intrusive medical procedures.*

INTRODUCTION: Young, chronically ill children who experience repeated or prolonged hospitalization struggle not only with developmental stress, but also with the anxiety of the illness and hospitalization. These children have been found to be at considerably increased risk for social and emotional difficulties. A series of play interviews were implemented to determine differences in the expression of issues of healthy children, acutely ill children, and chronically ill children. The play of the chronically ill children focused on issues of intrusion.

RESEARCH METHODS & DESIGN: The research sample included six boys and four girls who had been diagnosed with a chronic illness and whose hospital stay had a duration of at least twenty-one days. The children had several previous hospitalizations and seven had previous surgeries. Six of the children were 2 to 4 years of age and four were in the 4- to 6-year age range.

Play interviews were conducted every five to seven days with each child until discharge from the hospital or when a maximum of six interviews was reached. A total of forty-nine interviews were conducted. Data were collected using a specific play interview procedure and specific materials. The children were presented with a suitcase containing a variety of toys, including familiar toys, family figures, and medical/hospital equipment. They were free to take the lead and play while the researcher took notes.

INTERVENTION: In the initial play interview the researcher picked up and identified each toy in the suitcase. The child was then permitted to play with the toys while the researcher took notes. The play session was nondirective, and requests by the child for the researcher to participate were declined. Each play interview lasted for forty-five minutes and the child was free to refuse to play. All behaviors identified as intrusive constituted the database for the study and were content analyzed.

RESULTS: Nine of the ten chronically ill children played out intrusion themes during the play interviews. For five children more than 25 percent of the total play was related to intrusion. Four types of intrusion behaviors were identified in the content analysis: (1) injection play (55 percent of the intrusive play), (2) medications (23 percent), (3) temperature taking (17 percent), and (4) tube-feeding (4 percent).

Playing out injections was clearly a major concern for the children. The level of injection play appeared to parallel the children's experience in the hospital: 33 percent of the children's play with the syringe was exploratory, learning how the materials operated. The children's play was an accurate replication of the intrusion experience in the hospital 93 percent of the time during the first interview; 78 percent of their play activities were accompanied by verbalizations.

COMMENTARY: All nine of the children playing out intrusion themes played with the injection materials. Receiving injections continues to be a significant issue for hospitalized children. Some 40 percent of the intrusion behaviors displayed represented temperature taking and medications. This suggests that although these procedures are routine for hospital staff, they can be potentially devastating for the pediatric patient. It is imperative that hospitalized children have the chance to express their fears, especially those related to intrusion. This study amply demonstrates children's willingness to communicate their concerns through play.

SOURCE: Ellerton, M. L., Caty, S., and Ritchie, J. A. (1985). Helping young children master intrusive procedures through play. *Children's Health Care* 13(4):167–173.

POSSIBLE *DSM-IV* DIAGNOSIS:

Insufficient information provided in the study.

THERAPEUTIC PLAY FOR ANXIETY ISSUES

AUTHOR: **Patricia A. Garot**

FOCUS: *Development, implementation, and evaluation of a therapeutic play program for a 5-year-old girl hospitalized with an infected lymphangioma and experiencing fear and stress.*

INTRODUCTION: Brandy was admitted to the hospital for antibiotic treatment of lymphangioma. The IV treatments caused her to have high levels of anxiety, and she was very fearful of separation from her parents. Therapeutic play was a part of the prescribed treatment regimen.

CASE STUDY: Brandy was described as a relatively healthy girl aside from her diagnosed condition. She lived at home with her parents and a 14-year-old stepbrother. Her mother was German and spoke German to her, and her father spoke English. Brandy talked more often and more affectionately about her father. When Brandy's mother brought her to the hospital, she talked about Brandy as if she were not there. At one point in the interview Brandy cried while her mother told a story about her, and the mother did not notice or seem concerned about this emotional response. Brandy was reported to be polite but very quiet and withdrawn with hospital staff.

Brandy's treatment regimen while in the hospital included (1) one intravenous medication every six hours, (2) another intravenous medication every six hours, (3) a heparin lock, (4) hot soaks to the left cheek three times a day, (5) a clear liquid diet, (6) activity as desired, and (7) age-appropriate play.

INTERVENTION: The therapeutic play plan established for Brandy included (1) setting up a play session in the playroom to assess her level of understanding about her inpatient treatment; (2) providing various play materials, including a play hospital with characters and equipment and art materials; (3) asking Brandy to draw a picture of herself; (4) encouraging Brandy to draw a picture about her being in the hospital; and (5) encouraging Brandy to process her hospitalization by role playing with the dolls and play equipment.

This play plan was implemented in two forty-five-minute play sessions. Four diagnostic issues were identified, including anxiety related to the IV therapy, separation anxiety, a knowledge deficit related to the reasons for hospitalization, and low self-esteem related to an altered body image due to Brandy's swollen cheek. Goals were established to specifically address these four issues.

The therapeutic play sessions were reported to successfully address the identified issues. Brandy was able to verbalize her fears as she role-played starting and restarting the IVs, irrigating the heparin lock, and infusing medication. She verbalized her fear about her parents leaving as she successfully role-played her parents visiting and returning to the hospital. Brandy displayed her understanding of the hospitalization procedure as she talked to one of the dolls about the infection in her cheek and how medication was necessary to get well. Brandy was able to gain a better perception about her body image as she verbalized to a doll that it was acceptable to look different.

COMMENTARY: Play therapy was shown to be effective in conjunction with the nursing process. Stress and anxiety related to the hospitalization were significantly reduced, and self-acceptance was enhanced. The prescriptive approach involving the provision of specific play materials and the initial direction of the play therapist proved beneficial in meeting focused therapeutic goals.

SOURCE: Garot, P. A. (1986). Therapeutic play: work of both child and nurse. *Journal of Pediatric Nursing* 1(2):111–115.

POSSIBLE *DSM-IV* DIAGNOSIS:

293.89   Anxiety Disorder Due to a General Medical Condition

TREATMENT OF HOSPITALIZED CHILDREN FOR ACUTE ILLNESS

AUTHORS: Carol A. Daniel, William A. Rae, Jacqueline H. Sanner, Jan Upchurch, and Frances F. Worchel

FOCUS: *Hospital fears experienced by pediatric patients hospitalized for acute illness.*

INTRODUCTION: The investigation involved the effects of play on the psychosocial adjustment of children hospitalized for acute illness. The psychosocial adjustment of acutely ill children has been determined to be a crucial variable in their healing process. Questions to be answered have revolved around the issues of the kind of play and the medium of verbal communication. This study attempted to isolate and evaluate the effect of these variables on a variety of dimensions, including adjustment, fear, and stress.

RESEARCH METHODS & DESIGN: The subjects were sixty-one children aged 5 to 10 who were admitted to the pediatric ward of the Scott and White Memorial Hospital in Temple, Texas. The criteria for inclusion in the research included (1) absence of mental impairment or communication dysfunction according to parents, (2) age (5 to 10 years), (3) no history of contact with a mental health professional according to parents, (4) no more than four previous hospitalizations, and (5) a planned hospitalization of at least three days. Of the original sixty-one subjects fifteen had incomplete data; thus forty-six subjects made up the final sample. The sample was stratified based upon age, sex, and number of hospitalizations, then randomly assigned to one of four groups: therapeutic play, diversionary play, verbal support, and no treatment.

The pre- and post-instruments used included the Missouri Children's Picture Series (MCPS), the Fear Thermometer (a pictorial version of the Medical Fears subscale of the Fear Survey Schedule for Children), the Stress Inventory (filled out by the parents), the Zuckerman Adjective Checklist (measured by parents and nurses), and the Vernon Post-Hospitalization Behavior Questionnaire (PHBQ; filled out by the parents).

INTERVENTION: After pretesting, the children were assigned to one of the experimental groups or to the control group. Nurses and other hospital personnel were blind to the children's group assignment. All interventions were administered by a single research assistant who was trained by the study's designer in each of the experimental interventions. The assistant's progress notes were checked carefully to monitor compliance with the research design.

Under the verbally oriented support condition the children discussed their concerns, anxieties, and fears with the research assistant. Although any topic the child suggested was discussed, the child was not allowed to engage in any play behavior. The diversionary play condition involved the children being allowed to play with toys. Fantasy play was discouraged, and activities included games and puzzles; the research assistant did not engage in any verbally or therapeutically supportive activities. Under the therapeutic play condition the children were involved in nondirective child-centered play therapy. The children played with toys of their own choosing, with hospital-related materials provided. In the control condition the children had no contact with the research assistant other than the pre- and post-assessments.

On the third day of the children's hospital stay they were post-tested.

RESULTS: Statistical analysis showed no differences among the children related to sex, age, or the other inclusion criteria. Significant differences were shown on the Fear Thermometer between the results of children participating in the therapeutic play condition and those participating in all other groups. Children who participated in the therapeutic play (child-centered play therapy) showed a significantly lower level of fear. There were no significant differences in the results for the three other groups. The MCPS suggested an increase on the somatization scale for children involved in therapeutic play when compared to the other groups. There were no significant differences between the groups on the results of the other assessment scales.

COMMENTARY: The authors concluded that the results demonstrated support for the use of therapeutic play in a hospital setting. The significance demonstrated on the Fear Thermometer appear even more important because this specific assessment measures children's self-perceptions directly related to hospitalization. When children feel less fearful about the hospital experience, it may well be postulated that they experience less psychological distress and greater emotional well-being. The difference in significance in the results of the children's self-report and parents' ratings is consistent with previous studies. The authors also suggest additional mitigating factors. The efficacy of the intervention, however, is perhaps best measured by self-report rather than an observer's report. This study does document the effectiveness of child-centered play therapy intervention in decreasing the level of self-reported fears for pediatric patients.

SOURCE: Daniel, C. A., Rae, W. A., Sanner, J. H., Upchurch, J., and Worchel, F. F. (1989). The psychosocial impact of play on hospitalized children. *Journal of Pediatric Psychology* 14(4):617–627.

POSSIBLE *DSM-IV* DIAGNOSES:

293.89   Anxiety Disorder Due to a General Medical Condition
309.24   Adjustment Disorder with Anxiety

PLAY THERAPY IN A PEDIATRIC HOSPITAL DEPARTMENT

AUTHOR: **K. Zilliacus and S. Enberg**

FOCUS: *The effectiveness of a hospital-based play therapy program was evaluated through survey research.*

INTRODUCTION: Children who experience hospitalization must deal with concomitant fears and anxiety. While the efficacy of play therapy interventions with children who have already been admitted to the hospital has been determined, bringing a therapeutic play experience to children in the hospital waiting room is an innovative treatment intervention. The effectiveness of a play therapy program based in the outpatient department waiting room of the Children's Hospital in Helsinki, Finland, was investigated.

RESEARCH METHODS & DESIGN: The subjects involved in the survey research included 100 parents whose children had participated in the organized play therapy program at the hospital and twenty-one members of the hospital staff. Interviews were conducted to assess the effectiveness of the program by studying the respondents' attitudes. The age range of the children whose parents participated in the study was 2 to 16 years, with a mean of 6.8 years.

INTERVENTION: The play therapy program consisted of a well-supplied play area in the waiting room of the pediatric section of the hospital. A trained adult "play leader" was present during the day. In addition to the waiting room play therapy, the authors noted that there were six play leaders working on ten wards with an average of twenty patient beds. Children visiting the hospital for outpatient services or children being admitted to the hospital were able to take advantage of the play activity.

A variety of play materials was offered, including a kitchen set, dolls, cars, and building modules. Games, books, and music were available for the older children. Art and craft materials were also provided. The play leader provided direction to the play activity, but the children were free to participate or not or to choose an alternate activity. Play therapy was conducted in a corner of the waiting room, with the intent of involving the children and their parents in the process. Interested parents were informed about the process, and encouraged to continue play activities at home. Siblings were also encouraged to be involved.

RESULTS: Both parents and hospital staff responded to the interviews with positive feedback for the play therapy program. In response to a question about whether the play activity reduced the children's tension, 35 percent of the parents answered "very much," 47 percent answered "somewhat," and 18 percent saw no reduction in tension. Thus 80 percent of the parents considered the play therapy to be effective in reducing fear and anxiety. The parents were also asked, "How do you feel when your child is taking part in the play activity?" Ninety-one percent answered "more relaxed" and 9 percent reported "no change." To the question about whether the parents themselves received ideas from the play activity, 88 percent answered positively. In an examination of what the children involved in the play therapy program talked about both before and after the hospital visit, it was found they talked twice as much about the play as about the waiting and treatment, and nearly 5 times more about the play than about the pain.

     The hospital staff noted that the children appeared more relaxed, and that making contact with the parents was easier. Ninety percent of the staff respondents noted that the play therapy influenced their work (from "very much" to "some extent"). To the question "Is there any difference between children who have been occupied at the play table compared with those who have not?," 19 percent answered "yes, very much," 33 percent answered "yes, a lot," 43 percent answered "yes, to some extent"; 5 percent saw no difference.

COMMENTARY: The authors suggested that organized play in the hospital should be tension relieving and fear reducing and give the child an opportunity to live out feelings. Providing children with the opportunity to express their emotional and behavioral needs and concerns in such a challenging setting has been demonstrated to be effective with pediatric hospitalized children in many settings. The play therapy program in the waiting room facilitates both the treatment process for outpatient children and the admitting process for children to be hospitalized. The authors appropriately asserted that as more sick children are being treated at a hospital on an outpatient basis, organized play therapy activities in the waiting room and in the outpatient department are crucial additions to the overall treatment program.

SOURCE: Zilliacus, K., and Enberg, S. (1980). Play therapy in the pediatric out-patient department. *Paediatrician* 9:224–230.

POSSIBLE *DSM-IV* DIAGNOSES:

309.24   Adjustment Disorder with Anxiety
293.89   Anxiety Disorder Due to a General Medical Condition

14

Learning-Disabled Children

Children with learning disabilities may be found in almost any group of children, and such difficulties are not likely to exist in isolation. Children's problems must always be viewed from a global perspective. Although causality cannot always be established, we do know that such problems typically exist in an interrelated nature. Just as ripples travel the entirety of the pond, disturbances reverberate throughout the child's organism, especially impacting the emotional state of the child. This in turn exacerbates the identified learning difficulty, resulting in a vicious cycle. Published accounts in the literature indicate that play therapy is a viable approach for intervening in this cycle in a manner that frees the child to focus internal resources on correcting the problem. Play therapy, in fact, may be the only experience that allows these children to experience the emotional success that is necessary for them to begin the process of correcting identified problems. Success of any kind has usually been lacking in the lives of these children, and in the playroom they can create their own success.

PLAY THERAPY FOR CHILDREN WITH LEARNING DISABILITIES

AUTHOR: **Claire Lynn Fleet Siegel**

FOCUS: *Play therapy and parental counseling with learning-disabled children.*

INTRODUCTION: Serving learning-disabled children in the educational setting is an important and often difficult task. It includes finding ways to increase a child's cognitive, affective, psychomotor, and environmental dimensions. In this study combinations of play therapy and parental counseling were found to significantly impact the educational dimensions as well as parents' attitudes and the parent–child relationship.

RESEARCH METHODS & DESIGN: Forty-eight second to fifth grade children with learning disabilities participated in this yearlong study. The children were randomly placed in two educational settings: twenty-four children in a special class and twenty-four in regular classes with tutorials, forty minutes a day, five days a week. Twelve children in each class received therapeutic intervention and twelve served as the control group, with no treatment.

Pre- and posttests were given to measure changes in the areas of cognitive, affective, psychomotor, and environmental dimensions. Three constructs derived from factorial analysis of the foregoing dimensions were also analyzed: (1) interaction between parent attitude and child achievement, (2) interaction between child and parent adjustment, and (3) interaction between psychomotor functioning and intelligence. The study ran for a full school year.

INTERVENTION: The treatment group in each class was divided into three groups of four children each. The first group received play therapy, the second group's parents received parental counseling, and the third group received play therapy with parental counseling. All the parents agreed to a minimum of ten counseling sessions.

RESULTS: This yearlong study found that learning-disabled children who received therapeutic interventions significantly improved in all four dimensions: cognitive, affective, psychomotor, and environmental. The children also improved at a statistically significant level in the three constructs, which included the four dimensions identified above: (1) interaction between parent attitude and child achievement, environmental and cognitive (p = .001); (2) interaction between child and parent adjustment, affective and environmental (p = .001); (3) interaction between psychomotor functioning and intelligence, psychomotor and cognitive (p = .05). The children who received none of the therapeutic interventions actually had a decrease in posttesting scores in the psychomotor and cognitive areas, while those receiving therapeutic intervention had increased scores.

There was no significant difference in whether the children were in the special classroom of all learning-disabled children or in a regular classroom receiving additional tutoring.

COMMENTARY: It is apparent that learning-disabled children benefit greatly with the addition of therapeutic interventions to their classroom experiences, regardless of the type of classroom setting. One might expect play therapy and/or parental counseling to improve child–parent interactions, but the added growth and development in areas of cognitive and psychomotor skills is an exciting finding.

SOURCE: Siegel, C. L. F. (1970). The effectiveness of play therapy with other modalities in the treatment of children with learning disabilities. *Dissertation Abstracts International* 31(08):A3970.

POSSIBLE *DSM-IV* DIAGNOSIS:

Insufficient information provided in this study.

15

Mentally Challenged (Handicapped)

Mentally challenged children are first and foremost persons. They happen to have limitations and challenges, as do all persons, to which specific labels have been attached. Like other persons they experience intense emotions and feelings. Until very recently, treatment for mentally challenged children typically involved medication and behavioral control methodologies with little or no attention to their emotional or mental health needs. Estimates of the incidence of emotional problems in mentally challenged individuals range upward to 50 percent with depression, low self-esteem, anxiety, and socialization problems the most common. Play therapy is especially appropriate for these children because it provides a medium of communication and expression uniquely suited to the mental and developmental needs of the child, and the focus is on treatment for emotional problems rather than an exclusive goal of behavioral change. Although slow to become part of the therapeutic procedures used with mentally challenged children, a 1985 survey in the Netherlands found that play therapy was used in approximately 40 percent of the residential centers for mentally challenged persons.

GROUP PLAY THERAPY WITH MENTALLY CHALLENGED CHILDREN

AUTHOR: **Benjamin Mehlman**

FOCUS: *Group play therapy to facilitate the psychological adjustment of mentally challenged children.*

INTRODUCTION: A review of the literature found few references to the use of group play therapy with mentally challenged children. The consensus of the time was that "mental deficiency" was beyond limited psychotherapeutic assistance. This study recognized the importance of the emotional lives of children who are mentally challenged.

RESEARCH METHODS & DESIGN: The subjects for this study were thirty-two children from the Syracuse State School for the Mentally Retarded. The children's ages ranged from 86 to 140 months with a mean age of 120.8 months; the length of residence in the institution ranged from four months to forty-eight months, with a mean length of residence of eighteen months. The order of birth ranged from first to ninth.

Three groups took part in the study: (1) group play therapy, (2) group inactive, and (3) group movie. The group inactive had no contact with the treatment other than the pre- and posttesting. The group movie, in which children were shown short movies or were read stories for the duration of the experiment, was designed as a control for the disturbance of the institutional routine and the personality of the therapist. The play therapy group participated in biweekly nondirective play therapy group sessions. Each session was fifty minutes long, and a total of twenty-nine sessions were held over a sixteen-week period.

Pretesting was conducted during the six-week period prior to commencement of the play therapy group; posttesting was completed in the six-week period following completion of the treatment group. The following instruments were used: the Revised Stanford Binet (Form L), the Grace Arthur Point Scale of Performance Tests (Revised Form II), the Rorschach, the Haggerty-Olson-Wickman Behavior Rating Scale, and the California Test of Personality.

INTERVENTION: Mehlman described the group play therapy as nondirective, "along the lines described by Axline."[1] An attempt was made to have an observer present during each play session. This was administratively feasible for only eighteen of the twenty-nine sessions. The therapist completed reports of each session, which were compared with the notes taken by the observer.

RESULTS: The play therapy group evidenced positive behavioral and personality changes as compared to the other groups on the Haggerty-Olson-Wickman and on the F percent of the Rorschach. There were no statistically significant changes in intelligence measures.

COMMENTARY: Although the statistical significance of the outcome measures was limited, there appeared to be considerable qualitative benefit for the children who participated in group play therapy. Mehlman noted that a basic assumption in the study was that the mentally challenged child, despite intellectual limitations, can grow in play therapy because therapeutic benefit does not depend on intellectual ability. The benefits of the play therapy relationship and the resultant therapeutic progress, while observable on a qualitative level, did not show quantitative significance. Clearly, quality of life for the mentally challenged child extends beyond intelligence measures.

SOURCE: Mehlman, B. (1953). Group play therapy with mentally retarded children. *The Journal of Abnormal and Social Psychology* 48(1): 53–60.

POSSIBLE *DSM-IV* DIAGNOSIS:

319   Mental Retardation, Severity Unspecified

---

1. Virginia Axline, *Play Therapy* (New York: Ballantine Books, 1969).

THE EFFECT OF PLAY THERAPY ON IQ
AND EMOTIONAL AND SOCIAL DEVELOPMENT
OF MENTALLY CHALLENGED CHILDREN

AUTHOR: **Lydia Mundy**

FOCUS: *The use of individual play therapy to alleviate emotional disturbance and increase measured intelligence with mentally challenged children.*

INTRODUCTION: Mundy conducted her research on psychotherapy with mentally challenged children at a time in the field of psychology when psychotherapy was deemed inadvisable with this population. Mentally challenged children who were experiencing neurosis and behavioral disturbance were placed in nondirective play therapy to assess the impact on IQ and social adjustment.

RESEARCH METHODS & DESIGN: The subjects for this study were twenty-three children from the Fountain Hospital in London, England. These children represented the total treatment population, with a comparably matched control group pre- and posttested as well. The average age for children in the treatment group was 8.5 years and for the control group 8.0 years, with a range of 5 to 12 years in both groups. The average age at the time of first hospitalization was 4.5 years for the treatment group and 4.9 for the control group. The initial average IQ of the treatment group was 45, for the control group 44; the difference is statistically nonsignificant.

The assessment instrument utilized for pre- and posttesting was the Revised Stanford Binet (Form L). Qualitative assessment was conducted to measure social adjustment change.

INTERVENTION: Because of the regressed developmental condition of the children, play therapy was selected as the most appropriate medium for communication. The treatment intervention was described as nondirective play therapy "modified by an analytically oriented therapist." The play therapy was carried out over a period of nine to thirteen months, with posttesting conducted within six months. The members of the control group were tested on a similar timetable.

Case details on one child (Janet) were provided in the study because of the pronounced change in her presentation. Although there was no significant change in her intellectual functioning, the "alteration of her behavioral adjustment was so striking that her case seems worth quoting." Janet, who had been virtually nonfunctioning (unintelligible speech, frequent tantrums, poor reality contact), made remarkable progress, as evidenced by increased reality contact, decreased obsessional behaviors, increased comprehension and initiative, and markedly improved speech.

RESULTS: The quantitative results indicated relevant differences between the treatment and control group in terms of IQ measurement. The mean IQ of the treatment group increased nine points in the posttesting versus two points for the control group. Mundy asserts that it could be "assumed with fair certainty that the significant alteration . . . was due to the treatment." In a qualitative assessment of social adjustment, the majority of children in the treatment group were considered ready and suitable for special academic programs for which they were previously deemed inappropriate. There were decreases in temper tantrums and uncooperative behavior as well as increased social cooperation and constructive behavior. One compelling observation was the noteworthy development of verbal ability in a group that initially appeared mentally incapable of verbalizing.

COMMENTARY: Mundy suggested that the most important finding in her study was that children who are mentally challenged exhibit minimal resistance to psychotherapy. The quantitative and qualitative measures support the provision of play therapy interventions with this challenging population. Mundy posited that the benefits of play therapy had far-reaching benefits for these children, noting that the improved social behavior that resulted from the therapy correlated with a greater desire for communication, which in turn produced increased speech and verbalization. The play therapy relationship effectively impacts children regardless of their limitations; mentally challenged children are no exception.

SOURCE: Mundy, L. (1957). Therapy with physically and mentally handicapped children in a mental deficiency hospital. *Journal of Clinical Psychology* 3–9.

POSSIBLE *DSM-IV* DIAGNOSIS:

318.0   Moderate Mental Retardation

PLAY THERAPY WITH MENTALLY CHALLENGED INSTITUTIONALIZED CHILDREN

AUTHORS: **Barbara L. Newcomer and Thomas L. Morrison**

FOCUS: *Individual versus group play therapy and directive versus nondirective play therapy with institutionalized children who were mentally challenged.*

INTRODUCTION: Play therapy interventions were used with institutionalized children who were mentally challenged to assess the impact on social and intellectual functioning.

RESEARCH METHODS & DESIGN: The subjects for this research were twelve children who were mildly and moderately mentally challenged and were institutionalized at a state facility. Their ages ranged from 5.1 to 11.75 years, with a mean age of 8 years. The children were randomly assigned to treatment groups, with four children receiving individual play therapy, four receiving group play therapy, and four forming a no-treatment control group.

The assessment instrument used was the Denver Developmental Screening Test, designed to measure subjects' developmental level. The test categories were (1) gross motor, (2) fine motor-adaptive, (3) language, and (4) personal-social.

INTERVENTION: The children assigned to group or individual play therapy received ten sessions of directive play therapy over a six-week period. Following this, they received ten sessions of nondirective play therapy over a six-week period. They then received ten more sessions of directive play therapy over the next six-week period. Control group members received no treatment. All children were evaluated with the Denver Developmental Screening Test before the commencement of treatment and after each six-week period.

During directive therapy the therapist assumed responsibility for the guidance of the play. In the nondirective therapy the therapist left the responsibility and direction to the child. The same play materials were used in all treatment groups, and the same activities were introduced in the individual and group directive play experience.

RESULTS: The mean scores of the children in the play therapy groups increased continuously over the thirty sessions (eighteen weeks) of therapy. The initial hypothesis that the play therapy intervention given to the children would have a beneficial effect on social and intellectual functioning was confirmed by analysis of variance of the data. The mean scores of the control group remained unchanged. Additional hypotheses regarding different results according to individual versus group play therapy and directive versus nondirective play therapy did not produce statistically significant results. Qualitative observations of the children involved also supported the quantitative results. The authors suggested in their qualitative analysis that directive play therapy seemed more beneficial than the nondirective approach.

COMMENTARY: Newcomer and Morrison suggested that a major benefit of the play therapy intervention was its unique response to the inherent social deprivation that occurs with institutionalization. The children involved in the treatment quickly became attached to the therapist and to the playroom. The authors additionally suggested that the play therapy intervention led to increased motivation on the part of the children involved in the treatment. These two elements may be significant factors in the measured increase in developmental level for the treatment subjects. The authors also posited that directive play therapy was perhaps more appropriate for this population because of the inherent disorganization of children who are mentally challenged. Although this was not shown to be significant in the quantitative results of the study, the more important issue appears to be the clear benefit of the play experience for an often disenfranchised population of children.

SOURCE: Newcomer, B. L., and Morrison, T. L. (1974). Play therapy with institutionalized mentally retarded children. *American Journal of Mental Deficiency* 78(6):727–733.

POSSIBLE *DSM-IV* DIAGNOSES:

317   Mild Mental Retardation
318.0   Moderate Mental Retardation

16

Reading Difficulties

Although the exact nature of the association of reading difficulties and emotional difficulties has not been established, the literature supports the hypothesis that a definite relationship exists. There is consensus that reading problems often stem from emotional maladjustment that has been contributed to by unmet needs. Historically, studies have shown that personality maladjustment frequently coexists with reading difficulties. Our society places such importance on reading achievement that failure in this area often has a negative impact on a child's self-concept. The feelings of frustration, failure, and discouragement that accompany reading difficulties may lead to emotional conflicts, and repeated failure in reading may contribute to making children regard themselves as failures. It is no wonder, therefore, that in such circumstances children feel helpless, hopeless, worthless, impotent, powerless, and unable to change their situation, and thus develop an external rather than internal locus of control. As demonstrated in the studies in this chapter, the unique nature of the play therapy relationship allows children to act out their feelings of frustration, anger, and powerlessness and returns control to children, thus building up their self-concept and empowering them—all necessary in the development of an internal locus of control.

TEACHER USE OF PLAY THERAPY PROCEDURES FOR POOR READERS

AUTHOR: **Virginia Axline**

FOCUS: *Teacher use of play therapy procedures in the classroom to facilitate children's reading readiness.*

INTRODUCTION: Children often have the capacity to learn but may not participate easily in the reading process. This lack of reading readiness is based on many factors, including the skill to translate printed symbols into meaningful words, social and emotional maturity, and life experiences that develop a verbal vocabulary. Teachers may be able to use play therapy procedures to alleviate such problems.

RESEARCH METHODS & DESIGN: The thirty-seven children selected to participate in this study were initially identified by teachers, who were asked to refer seriously maladjusted readers in their classrooms. All those so identified were given the Gray Oral Reading Test and Gray Primary Reading Test. The thirty-seven who received the lowest scores were selected and placed in the same classroom. Their IQ's ranged from 80 to 148. There were eight girls and twenty-nine boys, four children had serious vision problems, five were African-American, and thirty-two were Anglo-American.

   The children's behavior was recorded in several ways. Trained observers recorded the behavior in the classroom weekly. The classroom teacher also kept notes on one-to-one interactions. On the basis of the teacher's interactions, it was discovered that most of the children had serious emotional problems: parental divorce, absence of a parent due to military service (war), verbal and/or physical abuse at home, abandonment by a parent, a seriously ill parent, a murdered parent, and so on. This personal information was not initially known, and therefore not the basis for a child's being selected for this study. However, the researchers later identified emotional difficulties as key to the lack of reading readiness.

   The classroom environment was set up to encourage personal expressiveness. The children were encouraged to interact with the teacher on a one-to-one basis. The teacher responded with child-centered therapeutic responses that included focusing on the child, validating feelings, and respecting the child and the child's world. A variety of media for self-expression was made available in the classroom, including toys, puppets, musical instruments, and art materials. Puppet shows and dramatic play were encouraged. The goal was to assist the children not only to express self but to problem-solve, think through a situation, and clarify their perceptions.

In reading groups the children listened to stories, read stories, and told their own stories. None of them were required to come, but once they realized that reading groups were in fact an option, they came, ready and willing to participate.

Four children received thirty-minute individual play therapy sessions once a week for eight weeks. None of the children received any special remediation in the area of reading or any other intervention.

At the end of four months all the children were given the same reading tests and IQ test.

RESULTS: One child dropped out of the study, leaving thirty-six children. The children's reading skills were subdivided into words, sentences, and paragraphs. In the area of words twenty-one of the children improved beyond the typical growth expected. Their scores ranged from four months' to sixteen months' improvement. In the area of sentences twenty students improved, ranging from four and a half months to fifteen months. Twenty-two students improved over the expected level with reference to paragraphs; their scores ranged from four and a half months to seventeen months. Only six of the thirty-three children showed below-expected gains across all three reading skill areas.

In the area of IQ four children increased their scores by eighteen, twenty-four, thirty-two, and thirty-six points, respectively. Three of the four had received the individual play therapy sessions.

The fourth child who received play therapy sessions had an initial IQ score of 126 and did not show any dramatic increase; her reading scores, however, increased twelve months in words and sentences, and seventeen months in paragraphs.

COMMENTARY: It appears from this study that children can make advances in the areas of reading when provided with a classroom atmosphere in which the teacher is able to respond in a therapeutic manner and the child's self-expression is honored and encouraged. The addition of only eight thirty-minute play therapy sessions resulted in even more dramatic changes for all four children who participated. As Axline commented in this study, there may be a significant emotional factor involved in the lives of children who experience difficulties in reading. However, the emotional factor may not be easily identified, thus not treated.

SOURCE: Axline, V. (1947). Nondirective therapy for poor readers. *Journal of Consulting Psychology* 11:61–69.

POSSIBLE *DSM-IV* DIAGNOSES:

315.00 Reading Disorder

Other diagnoses varied by child:

995.5   Physical Abuse of Child
V61.20 Parent–Child Relational Problem
300.02 Generalized Anxiety Disorder
309.00 Adjustment Disorder
309.21 Separation Anxiety Disorder

BRIEF CLIENT-CENTERED PLAY THERAPY
TO INCREASE READING SKILLS

AUTHOR: **Robert E. Bills**

FOCUS: *The use of child-centered play therapy to improve reading skills in school-age children who were experiencing learning difficulties, especially in reading.*

INTRODUCTION: Bills studied third graders who had been identified as slow learners and who had delayed reading development. Child-centered play therapy was used to remediate the problem based on the belief that poor reading resulted from an inconsistent attitude on the part of a child and a conflict between the child's viewing him- or herself as a good or poor reader.

RESEARCH METHODS & DESIGN: A class of third graders, all identified as slow learners, were selected for this study. The slow learner designation was based on a child's inability to learn at an age-typical speed. None of the children had been placed in this special classroom because of emotional difficulties or limited intellectual factors. All twenty-two children in the selected class began the study, four dropped out for various reasons, leaving eighteen children from whom data were collected and analyzed. Eight children in the treatment group were selected based on intelligence quotient: four had very high intelligence (IQ 111–159) and four had average intelligence (IQ 99–111). The ten children who received no treatment formed a comparison group.

The study was designed to have three time periods: a control–baseline phase, the treatment phase, and the posttreatment phase to assess any lasting effects of the treatment. Each phase consisted of thirty school days. The first phase allowed the children to serve as their own control group and established a baseline for their reading skills. At the beginning and end of this period all the children were given oral and silent reading tests. In the second phase the eight selected children received one individual, client-centered play therapy session each week. A weekly client-centered group play therapy session was added during the last three weeks of this stage. At the end of the third stage all the

children received the oral and silent reading tests. No special intervention was given during this last stage.

RESULTS: The six individual and three group client-centered play
therapy sessions resulted in statistically significant gains in reading
by the children in the treatment group. All of the eight children in
the treatment group increased their reading skills at the end of the
second stage as compared to their scores at the end of the first phase.
Taken as a group, the change was statistically significant at the .001
level of probability. The children's reading skills continued to grow
during the third and final stage although no further intervention was
given. The group's gain during the third and final stage was statistically significant at the .01 level of probability.

The author indicated that the children were either learning at
a more rapid pace because of the play therapy or, more likely, the
play therapy allowed the children to maximize the information they
already had but previously had been unable to use effectively.

COMMENTARY: One of the most exciting findings of this study was that
statistically significant change occurred after only six individual play
therapy sessions and three group play therapy sessions. Also, although
these children were not selected on the basis of any emotional maladjustment, six of the eight also showed improvement in personal
areas. These findings demonstrate the effectiveness of play therapy
in facilitating change in the total child.

SOURCE: Bills, R. E. (1950). Nondirective play therapy with retarded
readers. *Journal of Consulting Psychology* 14:140–149.

POSSIBLE *DSM-IV* DIAGNOSIS:

315.00   Reading Disorder

PLAY THERAPY AS AN INTERVENTION FOR A READING PROBLEM

AUTHOR: **Ray H. Bixler**

FOCUS: *Use of play therapy with a 10-year-old boy with poor reading performance and behavioral problems.*

INTRODUCTION: William was initially referred for counseling because he was underachieving in school, specifically reading, and was at risk of failing the third grade. An IQ test indicated average intelligence, and an achievement test revealed he was working about one year behind his grade placement. His mother reported behavioral problems in the home, which included two brothers, one a year older and one aged 3½. His father was also in the home, and both parents were employed.

CASE STUDY: William began play therapy with a counselor with whom he developed a deep therapeutic relationship. After twenty sessions his first counselor left and a second counselor provided William's last eight play therapy sessions. Nondirective play therapy was used, with an emphasis on limit setting. William's mother was inconsistent in bringing him to his sessions, which often meant several weeks between sessions and prematurely terminated treatment. During the play therapy intervention it became apparent that William was having problems with sibling rivalry, which in turn led to scholastic problems.

During the first twenty sessions William often talked about problems at school. He stated that his school was "one of the rottenest" and that he hated the school. William also expressed his wish to be able to read better. In the eighth session he reported that his younger brother had broken his sailboat. In the ninth session his interaction referred to both brothers. In his final two to three sessions with his first therapist William struggled to work through the termination of that relationship. He threatened to lock up the therapist so he could not leave and to shoot pins at the new therapist.

In the first session with the new therapist William expressed his disappointment with having to establish a new relationship. During this process William tested the limits to see just what the new therapist would allow him to do and to identify the differences between the therapists. In the second session with the new therapist a great deal of aggressive play occurred, during which William communicated that he did not like it when things did not go his way. William also expressed, through play, that even though he was taking the role of the "bad guy," he would rather be the "good guy." This conflict between good and bad continued for several sessions.

William continued to express aggression during work with the new therapist. The therapist continued to set firm, appropriate limits. The ongoing theme appeared to be focused around how much destructive behavior the therapist would tolerate and still accept William, particularly when the aggression was aimed at the baby dolls. When the therapist correctly reflected back William's feelings, William ceased being destructive and engaged in constructive play. When the therapist missed the feeling, however, or became too interpretive, William's aggressive and/or destructive play escalated.

William's mother terminated play therapy when his behavior problems cleared up at home and he began passing subjects at school. William, who had correctly spelled words in several of his sessions, brought his spelling list into his final session and misspelled all of them. This seemed to be a clear expression that he did not feel ready to terminate.

COMMENTARY: Bixler used this case example to identify the importance of treating the child and not the presenting problem or diagnosis. Bixler stated that nondirective play therapy results in a speedier resolution to children's problems in that children are allowed to deal with what is of importance to them. As in William's case, if intervention had focused on the reading problems through tutoring, the real cause of his problems would never have been addressed.

Bixler also detailed excerpts from the new therapist's sessions. Each session is followed by Bixler's assessment of the therapist's responses, identifying strong, appropriate responses, and contrasting those that were off target with examples of better responses. This format is of additional help to the play therapist as it facilitates understanding of where one might easily go astray in a session.

SOURCE: Bixler, R. H. (1945). Treatment of a reading problem through nondirective play therapy. *Journal of Consulting Psychology* 9:105–118.

POSSIBLE *DSM-IV* DIAGNOSES:

315.00   Reading Disorder
V61.8   Sibling Relational Problem

17

Selective Mutism

Selective mutism, in which children remain silent in certain situations, is a relatively rare childhood disorder; some researchers estimate seven cases per thousand children. The 1994 *DSM-IV* changed the name of this disorder from Elective Mutism (*DSM-III-R*), which the committee felt was less descriptive and implied motivation, to Selective Mutism. The terms are used interchangeably in this chapter since the majority of articles in the literature refer to elective mutism. This condition is most frequently observed when the child talks at home but not at school, although there have been some cases in which the reverse is true. We are familiar with primary-grade children who will not talk in the classroom or read aloud in the reading circle but read at an advanced level at home. This can be an exasperating situation for the teacher who must give a grade for reading.

Children who are selectively mute tend to be oppositional, defiant, controlling, moody, aggressive, stubborn, sulky, strong willed, and distrustful, and to have temper tantrums. They can also be submissive, sensitive, weepy, insecure, frightened, passive, anxious, fearful, and dependent. Play therapy is the recommended treatment of choice for children who are selectively mute because there is no pressure or expectation to verbalize. Play allows them to safely express feelings about the self that they have felt was unacceptable. The play therapist's acceptance of these feelings allows the children to experience themselves in a more positive way. As these children are able to accept themselves, they can relinquish the silence that has defended their sense of self.

NONDIRECTIVE PLAY THERAPY WITH AN ELECTIVE MUTE CHILD

AUTHOR: **Virginia M. Axline**

FOCUS: *Use of nondirective play therapy with a 5-year-old boy with elective mutism and undersocialized behaviors.*

INTRODUCTION: Billy was referred for play therapy because of the threat of expulsion from kindergarten. Billy would not interact with other children and would not speak to anyone. He crawled around the room close to the wall, and when approached by another child rolled up into a ball and hid his face. He would not participate in any school activities and would not listen to stories. Billy had not been like this when he entered kindergarten six months earlier, however.

CASE STUDY: Billy's mother reported that his development appeared to be healthy until the age of 3 when he suddenly stopped talking, stopped walking, and regressed to a completely infantile stage. This change in behavior followed the mother's (recent) hospitalization for emergency surgery. She took Billy to a physician, who diagnosed him as "feebleminded." She reported that Billy's brother was "feeble-minded" (mentally retarded), and that she was fearful that Billy might also be. He was physically in good health, but had received a psychometrist's report of an IQ score of sixty-eight.

INTERVENTION: Billy entered the playroom with a blank stare, drooping figure, and shuffling gait. He went to the middle of the room and stared, and was told by the therapist that he could play with any of the toys if he wanted to. After standing for a long time, Billy played by sifting his hands in the sandbox for the entire session. He seemed more alert in the second session, playing again in the sand and occasionally looking silently at the therapist. During the third session he played with cars in the sand and made a few comments to the therapist, who replied each time Billy spoke. When Billy came in for his fourth session, there was a significant change in his behavior. He did not drag his feet, he was more alert, and he talked with the therapist. Billy's mother reported a noticeable change at home, with Billy talking more, appearing less tense, and the regressive behavior disappearing. During the fifth week the school called home to inquire about what was happening with Billy, as his behavior at school was also changing positively.

RESULTS: Billy continued to improve during the ensuing weeks of play therapy. He talked more with the therapist, and his play became more complex and imaginative and his demeanor more positive and free. The mother reported more assertive behavior at home and a greater willingness to venture out into the neighborhood. There were still some difficulties at school, however, where Billy had been labeled by the teachers and ostracized by the other students. The therapy was concluded with a series of group play therapy sessions that significantly reduced the social difficulties at school. One year after termination the mother reported that Billy had adjusted excellently to a new school situation, was doing well academically (a new IQ score put him well within the average range), and was a "happy, relaxed child."

COMMENTARY: Axline postulated that a child behaves as he perceives himself in relation to others, and that a child's behavior is dependent upon the current feeling of adequacy or inadequacy in coping with the particular circumstances. She believed that Billy's play therapy provided a freeing experience from the "chains of past experiences" and gave him a safe place in which to operate. It was in this environment that Billy was able to process his issues and express himself fully. The changes that occurred for Billy in the playroom naturally translated outside into his life at home and school. The safety and the relationship that Axline's approach offered Billy are conditions that the elective mute child seems to need in order to find the freedom so desired.

SOURCE: Axline, V. M. (1948). Some observations on play therapy. *Journal of Consulting Psychology* 12:209–216.

POSSIBLE *DSM-IV* DIAGNOSES:

313.23   Selective Mutism
300.23   Social Phobia, Generalized
317.0   Mild Mental Retardation

INDIVIDUAL AND SIBLING GROUP PLAY THERAPY WITH A SELECTIVE MUTE CHILD

AUTHORS: **Karen Barlow, JoAnna Strother, and Garry Landreth**

FOCUS: *Use of individual and sibling group play therapy to treat selective mutism and enuresis in a 5-year-old girl.*

INTRODUCTION: Amy refused to talk at school or in any situation away from the home, and exhibited excessive shyness, enuresis, and nighttime bedwetting. Amy's two brothers had also suffered from nighttime bedwetting. Previous research has shown high incidents of enuresis, excessive shyness, and immaturity among selective mute children.

CASE STUDY: Amy did not speak a single word during the first five months she was enrolled in the early childhood program at her school. She passed all the nonverbal items at the appropriate age level on an early childhood screening test and was put in a special education class. Amy's teachers observed her to be a passive little girl who sat and observed activity around her. Her social skills were virtually nonexistent. She did not play with groups of children, but preferred to play alone or with an adult. An unusual behavior was that Amy did not show pain even in extreme situations, such as having her pierced earrings pulled through her ears while playing or when she fell in the gymnasium at school, which caused her mouth to bleed.

INTERVENTION: Amy was seen in a combination of individual and sibling group play therapy once a week for nine months. During the initial session in play therapy she was totally nonverbal. She hid under the paint easel and gestured for forty-five minutes. In the second session Amy refused to enter the playroom without a friend who had accompanied her to the center. In this session Amy chatted and played contentedly with the friend. In later sessions Amy's friend was not available, and it was decided to add Ben, her 9-year-old brother, and Ned, her 2-year-old brother, to the sessions individually at different times. When Ben was in the playroom, he was the responsible one—

for himself and for Amy. Ben talked and played for both of them. When Amy played in the playroom with Ned, she was the teacher and helper, although Ned was independent. When Amy played alone in the playroom, she remained shy, yet verbal. A combination of sibling play therapy, individual play therapy, and brief family consultation was found to be the most appropriate approach.

A theme that continued for most of the play sessions was Amy's need to be in total control, and she used silence to accomplish this by demanding the play therapist be silent. As Amy became more independent, Ben dropped his role as protector and responsible member of the family. Amy's new confidence extended into the home and classroom as she began to express feelings more frequently and talking, singing, and participating in class became fun for her. As Amy became more verbal and participated more actively in her world, the enuresis occurred less frequently.

COMMENTARY: Because elective mute children have a purpose for their behavior, verbal prodding by adults usually reaps few benefits. Play therapy provides the child with a safe place where there is no pressure to talk. The authors conclude that lack of verbal communication skills and underdeveloped social skills were paralyzing Amy's efforts to function in society beyond her immediate family. Individual play therapy in this case seemed to bring faster results because the issues could be defined immediately, and work in sessions and at home could begin on the shift in the communication pattern. The sibling group play therapy sessions provided an intimate environment in which Amy could interact safely.

SOURCE: Barlow, K., Strother, J., and Landreth, G. (1986). Sibling group play therapy: an effective alternative with an elective mute child. *The School Counselor* 34(1):44–50.

POSSIBLE *DSM-IV* DIAGNOSES:

317.23   Selective Mutism
307.6   Enuresis

PSYCHOANALYTIC PLAY THERAPY WITH AN ELECTIVE MUTE CHILD

AUTHOR: **Morton Chetnik**

FOCUS: *Intensive treatment of a 6-year-old girl with elective mutism, using play techniques.*

INTRODUCTION: Amy was referred for treatment for elective mutism, together with noncompliance, multiple fears, and other parental concerns. The two years of Amy's psychoanalytic treatment included play therapy, doll play, and art and clay work.

CASE STUDY: Amy was reported to have had a "talking problem" all her life. In kindergarten she had not spoken to her teachers or peers for the entire year. At home she whispered occasionally with her parents or siblings and never to anyone else. Amy was generally described as stubborn, passive, and withdrawing, and was considerably noncompliant at home. She also had a number of fears, including a strong fear of dogs, bedtime fears, and a fear of being alone. Amy experienced occasional enuresis and soiling at times of increased anxiety. Her parents expressed concern about Amy's vivid fantasy life, which would sometimes be intense and aggressive.

Amy was from a large family, the fifth of six children. She became hostile and aggressive toward her younger sibling at birth, and the infant had to be protected from her. At age 3 Amy fell into a pool and had to be resuscitated after several minutes of unconsciousness. A resulting lung infection resulted in six weeks of hospitalization. She never spoke while hospitalized, and her eating and verbalization remained restrictive until the time of referral.

INTERVENTION: Treatment consisted of two years of intensive psychoanalytic play therapy. Amy was "totally silent" throughout the treatment process, although Chetnik reported many forms of "vivid communication" during the sessions. These included drawing, writing, intense play, body gestures, and, finally, sounds.

In the first few weeks of the therapy Amy would play in a corner of the room in a "compulsive" manner, primarily focused on using the clay. During this early play she was very distressed about messiness. Eventually she moved to the doll family, where the play consisted of separations of family members and loving reunions. Amy also played out several pediatric visits. Another theme during these early months of treatment was role-playing animals and play with the scissors. Interpretive comments by the therapist during this play resulted in Amy's becoming increasingly anxious and regressive in her play.

Chetnik also worked with the parents during the course of treatment and reported that Amy's mother in particular had considerable negative emotions about her daughter's situation. A pattern of lateness and unpaid sessions became an issue during this process.

Chetnik reported markedly improved adjustment for Amy during the second year of treatment. He described Amy's "control" of the process, using examples of how Amy would sing on her way to the playroom, but refuse to verbalize once in the room. She began to talk in most settings, but not in the playroom. During this second year her speech difficulties decreased and disappeared outside treatment. Amy began to participate in the classroom, made friends with several of her classmates, began to talk with neighbors, and greatly enjoyed talking on the phone. Chetnik also reported that Amy's relationship with her mother had shown remarkable improvement.

COMMENTARY: Play therapy provides a child with an opportunity to be in control regardless of the specific therapeutic approach. Amy was able to process her need for power and control in the play sessions, which resulted in the amelioration of her presenting symptoms. She "communicated" in a variety of ways during the treatment process, which led to increased communication outside therapy. Chetnik concluded his report of the process with a discussion of psychoanalytic issues in the play as well as diagnostic and prognostic concerns. Chetnik was able to keep in touch with the family and noted that Amy remained stable throughout her latency years. The psychoanalytic play experience was clearly beneficial for Amy, resulting not only in symptom reduction, but also in the opportunity to gain mastery and control in the play and in her life.

SOURCE: Chetnik, M. (1973). The intensive treatment of an elective mute. *Journal of the American Academy of Child Psychiatry* 12(3): 482–498.

POSSIBLE *DSM-IV* DIAGNOSES:

313.23   Selective Mutism
309.21   Separation Anxiety Disorder
313.81   Oppositional Defiant Disorder

18

Self-Concept and Self-Esteem

The terms *self-concept* and *self-esteem* are often used synony-mously and are therefore combined in this chapter. Self-concept is the internal measure of one's worth. The individual forms a sense of self based on external experiences and internal perceptions. Self-concept may be defined as *the perceptions individuals hold about them-selves* or as *a set of beliefs about self*—the evaluation a person usually maintains about self that suggests the degree to which an individual sees himself or herself to be capable, acceptable, successful, and im-portant. Play is a key factor in a child's development, learning, and self-concept. Research studies have demonstrated a significantly positive correlation between self-concept and parental acceptance, academic achievement, classroom adjustment, perception of oth-ers, sociometric choice status, emotional adjustment, and overall personal adjustment. Children express their thoughts and feelings primarily through play. Play also allows a child to practice activities and to master skills. The play therapy relationship provides the necessary freedom for introspection and development of an inner life that are the prerequisites for a positive self-concept. In this relationship, in which responsibility is returned to the child, the child can begin to gain mastery over the environment and the self. As is shown in this chapter, parents in the most adverse of circumstances can be taught to use play therapy skills to improve their children's self-concepts.

PLAY THERAPY INCREASES THE SELF-CONCEPT OF POOR READERS

AUTHOR: Judy Crow

FOCUS: *Children who are poor readers often have low self-esteem. This research study explored the use of play therapy to increase the self-esteem of poor readers.*

INTRODUCTION: School-based play therapy sessions were provided for children identified as poor readers who had been held back in first grade. Because of the school schedule, slight modifications to the usual forty-five- to fifty-minute session were necessary.

RESEARCH METHODS & DESIGN: The children for this study were initially identified as children who had been retained in the first grade and had the lowest scores on the Gates-MacGinite Reading Test or the Stanford Reading Achievement Test. Children from two schools participated in the study; students in one school were the experimental group, and the students in the second school were the control group. All the children completed a battery of instruments before and after treatment. The instruments used to collect data were the Gates-MacGinite Reading Test, Piers-Harris Children's Self-Concept Scale, and the Intellectual Achievement Responsibility Questionnaire.

INTERVENTION: For the following ten weeks, the twelve children in the experimental group received one thirty-minute play therapy session each week. The author was the play therapist. She had been trained specifically in play therapy in the graduate program at the University of North Texas. She also had one year of supervised clinical experience in play therapy.

After the ten sessions of play therapy ended, the same instruments used to collect the predata were administered again. One child in each group, experiential and control, had moved, leaving eleven in each group. The resulting data were statistically analyzed using the analysis of covariance (ANCOVA) to take into account any initial differences between the two groups. (ANCOVA is also sensitive to any differences among group members.)

RESULTS: The children who received play therapy improved in their self-concept as measured by the Piers-Harris Children's Self-Concept Scale. The increase in self-concept was statistically significant at the .0435 level. The Intellectual Achievement Responsibility Questionnaire was used to measure the locus of control. The children involved in play therapy improved their internal locus of control; the children in the control group did not. All twenty-two children made gains in their reading ability as assessed by the Gates-MacGinite Reading Test. There was no noticeable difference in the gains made between the children in the experimental or control groups.

The play therapist also identified changes in specific children over the course of the sessions. Several displayed play therapy behaviors that indicated an increase in attention span and the ability to focus. Another child, who never spoke during initial sessions, displayed greater self-confidence and frequently spoke in more complex sentences. A child who allowed her twin sister to initiate social and academic interactions developed her own sense of control and assertive skills during play therapy. A very aggressive boy, often identified as out of control, exhibited substantial aggression in the initial play therapy sessions. As his sessions continued he developed self-control as evidenced in his development of more appropriately timed speech patterns.

COMMENTARY: School-based play therapy has been found very effective for children in need of improvement in self-concept and a wide variety of other problems and concerns. It is encouraging that thirty-minute sessions appear to be effective interventions. These shorter sessions fit more easily into the school schedule and allow the school counselor to serve more children. The shorter sessions also indicate to play therapists in a nonschool setting that significant therapeutic responses can occur.

SOURCE: Crow, J. (1990). Play therapy with low achievers in reading. Doctoral dissertation, University of North Texas, 1989. *Dissertation Abstracts International* 50(09):B2789.

POSSIBLE *DSM-IV* DIAGNOSIS:

315.00   Reading Disorder

FILIAL THERAPY AS AN EFFECTIVE INTERVENTION FOR INCREASING CHILDREN'S SELF-CONCEPT

AUTHOR: **Nancy Miller Glass**

FOCUS: *Training parents in child-centered play therapy procedures as a methodology for increasing children's self-concepts.*

INTRODUCTION: Glass concluded from her literature review that the variables of parental acceptance and self-esteem are essential to positive parent–child relationships and that filial therapy provides advantages over traditional approaches to child treatment. Her study was conducted to determine the effect of filial therapy on parental acceptance, child and parent self-concept, parent–child relationships, and family environment as assessed by both parents and children.

RESEARCH METHODS & DESIGN: The subjects for this study included twenty-seven parents and twenty children who had voluntarily applied for filial therapy at a counseling center. The experimental group consisted of the first fifteen parents who contacted the center requesting the therapy; the control group, the remaining twelve parents. (These parents were placed on a waiting list to receive filial therapy at a future date.) The children who participated in the study were between the ages of 5 and 10 and were described by their parents as displaying behavior that was a source of concern to them. The measurement instruments used included the Porter Parental Acceptance Scale, the Coopersmith Self-Esteem Inventory, the Primary Self-Concept Inventory, the Madanes Family Hierarchy Test, the Family Environment Scale, and the Children's Version of the Family Environment Scale. The experimental design of the study was a nonrandomized, pretest–posttest, control group design.

INTERVENTION: Filial therapy was originally conceptualized by Bernard Guerney (1964)[1] as a structured treatment program for children

---

1. Bernard G. Guerney, Jr., "Filial Therapy: Description and Rationale," *Journal of Consulting Psychology* (1964), 28:304–360.

ages 3 through 10 with emotional problems. Parents are trained to apply the concepts and techniques of child-centered play therapy with their own children. Training is conducted in a small group format through didactic instruction, videotapes, role playing, and supervision. The program structure includes regularly scheduled parent–child special play sessions at home in which the parent rather than a professional therapist is the therapeutic agent. Parents receive supervision for these play sessions from an experienced filial therapist and have the opportunity to discuss their experiences with other parents during weekly group meetings.

For this study experimental group parents were divided into three filial groups that met weekly in two-hour sessions for ten consecutive weeks. Parents were trained to conduct weekly thirty-minute play sessions with their children at home while they continued their weekly training group meetings. Control group parents and children met only for administration of the pre- and posttests.

RESULTS: The mean difference for pre-post scores on measures of self-concept for both children and parents in the experimental group showed positive, although not statistically significant, change as compared to scores for the control group. The mean difference for pre-post scores on the Porter Parental Acceptance Scale did show significant positive change as compared to the control group scores. Since self-concept of the child has been shown to be highly related to parental acceptance or rejection, the increase in parental acceptance resulting from the filial therapy training could be expected to affect the child's self-concept over time.

COMMENTARY: Although results from the various instruments did not always indicate significant change, the clearly positive trends reported in Glass's study lend support for the use of filial therapy as an effective intervention for parents and children. Filial therapy affects the parent–child relationship from both sides. Increased self-concept in children contributes to less inappropriate behaviors. Increased acceptance by parents reduces the negative impact of problem behaviors in children. An additional benefit of filial therapy is the empowering of parents to actively intervene in their children's lives rather than defer to an expert.

SOURCE: Glass, N. M. (1987). Parents as therapeutic agents: a study of the effect of filial therapy. Doctoral dissertation, University of North Texas, 1986. *Dissertation Abstracts International* 47(07):A2457.

POSSIBLE *DSM-IV* DIAGNOSIS:

Insufficient information provided in the study.

ACTIVITY PLAY THERAPY TO INCREASE ELEMENTARY STUDENTS' SELF-CONCEPT

AUTHOR: **Myrna Frank Gould**

FOCUS: *Using group play therapy to improve the self-concept of elementary school students.*

INTRODUCTION: Research was conducted within a school system to discover the feasibility and effectiveness of providing group play therapy and discussion group experiences for children within that environment.

RESEARCH METHODS & DESIGN: The Piers-Harris Children's Self-Concept Scale (CSCS) was administered to eighty-four elementary school children identified by teachers as having low self-image although not suffering from significant maladjustment. The children were then randomly assigned to experimental, placebo, and control groups with twenty-one children in each group. Pretest and posttest scores from the Piers-Harris CSCS were compared for all groups using analysis of variance and t tests.

INTERVENTION: The children from the experimental group were divided into groups of three or four and participated in nondirective group play therapy once each week for twelve weeks. Children in the placebo group were divided into three groups of seven and participated in discussion groups under the same schedule. Half the children in the control group met only for administration of the pre- and posttests; the remainder met only for administration of the posttest.

RESULTS: The mean difference for pre-post scores on the Piers-Harris CSCS for both the play therapy group and the discussion group showed positive change. The strongest positive change was noted for the children who participated in group play therapy. No significant change was noted for the control group.

COMMENTARY: Gould suggested that the school is in a unique position to make a valuable contribution to the mental health of children.
The opportunity to interact with each other in group play therapy
and/or discussion groups provides children with the chance to learn
and practice new social skills within a controlled environment, resulting in a measurable increase in self-concept. Gould suggests that both
play therapy and discussion groups be conducted as part of the regular planned school program. It was the researcher's belief that *all* children could benefit from therapeutic interventions, which historically
have been assigned and relegated to those defined as "at risk."

SOURCE: Gould, M. F. (1980). The effect of short-term intervention
play therapy on the self-concept of selected elementary pupils. Doctoral dissertation, Florida Institute of Technology, 1980. *Dissertation
Abstracts International* 41 (03):B1090.

POSSIBLE *DSM-IV* DIAGNOSIS:

Insufficient information provided in the study.

CHILD-CENTERED GROUP PLAY THERAPY AS AN INTERVENTION TO INCREASE SOCIOMETRIC STATUS AND SELF-CONCEPT

AUTHOR: **Reese Milton House**

FOCUS: *Using child-centered group play therapy to bring about desired changes in self-concept in children identified as underchosen on a sociometric test.*

INTRODUCTION: After conducting a review of the literature, House concluded that the effectiveness of child-centered group play therapy had not been validated. His study was designed to investigate the effects of child-centered group play on the self-concept and sociometric status of selected second grade children in a public school setting.

RESEARCH METHODS & DESIGN: Thirty-six children were selected for the sample. Twelve children each—six boys and six girls—were randomly assigned to the experimental group, control group one, and control group two. The Scamin Self-Concept Scale and a sociometric test were administered to the subjects before and at the conclusion of treatment. A two-factor mixed design with repeated measures on one factor analysis of variance was used to compare experimental and control groups on each instrument.

INTERVENTION: Members selected for the experimental group participated in child-centered play therapy in groups of six for twenty thirty-minute sessions conducted by the researcher over a period of ten weeks; members selected for control group one participated in a specialized reading program under the same regimen. Members assigned to control group two received no treatment other than pre- and posttests.

RESULTS: The self-concept of members of the experimental group increased significantly over the ten-week period while the self-concept of members of both control groups decreased slightly, although not significantly. All three groups demonstrated a significant increase in sociometric status. House noted that since the stability of sociometric relationships is probably not firmly established by mid-October of the second grade, developing and changing relationships in the classroom may cause sociometric status to change at this age level. The experimental group did show a greater score gain in sociometric status than the control groups, though the difference was not significant. Since the teachers were aware of the underchosen members, perhaps they facilitated some changes in sociometric status through their attitudes toward these children. In the case of the two control groups an increased status position apparently does not positively influence one's view of self, as measured by the Scamin Self-Concept Scale. However, the self-concept of members of the control groups may increase eventually, especially if their higher sociometric status is maintained.

COMMENTARY: Participation in child-centered group play therapy provides a climate for change in which a child can learn to express feelings in appropriate ways, resulting in the development of positive regard for self and others. This change supports the premise that an individual has a strong capacity for growth toward mature behavior if given the freedom to do so. The value and importance of a healthy self-concept has been established in our society. Implications for the use of child-centered group play therapy in the public schools seem to be clear. Since two half-hour group play therapy sessions per week significantly enhanced the self-concept of children identified as underchosen, initiating an extensive program of child-centered group play therapy as part of any elementary counseling program would be highly recommended.

SOURCE: House, R. M. (1970). The effects of nondirective group play therapy upon the sociometric status and self-concept of selected second grade children. Doctoral dissertation, Oregon State University, 1970. *Dissertation Abstracts International* 31 (06):A2684.

POSSIBLE *DSM-IV* DIAGNOSIS:

Insufficient information provided in the study.

FILIAL THERAPY AS A TREATMENT MODALITY TO IMPROVE PARENT–CHILD RELATIONS AND INCREASE SELF-ESTEEM IN YOUNG CHILDREN OF INCARCERATED FATHERS

AUTHOR: **Frank Alan Lobaugh**

FOCUS: *Incarcerated fathers were trained to use child-centered play therapy procedures in thirty-minute play sessions when their children visited the prison.*

INTRODUCTION: Incarceration places emotional as well as physical distance between inmates and families. Filial training was introduced as an intervention to enhance the parent–child relationship and to positively impact the self-concepts of children whose fathers were incarcerated.

RESEARCH METHODS & DESIGN: Thirty-two incarcerated fathers randomly selected from volunteers who had been screened for English literacy and previous parenting classes were divided into an experimental group of sixteen and a control group of sixteen. Fathers in the control group were informed that they would receive training after the first training group was completed. All of the fathers completed instruments in a pre- and posttest setting. The instruments included the Porter Parental Acceptance Scale, the Parenting Stress Index, and the Filial Problems Checklist. All of the children completed the Joseph Preschool and Primary Self-Concept Scale in a pre- and posttest setting. Data gathered from the pre- and posttest instruments were evaluated using analyses of covariance.

INTERVENTION: For this study fathers in the experimental group met weekly for ninety-minute filial training sessions for ten weeks. In addition, each father in the experimental group was required to conduct special thirty-minute play sessions once a week with one of their children previously identified as the child of focus. Fathers in the control group received no training and agreed to see their child of focus during visitation in a playroom setting at least ten times.

RESULTS: Children of fathers in the experimental group showed significant increase in their scores on the measure of self-concept. Experimental-group fathers showed significant increases in their scores on unconditional love for their children, acceptance of their children's feelings and their children's right to express those feelings, acceptance of their children's unique makeup, and recognition of their children's needs for autonomy and independence. Parental stress decreased significantly for fathers in the experimental group, and the fathers reported significantly fewer perceived child behavior problems on the Filial Problems Checklist.

COMMENTARY: Filial therapy was shown to make a significant impact in the lives of incarcerated fathers and their children. The stress on both parent and child when the parent is incarcerated permeates every aspect of a child's life. An intervention that helps to support the parent–child relationship and measurably improves a child's self-concept relieves some of that stress and increases the child's ability to cope. The key ingredients that facilitated the parent-child relationship seemed to be the focused attention on the individual child and the use of newly learned play therapy skills that parents used within a special playtime environment. Equally significant results would seem to be just as likely with a less difficult population.

SOURCE: Lobaugh, F. A. (1992). Filial therapy with incarcerated parents. Doctoral dissertation, University of North Texas, 1991. *Dissertation Abstracts International* 53(04):B2046.

POSSIBLE *DSM-IV* DIAGNOSIS:

V61.20   Parent–Child Relational Problem

19

Social Adjustment Problems

Perhaps more than any other single indicator, social interactions—or the lack thereof—provide essential clues to children's emotional growth and adjustment. When poor relationships exist with peers or siblings, underlying needs of children should be examined. Likewise, socially immature, shy, or withdrawn behavior should call attention to children's poor self-concepts, feelings of inadequacy, need for nurturing, lack of acceptance in their lives, or intense interpersonal conflicts. These children often exhibit poor impulse control or quietly withdraw into themselves. For children who perceive themselves as different from their peers, or who have poor social interactions, group play therapy provides an especially effective modality for them to learn new social skills, to discover that they are capable, to receive the peer acceptance that is so crucial, and to develop self-control and self-acceptance. Group play therapy would especially be indicated in day care centers, kindergartens, school settings, and residential treatment centers. Play therapists are cautioned to equip themselves with the necessary training and supervision in group play therapy before using this approach.

GROUP PLAY THERAPY AS AN INTERVENTION FOR CHILDREN WITH PEER AND SIBLING RELATIONSHIP PROBLEMS

AUTHOR: **Claire M. Bloomberg**

FOCUS: *The use of group play therapy to improve peer relationships during group activities at school and relationships with siblings at home.*

INTRODUCTION: The majority of children who have difficulty interacting with peer groups at school were also found to have problems with sibling rivalry. Group play therapy provided the setting for these children to deal with their interactional problems.

RESEARCH METHODS & DESIGN: Two groups of five children were selected on the basis of Rorschach tests, teacher input, and therapist observations to participate in group play therapy sessions. The groups met once a week for an hour throughout the school year. The same play therapist worked with both play therapy groups using, as inferred from the description, a nondirective approach.

INTERVENTION: The children were free to choose the toys they wanted to play with; play activities were not suggested. Snacks, crackers, and juice were available whenever the children wanted them during the session. The play therapist allowed a wide range of behavior, including dumping water on the floor and smearing clay on the walls.

The play therapist indicated that the group members served as pseudosiblings and she as the pseudomother. Her approach was to reflect relationship interactions, such as, "I wonder if you know what you're fighting about? Are you fighting because you think I can't love more than one person at a time?"

Themes of the play included redefining the relationship between self and the sibling. Initially the play was ambivalent—sometimes nurturing, sometimes aggressive. One child killed the baby doll and then brought it back to life just before the end of the session. As termination approached, the play was more nurturing and positive.

Another theme was the interaction between the children and the play therapist. At one stage the children banded together against the play therapist. The play therapist saw this as the children, in reality, trying to work through their feelings regarding their mothers. Eventually all the children were able to express positive feelings toward the play therapist.

The play therapist met twice with the parents during the year to assist them in identifying the purpose of their child's behavior. The therapist indicated that two meetings were not sufficient to establish a working relationship with the parents.

RESULTS: The author briefly discussed the positive benefit of the group play therapy in qualitative terms. The children were described as more collaborative and less negative in their family and social interactions. A primary benefit of the group play approach was that the children discovered they were not alone in having "bad feelings." Increased positive affect and self-esteem were also noted.

COMMENTARY: Children who had problems interacting with their siblings had similar problems interacting with peers at school. Nondirective group play therapy appears to have been an effective intervention for these children. The establishment of a pseudofamily to assist these children in learning to handle a wide variety of emotions in the presence of an accepting adult had positive and therapeutic results for these children. When children's needs are met in a supportive group, coping skills are released to develop more positive relationship skills.

SOURCE: Bloomberg, C. (1948). An experiment in play therapy. *Childhood Education* 177–180.

POSSIBLE *DSM-IV* **DIAGNOSES:**

V61.20   Parent–Child Relational Problem
V61.8   Sibling Relational Problem
V61.81   Relational Problem NOS

SELF-DIRECTIVE PLAY THERAPY AS A TREATMENT FOR SOCIALLY IMMATURE KINDERGARTEN CHILDREN

AUTHOR: **Lee Edward Pelham**

FOCUS: *Group and individual play therapy as an intervention for socially immature kindergarten children.*

INTRODUCTION: The purpose of this study was to determine whether self-directive play therapy would be effective in increasing the social maturity of kindergarten students who had been identified by their teachers as socially immature.

RESEARCH METHODS & DESIGN: Nine kindergarten teachers referred fifty-two children characterized as "socially immature." Eighteen were randomly selected for membership in a control group that received no treatment. Of the thirty-four remaining students, seventeen received parental permission to participate in the study. Nine of the seventeen were assigned to receive group play therapy in three groups of three. The remaining eight were assigned to receive individual play therapy. Instruments used to test the hypothesis included the Missouri Children's Picture Services (MCPS), the Children's Self-Social Constructs Tests (CSSCT), and the Behavior Problem Checklist (BPC). Comparisons were made regarding the relative effectiveness of group and individual play therapy. Statistical analysis of the data was completed using analysis of covariance with the pretest scores used as the control variable.

INTERVENTION: Each child received six to eight forty-five-minute self-directive play therapy sessions conducted by the author. Nine children received group play therapy and the remaining eight participated in individual play therapy sessions.

RESULTS: Children who received either individual play therapy or group play therapy made positive gains in social maturity when compared to the control group. There was no significant difference in the amount of increase between the two groups. The children in these two groups scored more positively on the complexity scale of the CSSCT, which was used as a measure of self-concept and was also related to a person's ability to be flexible in response to new experiences. Teacher ratings of the BPC indicated that children receiving group and individual play therapy improved significantly in classroom behavior when compared to children in the control group. In retrospect the author found the MCPS did not measure maturity as identified by teachers and may not have been a valid measure of maturity for the younger children.

COMMENTARY: Play therapy, either individual or group, proved to be an effective intervention for immature kindergarten children. Improvements were seen in classroom behavior, self-concept, flexibility in new situations, and social maturity after only six to eight forty-five-minute sessions. Since more children can be served in a group play therapy format, this may be the most efficient use of time and resources in the school setting for this particular concern. Ineffective behaviors learned outside the play therapy group can be unlearned in the group.

SOURCE: Pelham, L. E. (1972). Self-directive play therapy with socially immature kindergarten students. Doctoral dissertation, University of Northern Colorado, 1971. *Dissertation Abstracts International* 32(07): A3798.

POSSIBLE *DSM-IV* DIAGNOSIS:

V62.81   Relational Problem NOS

PLAY THERAPY FOR CHILDREN
WITH SCHOOL ADJUSTMENT PROBLEMS

AUTHOR: **Randall L. Quayle**

FOCUS: *Play therapy for young children having problems adjusting to school.*

INTRODUCTION: Early elementary school children are frequently identified as being at risk for not making a satisfactory adjustment to the school setting. Without intervention it is believed these children will become increasingly maladjusted, increasing the child's risk of dropping out of school and developing emotional and psychological problems.

RESEARCH METHODS & DESIGN: Fifty-four children, 5 to 9 years of age, were identified as being at risk for school adjustment through the use of the teacher-completed AML Behavior Rating Scale–Revised. The scale produced scores for acting out, moodiness, and learning problems.

The thirty-five boys and nineteen girls were divided into three groups. The treatment group received individual play therapy sessions; a second, comparison group received individual attention in the form of tutoring; the third group, the control group, received no special attention.

Pre- and postmeasures were accomplished through the use of three forms of the Child Rating Scale: Teachers, Associate, and Child. The teachers were not told which students were being taken for play therapy and which for individual tutoring. The child aides who provided both the play therapy and the individual tutoring attention completed the Associate form. The resulting scores were analyzed using analysis of variance (ANOVA) and analysis of covariance (ANCOVA).

INTERVENTION: Eighteen children received twenty thirty-minute individual play therapy sessions and eighteen received twenty thirty-minute individual tutoring sessions. Children in the latter group went to a study room for assistance with homework or reading activities. The eighteen children in the control group received no special attention and remained in the classroom. All the children filled out, pre- and post-, the child version of the Child Rating Scale.

The two child aides who provided both the play therapy and the tutoring sessions had participated in the Primary Mental Health Project in this same school for at least three years and had six three-hour training sessions on reflective listening and child-centered play therapy. During this study a play therapy session was periodically videotaped and reviewed during the aides' bimonthly supervision sessions.

RESULTS: Children in both the individual play therapy group and the individual attention group improved. Children participating in the former group showed more positive growth in a greater number of areas, six of fifteen areas. The children receiving special attention showed positive gains in four of fifteen. The control group experienced negative results in seven of eleven areas. The only area in which the control group children demonstrated positive growth was assertive social skills, as identified by the teachers. This may have been learned as a result of interactions with the children in the other two groups as they improved in that same area.

The teachers rated children receiving play therapy as improving in learning skills, assertive social skills, task orientation, and peer social skills. The child aides' responses indicated the children improved in interactive participation and self-confidence.

COMMENTARY: More significant results may have resulted if the individuals providing the play therapy had received more training. As indicated above, their training was less then the equivalent of one graduate class. Also, as the author indicated, having the same individuals provide both the play therapy and the individual attention tutoring may have confounded the results. The aide's same empathetic interaction may have resulted in greater improvement in the children receiving individual attention. Even with all these concerns, the children receiving individual play therapy experienced greater growth and improvement.

SOURCE: Quayle, R. L. (1991). *The primary mental health project as a school-based approach for prevention of adjustment problems: an evaluation.* Unpublished dissertation.

POSSIBLE *DSM-IV* DIAGNOSES:

309.XX   Adjustment Disorder
300.02   Generalized Anxiety Disorder
V62.81   Relational Problem NOS
312.9   Disruptive Behavior Disorder NOS
313.81   Oppositional Defiant Disorder

GROUP PLAY THERAPY AS AN INTERVENTION MODALITY FOR MODIFYING THE SOCIAL ADJUSTMENT OF PRIMARY-GRADE BOYS

AUTHOR: **Lauriane Tondow Smith**

FOCUS: *Which is more effective, directive or nondirective group play therapy, with socially withdrawn or aggressive children?*

INTRODUCTION: This study compared the effectiveness of nondirective group play therapy and directive, problem-focused group play therapy in modifying the social adjustment, sociometric status, and self-concept of early-latency-aged boys.

RESEARCH METHODS & DESIGN: The eighteen second and third graders in this study were 7½ to 9½ years old, from a white, upper-middle-class public elementary school in the San Francisco Bay area. Based on teacher reports, the sample represented students who were socially withdrawn or aggressive and appeared to have more difficulties in social adjustment in comparison to their peers. Three groups of six children were matched by age, grade, IQ, and type of behavior problem. Each group involved two socially aggressive and four socially withdrawn subjects. The subjects had experienced no form of psychotherapy. The intervention techniques were randomly assigned to two of the three groups: directive, problem-focused play therapy and nondirective play therapy. The third group served as the control group. A pre-post test control group design was used and data were processed through analysis of variance and post hoc t-tests. Scales were used to measure pre- and post-social status, social skills, and self-concept.

INTERVENTION: The children in the two play therapy groups received twelve, forty-five-minute sessions over a ten-week period. The children in the control group received no special attention or intervention.

Directive group play therapy was defined as an organized, structured set of developmentally appropriate activities based on specific tasks and needs of latency-aged children using Slavson's[1] framework. The directive and developmentally phased activities were designed with personality development theory in mind. The therapist provided specific developmental goals for the group, encouraged communication on an emotional level, and subtly emphasized the group process rather than production of a group outcome. Each session had three basic segments. First, subjects were given directions regarding the activities for the session. Second, the subjects worked on a project. The third element was a therapist-directed discussion centering on feedback gathered during the activity. Activities for the sessions focused on getting acquainted, recognizing and understanding feelings, developing social skills and respect for others, and improving each child's ability to define problems, suggest alternatives, and understand the consequences of the alternatives to everyone involved.

The second group of children received traditional nondirective group play therapy based upon the principles and guidelines of Rogers[2] and the techniques of Axline.[3]

RESULTS: Subjects receiving directive group play therapy scored significantly higher on a measure of social status than subjects who received either nondirective group play therapy or no intervention. Both intervention groups scored significantly higher than the control group on the measures of social adjustment and self-concept. On each scale subjects receiving directive group play therapy scored significantly higher than those who received nondirective group play therapy.

COMMENTARY: The results of this study indicated that developmentally based, directive group play therapy was the most effective in changing the social adjustment of the subjects. In addition, the results indicated that in primary-grade boys nondirective group play therapy was also an effective intervention in facilitating positive change in social skills and self-concept, although not as effective as the directive approach.

---

1. S. R. Slavson, *Child Psychotherapy* (New York: Columbia University Press, 1952).

2. Carl Rogers, *Client-Centered Therapy* (Boston: Houghton Mifflin, 1951).

3. Virginia Axline, *Play Therapy* (New York: Ballantine Books, 1969).

It is often the perception that early-latency-aged children exhibiting poor social behaviors are not in need of intervention as they will outgrow their social handicaps naturally. Children may or may not outgrow their problems, but an important implication of this investigation is that intervention moves faster than no intervention in effecting social adjustment and self-concept change. These results confirm the value of providing intervention for children with social adjustment and self-concept problems and suggest that the intervention should be directive in nature and developmentally rooted.

SOURCE: Smith, L. (1988). The relative effectiveness of two group play therapy approaches in modifying the social adjustment of primary-grade children. Doctoral dissertation, Pacific Graduate School of Psychology, 1987. *Dissertation Abstracts International* 48(07):B2112.

POSSIBLE *DSM-IV* DIAGNOSES:

312.9   Disruptive Behavior Disorder NOS
309.0   Adjustment Disorder with Depressed Mood
309.3   Adjustment Disorder with Disturbance of Conduct
V62.81   Relational Problem NOS

DEVELOPMENT OF SELF-CONTROL IN BILINGUAL CHILDREN THROUGH GROUP PLAY THERAPY

AUTHOR: **Susan L. Trostle**

FOCUS: *The use of group play therapy to develop greater social acceptance through increased self-control in young minority children.*

INTRODUCTION: Bilingual immigrant children frequently encounter social, language, and other adjustment problems when beginning school. Social acceptance of self and others is usually low, often resulting in aggressive behavior and lack of self-control. Group play therapy is explored as an effective intervention procedure.

RESEARCH METHODS & DESIGN: Forty-eight Puerto Rican children aged 3 to 6 years were used in this study. Their teacher had identified them as having been in the United States for at least six months and their primary language at home was Spanish. The children were randomly assigned to the experiential or control groups, matching only the number of boys and girls in each group. Twenty-four children were assigned to six play therapy groups. The control group consisted of twenty-four children who received unstructured free play with their classmates, using a set of toys similar to those in the play therapy groups. Each group had a forty-minute session weekly for ten weeks. Group play therapy provided the children with an opportunity to develop their social, representational, and adaptive skills in the group settings.

RESULTS: Posttest results indicated that the children assigned to the play therapy groups showed significant improvements compared to those in the control group. The areas of improvement were self-control and higher developmental-level fantasy and reality play behavior. Boys became more accepting of others than did either the girls in the play therapy groups or any of the children in the control group.

COMMENTARY: This study supports the findings of other studies that have indicated that play therapy affects how children display aggression, and increases their ability for self-control. Additionally, gains were made in developmental levels of both fantasy and reality play for these minority children. This developmental gain may afford children a greater ability to work out strong emotions through the use of play. As a result, self-confidence and self-esteem increase. This in turn allows children to be more accepting of others. For minority children, or other children who perceive themselves as different from their peers, group play therapy appears to be an effective option for increased self-control and self-acceptance.

SOURCE: Trostle, S. L. (1988). The effects of child-centered group play sessions on social-emotional growth of three-to-six-year-old bilingual Puerto Rican children. *Journal of Research in Childhood Education* 3(2):93–106.

POSSIBLE *DSM-IV* DIAGNOSES:

309.3   Adjustment Disorder with Disturbance of Conduct
309.4   Adjustment Disorder with Mixed Disturbance of Emotions and Conduct
V62.81   Relational Problem NOS

20

Speech Difficulties

In this chapter we are not concerned with children who experience simple articulation problems but rather with children who exhibit a matrix of unsatisfactory communication that usually interferes with social interaction, academic achievement, and/or feelings about self. Speech therapy for these children is generally designed to make interpersonal exchange more satisfying and more successful, but may not provide for the emotional development necessary for general language development. Delayed speech development and/or speech difficulties should call attention to the need to consider emotional factors as contributing to the difficulty. Children's problems do not exist in isolation, but rather reverberate throughout the child's organism. For example, difficulties in speech may be accompanied by aggressive or withdrawn behavior. Play therapy provides children with an opportunity to release negative, restricting feelings that may have been inhibiting normal adjustment, and to develop a positive self-image necessary for emotional development and growth. The permissive attitude of the play therapist, the opportunity to interact with peers without adult interference, consistent limit setting in a constructive and positive manner, and acceptance of the child provide the setting essential for children's growth and development, including speech.

NONDIRECTIVE GROUP PLAY THERAPY TO FACILITATE SPEECH AND LANGUAGE DEVELOPMENT IN PRESCHOOL CHILDREN

AUTHOR: **Kenneth R. Bouillion**

FOCUS: *This study was undertaken primarily to evaluate the comparative effectiveness, appropriateness, and efficiency of nondirective group play therapy as an intervention modality for preschool children with speech or language delay.*

INTRODUCTION: Speech and language delay in preschool children is a commonly found problem. This study compared four intervention/treatment modalities including group play therapy.

RESEARCH METHODS & DESIGN: Forty-three children were involved in this study. The children, who ranged in age from 3 years, 6 months to 6 years, 2 months, were functioning at least at the average intelligence level, and showed no evidence of hearing difficulties. All were capable of following directions to perform simple physical-motor tasks. Each child was diagnosed as speech or language delayed based on a one-year lag between the child's measured articulation or receptive skills and the child's chronological age.

The forty-three children were randomly assigned to one of four treatment programs. Ten children were assigned to group play therapy, eight to individual direct speech therapy, nine to group speech lessons, seven to physical-motor training, and nine to a control group. Each treatment group met five days a week, thirty minutes each day, for fourteen weeks.

Pre- and posttesting was accomplished through the use of standardized articulation and language instruments. The resulting scores were analyzed by analysis of variance and correlational statistics.

RESULTS: The children who participated in group play therapy achieved significantly higher scores than the other treatment groups in the areas of fluency and articulation. These same children showed the least improvement, however, in remediating receptive language deficits. Bouillion speculated that nondirective group play therapy may be most effective for the early stages of intervention when the emphasis is on developing a therapeutic relationship at the child's own pace. He hypothesized that the supportive play therapy environment resulted in decreased anxiety and more comfort in the intervention situation, increased self-esteem, and development of both linguistic and affective expressive abilities. The general conclusion of this study was that a more holistic approach to therapeutic speech remediations, in which several intervention modalities could be combined, would be the most beneficial to the child.

COMMENTARY: The findings of this study indicate that group play therapy proved more effective in the remediation of expressive rather than receptive language skills in preschool children. Understanding this, developmental speech programs can more effectively intervene appropriately, matching the intervention to the needs of the individual child.

SOURCE: Bouillion, K. B. (1974). The comparative efficacy of nondirective group play therapy with preschool, speech- or language-delayed children. Doctoral dissertation, Texas Tech University, 1973. *Dissertation Abstracts International* 35(01):B495.

POSSIBLE *DSM-IV* DIAGNOSES:

315.31   Expressive Language Disorder
315.31   Mixed Receptive-Expressive Language Disorder
315.39   Phonological Disorder

TREATMENT OF EMOTIONALLY BASED DELAYED SPEECH WITH PLAY THERAPY

AUTHORS: **Henry Dupont, Theodore Landsman, and Milton Valentine**

FOCUS: *Play therapy with an emotionally disturbed child exhibiting delayed speech development.*

INTRODUCTION: Emotional disturbance can be the result of a variety of life experiences. This case highlights an emotionally disturbed 8-year-old boy who had experienced maternal deprivation, neglect, and multiple rejections. The child responded with both a speech delay and aggressive behavior.

CASE STUDY: Johnny, the sixth of seven children, had been removed from his mother's home at age 4. At age 3, with his mother pregnant, his father was sentenced to prison. When his mother became increasingly unable to parent all the children, Johnny and an older brother were placed in foster care. After about a year they were moved into what was supposed to be a permanent situation. However, the new foster parents were unable to cope with Johnny's speech problems and both boys were removed to another foster home. It was surmised that Johnny's subsequent negative and aggressive behavior resulted from maternal deprivation, neglect, and feelings of multiple rejections.

Johnny was an average student scholastically but had been diagnosed with a developmental speech disorder. When he was first assessed, his speech level was approximately that of a 3-year-old, indicating that speech development ceased at approximately the time his mother began having parenting problems.

INTERVENTION: Johnny was seen in individual play therapy for approximately one year. In the first several sessions his behavior was a pattern of aggression and destruction. He took great delight in making a shambles of the playroom, laughing and yelling with apparent glee. Limits had to be set frequently. Care was taken to be clear about accepting Johnny and his feelings, but not his inappropriate behavior. In the final sessions Johnny spent the time talking to the thera-pist about the things he was doing as he played constructively with blocks, pounded nails, and painted. In the last session he built a sail-boat and discussed why he would not be coming to therapy anymore.

A speech therapist not involved in Johnny's treatment performed a phonetic analysis periodically during the course of play therapy. The initial analysis indicated garbled, unintelligible speech, with few attempts to talk. Most often his speech consisted solely of vowel sounds. The final analysis showed he initiated speech freely and frequently with almost completely intelligible speech.

COMMENTARY: Speech, as well as other developmental tasks, can be delayed by emotional factors. The use of play therapy has been found to be effective in allowing children the opportunity to deal with the negative feelings and resulting behavior while in the presence of an accepting, caring, and understanding therapist. Play therapy frees children's natural developmental processes to move toward healthy growth and development.

SOURCE: Dupont, H., Landsman, T., and Valentine, M. (1953). The treatment of delayed speech by client-centered therapy. *Journal of Consultative Psychology* 17(2):122–123.

POSSIBLE *DSM-IV* DIAGNOSES:

312.8   Conduct Disorder
313.81   Oppositional Defiant Disorder
315.31   Expressive Language Disorder
995.5   Neglect of Child

PLAY THERAPY INTERVENTION FOR REGRESSION OF SPEECH IN A YOUNG CHILD

AUTHOR: **Lydia Jackson**

FOCUS: *Play therapy intervention with a severely regressed child.*

INTRODUCTION: This child reacted to the birth of two younger siblings and a negative change in discipline from his mother in such a severe manner that he was initially misdiagnosed as mentally retarded. His regression was so severe that he gave no evidence of hearing or understanding what was requested of him.

CASE STUDY: Terry was described as a happy, pleasant baby until the birth of his first sister when he was 20 months old. He had begun to say a few words and was feeding himself. A maternal aunt who came to take care of him used "smacking" as a form of discipline and convinced his mother to continue this. Terry stopped talking and tried to take the new baby away from his mother. During the same period Terry was hospitalized for two days for a circumcision, and for the following six months he had nightly "screaming fits." When Terry was almost 3½, his youngest sister was born. Regression was again noted, as well as aggressive behavior toward younger children. Terry became very attached to his mother, and followed her everywhere. He was enuretic and encopretic and made no attempt to self-regulate toileting. Although he often did not respond to being talked to, at night he could be heard humming or singing softly in his bedroom. As Terry did not respond to an attempt to assess his intelligence, he was labeled mentally retarded. At this point his mother sought a second opinion.

INTERVENTION: Terry was seen weekly for forty-five minutes of play therapy for eighteen months. In the initial sessions he explored the playroom and became so absorbed in his activity that it was as though the play therapist was not even present. His manipulation of toys and materials was excellent, inconsistent with the ability level of a mentally retarded child. In an early session, after receiving the play therapist's permission to put a toy in the water tray, Terry often filled the tray with numerous toys. He responded positively to limits set on what he could put into the water. In the sixth session Terry began his first real constructive play: building a bridge in the water tray.

Terry continued to play at the water table, and in the eighth session the play therapist introduced a doll family, naming three of them after Terry and his two sisters. The play therapist then enacted a scene with the dolls arguing and the parent dolls taking the boy doll's side. Terry responded by throwing water on the dolls until they fell over. Each time the play therapist stood them up again, Terry's water play would "sink them."

In subsequent sessions the play therapist continued to introduce various scenarios with the dolls. In one scene she had a male doll pretend to urinate in the water tray. Terry took the doll and threw it to the other end of the room every time this scene was played out. After a few sessions of this play, however, Terry began to speak in bursts of "jargon talk."

After his fourteenth session Terry was enrolled in a nursery school specially selected for its tolerant headmistress. He quickly began to respond to toilet training and other self-help skills. After an initial aggressive phase, Terry became protective of younger children at the school.

In the seventeenth session Terry began to alternate between messy and constructive play. His behavior at home became very aggressive. He broke favorite items of his mother, threw his sisters' dolls in water, and frequently attacked the dolls, urinating on them and their beds. Supportive parent consultation was essential during this time. Following the aggressive phase, Terry's behavior was marked by mischievousness.

A two-month break in play therapy was necessary at this time because of minor illnesses and summer vacation. Upon returning to the clinic, Terry was very affectionate, to the point of needing to kiss everyone goodbye before leaving. His play became conflicted: building and destroying, dirtying and cleaning. In session twenty-four, for the first time, Terry whispered a direct answer to a question by the play therapist. The interpretation was that Terry no longer needed to hide behind his impenetrable defense of "not hearing." Indeed, his variety of play continued to expand, and although he was still very focused in his play, he no longer shut out the play therapist. In the twenty-ninth session Terry spontaneously looked up at the play therapist and smiled. His play continued to increase in healthy and positive content, while ambivalent and destructive play decreased. In the forty-first session, free verbal give and take between Terry and the therapist occurred and continued in subsequent sessions. Meanwhile, at home, all the previous problem behavior had ceased. In a joint session Terry and his sisters were very friendly and happily played together.

RESULTS: Play therapy was discontinued after sixty-four sessions. Terry continued to have brief contact with his play therapist when he was in the clinic for speech therapy and assistance in development of reading skills. At 7 years of age Terry was found to have an IQ of 149 and a mental age of 10 years, 8 months. Even though he still had language problems, such as telescoping sentences and cutting out conjunctions and prepositions, he presented himself as an attractive boy with lots of energy and good social skills.

COMMENTARY: This case reminds us of how powerfully a child can react to changes within the family. A child's view of his or her self and world can necessitate lengthy intervention. It is important that the play therapist continue to trust the process while advocating for the child with the parents and school. The safety of the play therapy relationship allowed this child to venture forth into a world he had decided to shut out.

SOURCE: Jackson, L. (1950). Non-speaking children. *British Journal of Medical Psychology* 23:87–100.

POSSIBLE *DSM-IV* DIAGNOSES:

299   Autistic Disorder
299.10   Childhood Disintegrative Disorder (if behavior had begun after 24 months, rather than 20 months, as in Terry's case)
299.80   Pervasive Developmental Disorder NOS
313.81   Oppositional Defiant Disorder
313.23   Selective Mutism

THERAPLAY WITH ARTICULATION DISORDERS

AUTHORS: **Phyllis Kupperman, Sally Bligh, and Marjorie Goodban**

FOCUS: *A special form of Theraplay used to remediate the articulation disorders of young children.*

INTRODUCTION: Speech Theraplay was studied to determine its effectiveness in working with young children who have not activated their articulation acquisition. This form of intrusive interaction intensifies and mirrors normal parent–child interaction that promotes communication development. The goal of the sessions was not to teach the phonemes, but to activate the interaction that develops the desire and ability to increase communication.

RESEARCH METHODS & DESIGN: Six children enrolled in a university speech clinic were selected for participation in this study. Four of the children were preschoolers, aged 3 years, 2 months to 4 years, 6 months. The other two were 6-year-olds who had made little or no progress during six months of traditional remediation treatment.

The clinicians were six undergraduate student clinicians who had participated in a twenty-hour training course and/or a supervised clinical practicum. The Theraplay training included role playing, lectures, videotapes, group discussions, and supervision.

Pre- and posttesting was accomplished by using the Fisher-Logemann Test of Articulation Competence. Specific phonemes were identified for each child either through the use of distinctive features or developmental rationale. These phonemes became the focus of the intervention sessions.

INTERVENTION: Each child had two half-hour speech Theraplay sessions a week for six weeks. During the sessions the child's attention was drawn to the targeted phonemes embedded within a meaningful interchange or as part of a play sequence. In Theraplay the repertoire of prespeech interactions includes smiling, cooing and gurgling responsively, singing, counting fingers and toes, playing peek a boo, and other such activities. These activities activate normal articulation acquisition, and therefore are used with children of all ages. No props or toys are used. The child and the clinician sit facing each other on a mat on the floor. Physical contact, in the form of stroking, touching, and cuddling, occurs often. The clinicians often give high affect responses to encourage the child and help the child feel good about self.

RESULTS: The number of misarticulated items was reduced by each of the six children. The average reduction of error in articulation was 10.8 items. The pattern of articulation acquisition varied for each child. The two 6-year-olds gained proficiency in sounds. The pre-schoolers varied in their gains: one gained word endings, another, nearly all consonant blends; another, voiceless phonemes. In several cases parents reported the child making articulation changes at home before they became evident in the sessions.

Given the short duration of the study, six weeks, the authors did not believe that maturation was the cause of the growth. They hypothesized that the intensity of the positive affect associated with the stimulation resulted in higher self-esteem. The unconditional clinician approval may have also motivated the children to communicate more precisely.

COMMENTARY: Theraplay appears to be effective in activating or re-activating a child's normal speech development. The significance of a nurturing relationship to a child's healthy development is evident. This is not to imply the parents were not nurturing. However, the Theraplay sessions provided intensive and somewhat exaggerated positive interactions. The fact that the children began demonstrating improvement at home, rather than in the sessions, indicates the children's positive response to their parents.

SOURCE: Kupperman, P., Bligh, S., and Goodban, M. (1980). Activating articulation skills through Theraplay. *Journal of Speech & Hearing Disorders* 45(4):540–548.

POSSIBLE *DSM-IV* DIAGNOSES:

315.39   Phonological Disorder
315.31   Expressive Language Disorder

GROUP PLAY THERAPY TO IMPROVE SPEECH, SOCIAL SKILLS, PERSONALITY ATTRIBUTES, AND INTELLIGENCE

AUTHOR: **Martin Sokoloff**

FOCUS: *Group play therapy with children who have cerebral palsy and associated speech difficulties.*

INTRODUCTION: Cerebral-palsied children often have problematic articulation due to paralysis, weakness, or incoordination of muscles (dysarthria). This research sought to discover which therapy, individual speech therapy or group play therapy was more effective in alleviating these speech problems. Possible changes in social adjustment, personality, and intelligence were also investigated.

RESEARCH METHODS & DESIGN: Twenty-four cerebral-palsied children, identified as nonseverely dysarthric speech-handicapped, participated in this research. Pre and post data were collected using the Ammons Full Range Picture Vocabulary Test (to identify an intelligence quotient), the Vineland Social Maturity Scale (to assess social adjustment), and a personality rating scale. The children were also audiotaped as they responded to Blackie Pictures by a panel of experts for rating of communicative abilities.

Random assignment was made to either group play therapy or individual speech therapy. The two groups were balanced for IQ (an average of 81.4), age (average of 5.55 years), and gender (eight boys and four girls).

INTERVENTION: Four children were assigned to each of three play therapy groups. The groups met for one hour twice a week for thirty sessions. Two play therapy groups were led by a clinical psychologist and the third was facilitated by a doctoral student.

The twelve children in individual speech therapy were seen twice a week for thirty minute for a total of 30 sessions.

RESULTS: The children who received group play therapy showed statistically significant improvement (p<.01) in the areas of Attention, Concentration, Responsiveness to Therapeutic Techniques, Social Confidence, Self-Confidence, and Appropriate Expression of Nonverbal and Verbal Hostility.

Social maturity scores indicated that the children receiving group play therapy improved at a statistically significant level (p<.05). The personality rating of the children in group play therapy also improved at a statistically significant level (p=<.01).

There was no statistically significant difference between the two groups as to IQ. However, the children who received group play therapy did have an increase in the group's average IQ, from 82.5 (pre) to 86.4 (post). The range of IQ scores for children in group play therapy changed from 47–110 to 47–130. The children who received speech therapy actually lost IQ points, from an average of 80.3 (pre) to 78.2 (post).

The panel indicated that the children who received group play therapy improved significantly in communicative abilities. These included, specifically, Articulation, Intelligibility, Voice, Vocabulary, and Language Level. There were also interesting differences in improvement according to the child's age group. Children aged 5–7 years improved most in Articulation, General Intelligibility, and Language and Vocabulary Level. Children aged 7–10 years were fairly equal in areas of improvement. Children aged 10–13 years were most improved in Intelligibility, Vocabulary Level, and General Communicative Ability.

According to the author, significant factors in the group play therapy were the permissive attitude of the play therapist, the opportunity to interact with peers without adult interference, consistent limit setting in a constructive and positive manner, and the acceptance of the child.

COMMENTARY: Group play therapy was found to be an effective means by which certain cerebral-palsied children could improve speech skills, social adjustment, and their view of self. These results, many at a statistically significant level, were found after fifteen weeks of intervention. It would be interesting to see the possibilities of change for these children if group play therapy could be a standard part of the scholastic routine. One might postulate there would be an eventual plateau of gains, but to date it appears no one has discovered what these limitations might be.

SOURCE: Sokoloff, M. A. (1959). A comparison of gains in communicative skills, resulting from group play therapy and individual speech therapy, among a group of non-severely dysarthric, speech handicapped cerebral palsied children. Doctoral dissertation, New York University. *Dissertation Abstracts International* 20(02):B803.

POSSIBLE *DSM-IV* DIAGNOSES:

315.31   Expressive Language Disorder
315.39   Phonological Disorder

21

Traumatization

In this chapter we use the term *trauma* to refer to the broader, more inclusive context of children's experiences that may be stressful and traumatic as defined by David Levy. *Psychological trauma* is an extremely stressful event or happening that is usually atypical in the life experiences of the child and is distressing to the point of being overwhelming, causing an inability to cope. Young children should not be expected to describe such experiences verbally because they do not have the facility required to do so; such experiences are usually too threatening for the child to consciously describe. The natural reaction of children is to reenact or play out the traumatic experience in an unconscious effort to comprehend, overcome, develop a sense of control, or assimilate the experience. This repetitive playing out of the experience is the child's natural self-healing process. Some of the aspects of posttraumatic play as identified by Lenore Terr[1] are appropriate here to help play therapists

1. Lenore Terr, "Play Therapy and Psychic Trauma: A Preliminary Report," in *Handbook of Play Therapy*, edited by C. E. Schaefer and K. J. O'Connor (New York: Wiley, 1983), pp. 308–319.

recognize such behaviors: "compulsive repetition; unconscious link between the play and the traumatic event; literalness of play with simple defenses only; failure to relieve anxiety; danger; use of doodling, talking, typing, and audio duplication as modes of repeated play; and possibility of therapeutically retracing posttraumatic play to an earlier trauma" (p. 308).

SAND PLAY AS AN INTERVENTION FOR A CHILD WHOSE FAMILY SITUATION CHANGED DRAMATICALLY

AUTHORS: **John Allan and Pat Berry**

FOCUS: *Using sand play to help a child work through unresolved issues possibly resulting from being moved to a new and unfamiliar family.*

INTRODUCTION: Through sand play a child is given the opportunity to work through trauma by externalizing fantasies and developing a sense of mastery and control over inner impulses. Sand play is the process, the sand tray is the medium, and the sand world is the product. The process begins when the therapist invites the child to choose from an assortment of miniatures to make a picture in the sand. Each object has its own symbolic meaning and each tends to trigger a fantasy reaction. The therapist provides a safe and protected place where the inner drama and healing potential of the child's psyche can unfold. Interpretation is not encouraged, but rather the respectful witnessing of the symbolic creation. Cycles of chaos, struggle, and restoration recur as the drama of sand play unfolds.

CASE STUDY: James, a second-grade boy, was referred to the school counselor because of impulsive, aggressive behavior and poor social skills in the classroom and on the playground. Two years earlier James had been moved several hundred miles to live with a father he did not know, a stepmother, and her two older daughters.

INTERVENTION: James was seen for ten sessions. He immediately became involved when introduced to the sand tray and miniatures. In the early sessions his sand worlds reflected turmoil and chaos with evidence of feeling controlled and trapped by external forces. James's first scene in the sand had many animals and vehicles precariously and chaotically piled at one end of the sand tray, held down by two snakes. At the bottom of the pile Pegasus, the winged horse, was trapped. As the sessions progressed, the counselor was able to see differentiation, regulation, and separation of various emotions as symbolized by various objects in the sand tray scenes. Pegasus moved from a position of helplessness to become a personal symbol of inner strength. The scenes in the sand showed more organization, with vehicles parked appropriately, a house with people, and a tree in the corner symbolizing growth. James's sessions culminated in a sand world depicting order and family identity. James showed a circle of his family members, the family truck, a house, and a jet plane. Pegasus was placed in the center of the family circle. Treatment ended at the close of the school year. Teachers reported that James's impulsive, aggressive behavior had diminished, his social skills had improved, and he was channeling his energy into art and soccer.

COMMENTARY: This child was provided with an opportunity to explore unresolved trauma through sand play. The type of sand play presented relies on the child's inner healing power and emphasizes the counselor's role as a supportive and accepting witness to the process of the play. In this process the child is presented a "world" that he can control.

SOURCE: Allan, J., and Berry, P. (1987). Sand play. *Elementary School Guidance & Counseling* 21(4):301–307.

POSSIBLE *DSM-IV* DIAGNOSES:

V71.02   Child or Adolescent Antisocial Behavior
312.9   Disruptive Behavior Disorder NOS
313.81   Oppositional Defiant Disorder
300.4   Dysthymic Disorder

CHILD-CENTERED PLAY THERAPY WITH A NEGLECTED CHILD TRAUMATIZED BY HOSPITALIZATION

AUTHOR: **Eliana Gil**

FOCUS: *Toy hospital equipment used in nondirective play provided the opportunity for a neglected child to work through feelings about a sudden hospitalization due to appendicitis.*

INTRODUCTION: Physical traumas are often misinterpreted by young children as rejection and punishment for misbehavior. In the following case, fears of abandonment were confirmed when the child's parents were not located until four days after her hospitalization. Child-centered play therapy was selected to give the child a sense of control over her environment. The issue of the hospitalization was not introduced until the child made reference to her surgery. At that point the therapist provided the toy hospital equipment and followed the child's lead as she used the toys to reenact her own hospitalization.

CASE STUDY: Laurie, aged 7, was referred for "reunification" treatment. She had been in foster care for eighteen months while her parents completed a drug rehabilitation program. Her parents had been successfully drug-free for eighteen months and were continuing in therapy. Laurie had been made a dependent of the court at the time of her hospitalization since her parents could not be located. She was described as a classic victim of neglect, suffering from malnourishment, minor infections, impetigo, and an untreated visual problem. During foster placement Laurie developed a strong positive attachment to her foster family. Her foster parents described her as compliant, helpful, and at times almost invisible.

INTERVENTION: Laurie had been reunited with her biological parents before play therapy began, and was seen for a period of nine months. The treatment plan described by the therapist included using non-directive play sessions to establish a strong therapeutic alliance; the sessions became directive at points by talking about Laurie's life with her biological parents and about her surgery. Conjoint family sessions were also scheduled to discuss parenting issues and problems surrounding the reunification. A plan for making contact with the foster parents was formed to help reduce animosity and help Laurie with her separation issues.

During initial sessions Laurie chose to color or read quietly. The therapist engaged in parallel play, which seemed to help Laurie relax. Because of Laurie's expressed interest in reading, the therapist made available a book written for children in foster care. Eventually Laurie moved to the dollhouse and doll family, recreating scenes with her former foster family and describing the fun she remembered having with them. Laurie's parents had continued to show animosity toward the foster parents, even refusing to let her talk about them. A meeting arranged between the parents and foster parents successfully alleviated the antagonism and displaced anger, resulting in a positive alliance between both sets of parents.

Laurie's first self-portrait, done at the request of the therapist, showed a very small child with no hands or feet and a hole in the middle. As Laurie became more comfortable with the play therapy room and with her parents, her play changed. She frequently played with the dollhouse, showing her "ideal family." She also played ball with the therapist, displaying confidence and pride as her catching skills improved. Her self-portrait also looked different. The hole in the middle was gone and Laurie said it was getting better. This was the first time she had referred to her surgery, and the therapist took this opportunity to bring out the toy hospital equipment, which became Laurie's primary source of play. For the next eight weeks Laurie depicted scenes of a little girl being taken to a hospital in an ambulance and undergoing an operation. Her posttraumatic play was constricted and robotlike. The play was repetitive and anxiety remained constant. The parents reported regressive behavior at home, thumb sucking, and nightmares. At the ninth session the therapist intervened by providing a commentary on the events throughout the play. At first Laurie seemed surprised, but then paced herself to the therapist's commentary and added her own, eventually responding to the therapist's occasional questions about the child's feelings. This commentary seemed to enable her to observe, while experiencing and processing the difficult and frightening negative feelings associated with the traumatic event. After many weeks the therapist began to refer to the girl doll as "Laurie." In the final elaboration of her play the therapist asked Laurie to put the little girl's feelings into words and tell the ambulance people, the doctors, the counselor, the social worker, and her parents how she felt. The most difficult was for Laurie to tell her parents; she did not know how they would respond. Rather than answer her questions during play, the therapist helped Laurie ask her parents in a joint session directly why they had left her. After being prepared for the meeting by their therapist, the parents were able to reassure Laurie that her feelings of abandonment, fear, sadness, and anger were valid. The final phase of treatment involved Laurie's working through the painful process of understanding her feelings of anger toward her parents.

COMMENTARY: Laurie had successfully developed coping strategies to deal with her parents' severe neglect, but the trauma of hospitalization, surgery, and resulting foster placement completely disrupted her life. The successful multidimensional treatment provided for this family underscores the importance of creating a safe place for a child not only in the playroom, but in the home too. This child's need to take care of her parents interfered with her working on her own issues of fear around the hospitalization, sadness at losing her foster family, and anger toward her parents for abandoning her. The nonintrusive style of play therapy allowed the child to deal with her issues in the order that worked best for her. Separation from her foster family and development of some confidence in herself arose first, although the trauma of the hospitalization most deeply affected Laurie's relationship with her parents.

SOURCE: Gil, E. (1991). *The Healing Power of Play: Working with Abused Children*. New York: Guilford.

POSSIBLE *DSM-IV* DIAGNOSES:

309.81 Posttraumatic Stress Disorder
309.28 Adjustment Disorder with Mixed Anxiety and Depressed Mood
V61.20 Parent–Child Relational Problem
995.5   Neglect of Child

INTENSIVE PLAY THERAPY WITH CHILD WITNESSES OF DOMESTIC VIOLENCE

AUTHOR: **Sarina Kot**

FOCUS: *The effectiveness of intensive child-centered play therapy on improving self-concepts, internalizing and externalizing behaviors, problem behaviors, and playroom behaviors of child witnesses of domestic violence.*

INTRODUCTION: Child witnesses of domestic violence exhibit a broad range of emotional and behavioral difficulties. The effectiveness of intensive child-centered play therapy for such children was investigated in (1) improving self-concept; (2) reducing internalizing behavior problems such as withdrawal, somatic complaints, anxiety, and depression; (3) reducing externalizing behavior problems, such as aggression and delinquency; (4) reducing overall behavior problems including internalizing and externalizing behavior problems and social problems, thought problems, and attention problems; and (5) improving play behaviors in the areas of affection, contact, physical proximity, self-direction, aggression, mood, play themes, and food nurturing themes.

RESEARCH METHODS & DESIGN: A pretest-posttest control group design was used. Twenty-two children aged 3–10 were recruited from three domestic violence shelters. The children were placed in two groups—an experimental group that received play therapy and a control group that did not. Children in both groups received basic shelter services that included three educational and/or recreational groups per week. Both experimental and control group children participated in pre- and postplay therapy sessions that were videotaped. The videotapes were rated using the Children's Play Session Behavior Rating Scale. All the children completed the Joseph Pre-School and Primary Self-Concept Screening Test. The mothers completed the Child Behavior Checklist.

INTERVENTION: The experimental group—eleven child witnesses of domestic violence—received twelve play therapy sessions within a two-week period. Each session lasted forty-five minutes. Trained counselors, two at the master's degree level and one at the doctoral level, provided the play therapy.

RESULTS: Analyses of covariance revealed that the child witnesses in the experimental group demonstrated (1) significant improvement in their self-concept, (2) significant reduction in their externalizing behavior problems, (3) significant reduction in their total behavior problems, and (4) significant improvement in the play behaviors of physical proximity and play themes. Insignificant results were found in internalizing behavior problems and the play behaviors of affection, contact, self-direction, aggression, mood, and food nurturing themes.

COMMENTARY: This study supports intensive child-centered play therapy as a viable intervention for treating certain problem areas exhibited by child witnesses of domestic violence. Intensive play therapy can be used to deal with the traumatic aspects of witnessing interparental violence. The short time duration required for completing the intensive play therapy fits particularly well with the unstable and transient life situations of families suffering from domestic violence.

SOURCE: Kot, S. (1995). *Intensive play therapy with child witnesses of domestic violence.* Unpublished dissertation, University of North Texas, Denton.

POSSIBLE *DSM-IV* DIAGNOSES:

309.4   Adjustment Disorder with Mixed Disturbance of Emotions and Conduct
309.81   Posttraumatic Stress Disorder

PSYCHOANALYTIC PLAY THERAPY WITH A CHILD SUFFERING FROM TRAUMATIC NEUROSIS

AUTHOR: **G. Maclean**

FOCUS: *Psychoanalytic play therapy with a 3½-year-old boy suffering from traumatic shock.*

INTRODUCTION: Freud was concerned with the characteristic of psychic trauma throughout his professional career. He posited a sequential set of components to describe the process and outcome of psychic trauma. The precipitating stimulus is followed by an intrapsychic process that consists of a breakthrough of the protective stimulus barrier between the conscious and the unconscious, resulting in a state of psychic helplessness and consequently painful and unpleasurable affect. The outcome of any given case is dependent upon the context and intensity of the original trauma, the strength of the traumatized person's ego, and that person's subsequent life experiences.

CASE STUDY: The child was referred by his father five months after they both had been attacked by a leopard in a pet store. He was the only child of an upper-middle-class family. The parents were described as industrious, successful people with a good relationship and an interest in parenting as well as the ability to parent. Jason (the reviewer's chosen name) was suffering from frequent nightmares about "animals and monsters." He exhibited extreme anxiety and reluctance about being apart from his mother and excessive concern regarding the whereabouts of both parents. These symptoms appeared as a marked regression from Jason's formerly normal development.

INTERVENTION: Jason was diagnosed with traumatic neurosis and received individual play therapy once each week for a period of eight months, with at least one conjoint interview each month that included the parents. Throughout the sessions the reenactment in play of the traumatic event was a major theme. Jason would review every detail of the leopard attack verbally or symbolically, often over and over.

During the first few sessions Jason focused primarily on reenacting the attack. Several times he adopted the appearance of the leopard and attacked the therapist. Following these attacks, Jason asked to leave the playroom, therefore cutting the sessions short. The therapist interpreted this as Jason's fear of retaliation for the attacks. Another major issue of transference became Jason's anger at his parents, especially his father, for allowing the attack to occur. After setting up a situation in which the toys were attacked by the vicious toy leopard, Jason would angrily accuse the therapist of not protecting them. The therapist interpreted these accusations in the context of the original leopard attack, and took on the role of the father who did not protect Jason in the pet shop. At times Jason's initial response to this interpretation was an escalation in anger. When the interpretation was repeated, he would begin to play quietly, possibly needing to make recompense for his angry outburst.

Jason expressed a wide range of emotions during the therapy; each would surface, then rapidly disappear. He had a variety of defenses for dealing with these feelings and the conflict that often ensued. He dealt with his fear and anger by identifying with the aggressive leopard and attacking the therapist. He also exhibited the defense of identification by acting like a mother, father, or therapist, often assuming the role of his father during the reenactment. As Jason began to project his anger onto the environment, his fear of retaliation often surfaced. For example, if Jason identified with the leopard and swatted the therapist across the neck, this would immediately be followed by his entertaining the therapist. Over the eight months of therapy the child's symptoms decreased and at the time of termination they had disappeared.

COMMENTARY: This case illustrates the use of psychoanalytic play therapy to treat the phenomena of trauma. Maclean described how a definable traumatic event interrupted the process of an otherwise normally developing child. The shock of the leopard's attack overwhelmed the ego, as it produced feelings of abandonment, separation anxiety, anger, and expected punishment. These emotions were congruent with identical, preexisting emotions of fear, anger, and guilt derived from the age-appropriate oedipal conflict. Working through these conflicts and reestablishing the boy's normal development was accomplished in play therapy with the internal meaning of the traumatic event moving from unconscious to conscious awareness.

SOURCE: Maclean, G. (1977). Psychic trauma and traumatic neurosis: play therapy with a four-year-old boy. *Canadian Psychiatric Association Journal* 22(2):71–76.

POSSIBLE *DSM-IV* DIAGNOSES:

309.81   Posttraumatic Stress Disorder
309.21   Separation Anxiety Disorder
307.47   Nightmare Disorder
309.4   Adjustment Disorder with Anxiety

RACIAL DIFFERENCES CAUSE EXTREME REJECTION IN PLAY THERAPY: AN ISSUE FOR THERAPIST AND CHILD

AUTHOR: **May Tung**

FOCUS: *Acknowledging personal fears of what is different and unknown begins a boy's process from acute paranoia to healthy curiosity in play therapy.*

INTRODUCTION: A Caucasian child reacted with extreme rejection to a Chinese therapist. The therapist struggled with countertransference issues related to racial difference, resulting in self-awareness that greatly enhanced the relationship.

CASE STUDY: When John first came to the clinic, he was almost 10 years old. He was short, overweight, behaved much younger than his chronological age, and walked pigeon-toed. The presenting problems included temper tantrums, talking and laughing to himself, and peer difficulties. John lived with his mother and younger sister. John's mother was short and obese, and her conversation was interrupted by explosive and inappropriate laughter. John's father had suffered years of emotional disturbance and been frequently hospitalized until his suicide when John was 8. John's mother related that John's father had not wanted children and was physically and verbally abusive to John until shortly before the suicide. Since that time the family's life had been somewhat unstable, with frequent moves. Psychological testing revealed an extremely constricted and barren world in which John protected himself from the things that frightened him by not moving, not thinking, and not feeling.

INTERVENTION: Individual play therapy sessions were held approximately once a week for a period of eleven months. John's therapy progressed through a pattern of six stages: (1) distrust and distancing, (2) ambivalence, (3) reality testing of the nature and meaning of the apparent racial differences, (4) finding out if Tung could help him, (5) showing positive feelings toward Tung, and (6) accepting of Tung as a helping figure.

In the initial sessions John's distrust of the therapist was observed in the absence of significant content in his play. John would rarely accept anything from the therapist, including cookies. Tung honored John's need for physical and emotional distance by sitting in a corner of the room while John played on the floor, making his presence known by asking occasional questions or handing John a toy.

John had acknowledged that Tung was Chinese by making specific comments about Chinese people in the first two sessions. The topic did not come up again for four months. In the fifth month of therapy and for the following six months, the topic was raised in every session. John seemed to use Tung's ethnicity as his vehicle for developing trust. At first Tung's being Chinese appeared to frighten John and be too unusual for him to accept. Could such a person be trusted? Would such a person get as angry and hurtful as John's father? Would this person go back to his own people, abandoning John? John's solution before the development of trust was to kill all the "Chinks" so that Tung would have no one to go home to. Tung interpreted John's fears that people who look and speak differently can be frightening, that not knowing whether or not someone will hurt you when they are angry is frightening. He reassured John that he did not intend to leave him.

It was during this trust-building period that countertransference issues were most evident for Tung. Repeatedly hearing the term "Chinks" as John killed all the Chinese in his imaginary play caused Tung to be both uncomfortable and resentful. At the point that John's feelings of ambivalence toward Tung were most acute, Tung recognized John's pain and confusion. During this time the possibility of Tung's leaving the clinic came up and Tung began to feel personally responsible for causing or at least exacerbating John's pain. At this point Tung sought consultation. The greatest insight Tung developed through these consultations included acknowledging his own feelings of guilt for possibly damaging a child and also accepting that sadness is a part of life and belongs in the realm of the therapeutic relationship. This crisis period for Tung lasted about a month. Resolution coincided with Tung's not leaving the clinic and the beginning of the last stage of John's play therapy experience.

COMMENTARY: In this case study a young boy reacted negatively and with fear to the most obvious feature of the therapist, his ethnicity.

The therapist was a nonintruding and interested adult who accepted John's initial fears and gave John the time and support to go through his own healing process. This case demonstrates the very personal nature of the play therapy relationship and the importance of therapist self-awareness. Patience and understanding by the therapist in the face of personal rejection facilitates children's understanding and acceptance of themselves, thus enabling children to be accepting of others.

SOURCE: Tung, M. (1981). On being seen as a "Chinese therapist" by a caucasian child. *American Journal of Orthopsychiatry* 5(4):654–661.

POSSIBLE *DSM-IV* DIAGNOSES:

300.4   Dysthymic Disorder
V62.81   Relational Problem NOS
995.5   Physical Abuse of Child
300.0   Anxiety Disorder NOS

TRAUMATIC BIRTH SYMBOLIZED IN PLAY THERAPY

AUTHOR: **D. A. van Zyl**

FOCUS: *Using the ideas from primal theory in play therapy to understand a child's behavior subsequent to a traumatic birth.*

INTRODUCTION: Although van Zyl does not claim to be a primal therapist, the case presented is suggested as an example of the practical use of primal theory to interpret a child's behavior with the hypothesis that a traumatic birth is an important and enduring cause of neurosis.

CASE STUDY: Fritzie was referred for treatment at the age of 4½ because of hyperactivity, fearfulness, and complaints of loneliness that, according to his parents, Fritzie associated with death. This pattern had been apparent for some time, but intensified after a particular incident at kindergarten. Fritzie's mother inadvertently left him at the school after his class had already departed on a field trip. He was later found crying hysterically and shouting in an empty classroom. Subsequent to this incident Fritzie became enuretic and afraid of going to school. There were no other apparent instances of overt rejection or being left alone. Fritzie's mother was described as overprotective. Both parents were apparently strict disciplinarians and expected Fritzie not to get dirty, not to be overly active, and never to show anger.

INTERVENTION: Fritzie was seen in individual play therapy once each week for fifteen to twenty sessions. During the initial sessions Fritzie played with paints and the dollhouse. He would begin an activity in an orderly fashion, possibly imitating the structure seen in an adult world, then would gradually become more animated and break all boundaries, immersing his hands in the paint and splashing it on the paper. At the dollhouse Fritzie would introduce a story theme in which all the adults in the household would be killed and the boy would be happy and fly away.

The next few sessions were characterized by a theme of greater destruction, with dramatic situations such as people and animals dying, suffocating in the mud of the sandbox. These sessions prompted the therapist to hypothesize possible birth trauma and to consider primal theory. This hypothesis seemed to be confirmed when Fritzie's mother described an abnormally long labor in which the doctor had to use instruments to facilitate the process. She reported being able to feel Fritzie screaming while still in the birth canal. He was screaming upon delivery and the mother reported hearing him screaming in the hallway for "ages" before he was taken to the nursery.

Fritzie began a cycle of symbolic play in which animals and eventually a baby doll were trapped and Fritzie worked urgently to release them. At this point, although the therapist did not recommend it, Fritzie's parents terminated therapy. They reported that Fritzie could now accept being left alone. In addition, his hyperactivity had decreased and his enuresis had improved.

COMMENTARY: Although the author suggests that birth trauma may be the cause of Fritzie's undesirable behavior, the case history also indicates alternative hypotheses. The trauma of the birth may have affected Fritzie's mother more than she was aware of resulting in overprotective and smothering behavior on her part and limiting Fritzie's opportunity to develop a sense of competence. In the playroom Fritzie was allowed to experience feelings of power over his environment. Learning that he could exert control possibly gave Fritzie the confidence to take control of some aspects of his life outside the playroom. This case demonstrates the facilitative dimension of symbolic play in allowing the child to distance his or herself from the reality of an experience.

SOURCE: van Zyl, D. A. (1977). Traumatic birth symbolized in play therapy. *Journal of Primal Therapy* 4(2):154–158.

POSSIBLE *DSM-IV* DIAGNOSES:

309.24   Adjustment Disorder with Anxiety
307.6   Enuresis
309.81   Posttraumatic Stress Disorder

22

Withdrawn Children

Shy, quiet, withdrawn children can be a real challenge for play therapists who want to achieve results quickly. Efforts to entice, coax, encourage, or maneuver withdrawn children into some kind of response or activity with the play materials are usually met with resistance and result in immediate defeat. Withdrawn children are especially sensitive to such efforts, and seem determined to remain on their chosen course of noninvolvement. They may interpret the play therapist's struggle as rejection since the play therapist seems to be working hard to have them change. As is demonstrated in Virginia Axline's work in this chapter, persistent patience frees the child from the restrictions of past experiences, including perception of self in relation to those experiences, and provides the child a safety zone in which to experiment with new perceptions of self and thus new behaviors in a relationship of acceptance.

For some withdrawn children, group play therapy is especially effective because it is less threatening for them to enter new experiences in the company of two or three children. The presence of several children seems to speed up the development of a relationship between the play therapist and each child. It may be that the group accelerates the child's awareness of the permissiveness of the setting and also provides an opportunity for vicarious experiences.

CHILD-CENTERED PLAY THERAPY WITH AN EXTREMELY WITHDRAWN BOY

AUTHOR: **Virginia Axline**

FOCUS: *Helping a young withdrawn child release anxiety through child-centered play therapy.*

INTRODUCTION: Virginia Axline, founder of child-centered play therapy, describes her relationship with a withdrawn child and discusses her profound belief in allowing the child to express here-and-now feelings, attitudes, and issues. As this is allowed to occur, the child comes to know self better, and experience self-acceptance and the freedom to develop self-confidence and self-adequacy. The playroom and therapeutic relationship provide the space within which the child can safely explore a personal world.

CASE STUDY: Five-year-old Billy was facing possible expulsion from kindergarten because of his extremely withdrawn behavior at school. He would not talk or interact with other children, and if another child attempted to initiate contact, Billy would cover his face with his hands and arms and roll up into a ball. He would not respond to instructions from the teacher. The school-administered Stanford-Binet indicated an IQ of 68.

Billy's mother reported normal childhood development until age 3 when he stopped walking and talking and began to exhibit infantile behavior. Just before this sudden change she had been extremely ill and required emergency surgery. When she sought help for Billy, she was told he was retarded; unwilling to accept this diagnosis, she spent a great deal of time with him, teaching him to name colors, count, cut and paste, write his name, and so on.

INTERVENTION: Billy participated in forty-five-minute individual, child-centered play therapy sessions weekly. He entered the initial session with a shuffling gait and stood in the middle of the room with drooping posture and a blank stare. Eventually he went to the sandbox, where he spend the remainder of the session and ran sand through his fingers. During the next four sessions he added small elaborations to his play, such as moving cars in the sand, and adding a few comments. He appeared increasingly more alert and his walk had more energy. After the fourth session his mother indicated having observed significant improvement. Billy's regressive behavior had decreased and he was talking more and appeared less tense. After the fifth session Billy's teacher noted that although he still did not fully participate in classroom activities, his social interaction had increased.

Continued improvement was shown in the sixth through tenth sessions. Billy's play became more imaginative and complex, and he was more spontaneous and increased his verbal interaction. In the waiting room he talked easily with others, moved with a quick firm step, and displayed bright facial expressions. In preparation for termination several sessions of group play therapy assisted Billy in continuing his growth in social skills.

A one-year follow-up revealed that Billy continued to be happy and relaxed, with vivid and spontaneous expressive skills. He had several friends in his new school and testing had revealed an IQ of 105.

COMMENTARY: As demonstrated in this case, withdrawal may be severe enough not only to affect social relationships but also to place the child in jeopardy of possible, but incorrect, diagnosis of mild mental retardation. Without a therapist-driven agenda, this child was able to meet his own needs in play therapy and in the process free natural developmental coping skills.

SOURCE: Axline, V. (1948). Some observations on play therapy. *Journal of Consulting Psychology* 12:209–216.

POSSIBLE *DSM-IV* DIAGNOSES:

300.23   Social Phobia, Generalized
313.23   Selective Mutism
317.0   Mild Mental Retardation

THE USE OF OPERANT CONDITIONING IN NONDIRECTIVE GROUP PLAY THERAPY WITH WITHDRAWN THIRD-GRADE BOYS

AUTHORS: **Paul W. Clement and D. Courtney Milne**

FOCUS: *Behavioral techniques in group play therapy to bring about changes in withdrawn, introverted, and friendless 8- and 9-year-old boys.*

INTRODUCTION: Children, if quiet and subdued, rarely receive intervention, especially if the social withdrawal does not affect scholastic performance. However, helping such children learn skills to interact socially is always an important consideration. Group play therapy affords that opportunity.

RESEARCH METHODS & DESIGN: Eleven boys were selected from 2,761 third-grade children. Teachers identified boys in their classrooms who were socially withdrawn, introverted, very quiet, friendless, and lacked spontaneity. The eleven were selected from a pool of boys whose parents consented to participate in the study. The boys had psychological evaluations that included the Bender-Gestalt, the Children's Manifest Anxiety Scale, the California Test of Mental Maturity, and selected Rorschach cards. The subjects had an IQ range of 80–123. The boys were then randomly assigned to a token group, a verbal group, and a control group.

INTERVENTION: Each group met for one fifty-minute session per week for fourteen weeks. The token group was based on group play therapy methods of Ginott.[1] Brass tokens were given in the sessions for social-approach behavior. At the end of each session the tokens could be traded for small toys and candy. The verbal group was run the same way as the token group, except that verbal reinforcement rather than the token was given. The senior investigator was the therapist for both groups. The control group met in the same play therapy room but

---

1. Haim Ginott, *Group Psychotherapy with Children: The Theory and Practice of Play Therapy* (New York: McGraw-Hill, 1961).

without a therapist. This group was observed behind a oneway mirror to ensure the safety of the children. The mothers participated in concurrent guidance groups led by the junior investigator. These sessions were also based on the work of Ginott.

Pre-, mid-, and postdata were collected on the boys' productivity, anxiety, general psychological adjustment, and problem behaviors. The data included grades on report cards and standardized assessment instruments. Social adjustment was measured by observing the behavior of each boy during the group play therapy sessions.

RESULTS: The two treatment groups achieved statistically significant change in the area of social adjustment during the fourteen sessions. The boys in the token group improved in three areas; the boys in the verbal group improved in two areas, but got worse in one area. The boys in the control group showed no change. During the group play therapy sessions, the token group boys showed increases in verbal communication with each other ($p<.05$); in time spent in social play ($p<.01$); and in proximity, or getting closer to each other, during the group play therapy sessions ($p<.01$).

The boys in the verbal group displayed less dependence on the therapist by decreasing therapist-directed verbalization and increasing verbalization with their peers ($p<.01$); they also showed an increase in proximity ($p<.01$). The amount of time spent in social play, however, decreased for this group ($p<.01$).

The only change in problem behaviors occurred in the token group. The behavior problem checklist completed by the mothers indicated statistically significant improvement during the fourteen sessions ($p<.05$).

As measured by report card grades, performance showed no significant change. According to the authors, the preintervention data that indicated that all of the boys were average students with no reported scholastic problems accounted for this. The authors also indicated that anxiety, often reduced during play therapy, also showed no significant change during this study. In this case as well, the boys scored in the typical range of anxiety for their age range before this study began.

COMMENTARY: Group play therapy provides withdrawn children with the opportunity to develop social skills and process self-concept issues. Using a nondirective approach with the addition of operant conditioning through positive reinforcers resulted in significant improvement for the children participating in this study. The play therapy experience by itself provides positive reinforcement as children learn to accept themselves through the acceptance of the play therapist. The often-overlooked withdrawn child needs this experience.

SOURCE: Clement, P., and Milne, D. C. (1967). Group play therapy and tangible reinforcers used to modify the behavior of 8-year-old boys. *Behavior Research & Theory* 5:301–312.

POSSIBLE *DSM-IV* DIAGNOSES:

309.9   Adjustment Disorder, Unspecified
V62.81   Relational Problem NOS

TEACHERS PROVIDING PLAY THERAPY FOR WITHDRAWN STUDENTS

AUTHORS: **Bernard G. Guerney Jr. and Audrey Bach Flumen**

FOCUS: *Training teachers as play therapists for intervention with withdrawn school-age children.*

INTRODUCTION: Teachers were trained in filial therapy to provide play therapy for withdrawn children who were in the teachers' own classrooms. The teachers provided individual child-centered play therapy sessions outside the classroom with the goal of increasing assertive behavior within the classroom.

RESEARCH METHODS & DESIGN: Teachers received twenty weekly training sessions in filial therapy. The training included role playing, demonstration sessions, and participation in one play therapy session per week.

Fifteen children were identified as withdrawn based on their failure to communicate with other children, lack of interest in the classroom situation, and an unfulfilling approach to school. Nine children were assigned to the experimental group and the remaining six to the control group.

INTERVENTION: The nine children in the experimental group received forty-five-minute individual play therapy once a week for fourteen sessions. The children in the control group received no special treatment or attention of any kind. Pre- and postmeasures included trained observers coding the teachers' responses on an Empathy Rating Scale. The same observers coded the children's classroom behavior on a weekly basis.

RESULTS: The nine children who received play therapy showed a consistent pattern of increased assertiveness. None of the six children in the control group exhibited such a pattern. The children in the experimental group significantly increased initiation of peer interaction and talking with the teacher. The teachers were pleased with the resulting changes in the children, and also identified their own ability to generalize what they had learned regarding play therapy to other settings.

COMMENTARY: The teachers were able to learn sufficient play therapy skills to become therapeutic agents in the lives of the withdrawn children. Using teachers as therapeutic agents in conjunction with school counselors could have a dramatic effect on the needs of school-age children. Although the teachers were able to identify their ability to generalize the new skills to other settings, there was no attempt to see whether the children were able to do likewise. Positive changes were clearly identified in the children who participated in play therapy; further research is necessary to identify the extent of these behavioral changes in other settings.

SOURCE: Guerney, B. G., and Flumen, A. B. (1970). Teachers as psychotherapeutic agents for withdrawn children. *Journal of School Psychology* 8:107–113.

POSSIBLE *DSM-IV* DIAGNOSES:

309.9   Adjustment Disorder, Unspecified
V62.81   Relational Problem

BEHAVIORAL LEARNING THEORY APPLIED TO PLAY THERAPY AS AN INTERVENTION WITH A WITHDRAWN, NONEATING CHILD

AUTHOR: **John Graham White**

FOCUS: *The use of behavioral play therapy to facilitate the return of normal eating patterns in a child who had withdrawn from eating.*

INTRODUCTION: Children withdraw from normal patterns of living for various reasons. The child described in this study initially withdrew from other family members because of pampering by her father. After his death she increasingly withdrew in her eating behavior until she took in only liquids. The author described the application of learning theory to play therapy to resolve this child's withdrawal.

CASE STUDY: The child in this case was born five years after her older sister. Her father was away, serving in a war, during the first four years of the sister's life; the sister was identified as the mother's baby. After the father returned, the client child was born; she became identified as the father's baby. He fed her almost from the time she was born, played with her, and lavished care on her. When her father fed her, she would play with his shirt collar, and subsequently would not fall asleep unless she could hold onto a shirt collar.

By age 3 the child began demanding that her main meal of the day be fed to her by her father upon his return home from work. He would hold her on his knee during the meal, during which both of them ignored the mother and older sister. At bedtime she would not allow her mother to put her to bed, and screamed until her father came in and read several books. Finally she would fall asleep.

Just before she was 5 years old her father became very ill and spent seven weeks in the hospital. During this time the child could not see him, but still slept at night holding onto the collar of one of his shirts. When the father returned home, and until he died two months later, she spent the majority of her time in his room. After his death she still expected his return, as her mother told her he had gone "to God's hospital." When her mother began working, the child's appetite deteriorated despite the wide variety of games and entertainment various family members used to attempt to get her to eat. Once she commented to her mother that "Dr. B. says if I don't eat I'll never be a big girl. If I grow into a big girl my daddy won't recognize me, will he?" After six weeks of being bedridden, with a diagnosis of acute rheumatism, she stopped eating any solid food and was hospitalized.

INTERVENTION: This child's case was conceptualized from a behavioral learning theory perspective, identifying the father as the conditioned stimulus upon which the conditioned response of eating was based. The treatment plan was to provide a male psychologist as a stimulus-substitution of her father, later providing a generalization continuum to include members of the child's family.

The child was initially seen one hour a day during the first week of hospitalization. The sessions took place in a playroom set up like a large playhouse with child-size furniture, utensils for cooking, and a child's tea set. In the first session the therapist and child took care of the dolls, which included feeding them. In the next four sessions the child ate miniature cookies and drank milk from the small tea-cups, but refused to eat solid food on the ward. At the end of the first week she was discharged from the hospital.

Upon return to the hospital for outpatient treatment the following Monday, her mother reported that she had eaten a small amount of solid food during a visit to her paternal aunt and uncle. During the second week of daily play therapy sessions full-size cups and cookies were substituted for the doll-size ones. In midweek the mother reported having been embarrassed on one occasion when a neighbor chastised her for saying that this child would not eat, because the child had eaten two plates of food at the neighbor's home. Another neighbor, who had stopped by the child's house for a visit, reported to the mother that the child said, "I don't eat at this house. I don't eat for my mummy." Although there were no play therapy sessions over the next six days because of the Christmas holiday, the child sat down to meals with her mother and older sister even though she would not consistently eat with them.

During the next three weeks she had at least four play therapy sessions a week. The child began to prepare meals for herself and her therapist during these sessions. She also began taking the lead in other play activities. The therapist continued to play the role of her permissive, doting father. Six weeks after the play therapy sessions began, the child had the therapist drinking to the beat of her hammer pounding a pegboard. At this time the therapist decided to shift the pseudofather–daughter relationship from child-focused to more reality-focused. He began to retrain her from exploiting the relationship to being rewarded by responses to other stimuli. One example was having her assist the therapist in small, useful jobs around the clinic, in addition to participation in the playtime. At home she continued to eat better, including eating breakfast regularly and telling her mother when she was hungry. She continued to improve and suffered a brief relapse of only three to four days' duration when her mother returned to work.

Six months after her initial hospitalization, even with a six-week break because of measles and chicken pox, she continued to express an interest in food and developed some special favorites. Because she was now able to eat both at home and in the home of relatives, her eating was no longer the cause of concern.

At a three-year follow-up she continued to be eating normally. Nocturnal enuresis, which had been present at the time of hospitalization, cleared up twelve months after her eating problem was resolved. This child had suffered no relapse during the three-year period, even though her grandmother and a favorite uncle, who had become a father substitute, died. She was described as healthy and fairly well adjusted with her peers at home and at school.

COMMENTARY: This child's failure to transfer her stimulus response of eating from her father to others was resolved through the use of behavioral play therapy. The play therapy also provided the development of more assertive skills, as seen in her being allowed to become responsible for the direction of her play.

SOURCE: White, J. G. (1957). The use of learning theory in the psychological treatment of children. *Journal of Clinical Psychology* 15: 227–230.

POSSIBLE *DSM-IV* DIAGNOSES:

307.59   Feeding Disorder of Infancy or Early Childhood
309.9   Adjustment Disorder, Unspecified
V62.82   Bereavement
V61.20   Parent–Child Relational Problem

CHILD-CENTERED PLAY THERAPY WITH A WITHDRAWN CHILD

AUTHOR: **Virginia Axline**

FOCUS: *Child-centered play therapy with a socially withdrawn, selectively mute, emotionally disturbed child.*

INTRODUCTION: Axline's description of the case of 5-year-old Dibs has become a classic in the field of play therapy. Dibs's challenging behaviors ranged from mute and almost catatonic behavior in the classroom and at home to having violent temper tantrums. Although he did not attend a school for the mentally challenged or emotionally disturbed, Dibs was considered possibly both, or as having suffered some type of neurological damage. Nondirective or child-centered play therapy was employed.

CASE STUDY: Dibs was a puzzle to the adults in his life. His parents, teachers, the school psychologist, and the school pediatrician were unsure about the etiology or treatment for his bizarre behavior. Dibs had been in an exclusive private school for two years and exhibited severe withdrawn and mute behaviors. In general he did not talk and sometimes would not move. At time he crawled around the classroom on the floor, oblivious to teachers or other students. At other times he had violent temper tantrums. Often appearing to be mentally challenged, on occasion Dibs responded quickly and displayed flashes of superior intelligence.

His mother had used her influence with the private school to get him accepted into the program with the constant request that the teachers give him more time to change. His father was reportedly a gifted scientist and his younger sister was described as the "perfect child." Before entering treatment with Axline, the parents had concluded that Dibs was mentally challenged and requested referrals for programs to handle such children.

INTERVENTION: Axline observed Dibs in the classroom and had the initial play therapy session at his school. She described Dibs as seeming lonely and depressed: "There seemed to be no laughter or happiness in this child. Life, for him, was a grim business." Although there was limited interaction in the first session, Axline noted that she saw great potential and courage in Dibs. The following play therapy sessions were held at a local child guidance clinic.

A playroom with a wide variety of play materials was made available. Axline employed a nondirective or child-centered approach and left the direction of the therapy to Dibs, interacting with him at his request. As Dibs became more comfortable and explored the playroom, he began to be more emotionally expressive. Positive changes in his home and school behavior became evident as well. Although his parents initially asked not to be involved in the treatment process, Dibs's mother made an appointment with Axline to discuss the changes that were having an effect on the mother and the family, such as Dibs's coming out of his room more often, but also appearing very controlled and depressed. He began to enter and leave the therapy clinic in a much quieter and cooperative manner.

The positive changes in Dibs were reportedly having a positive effect on his family. The systemic effect included indications that Dibs was being treated with "more consideration, understanding, and respect at home." His playroom play became happier, and include positive artwork and songs he composed to sing. He began to express positive and negative emotions verbally in the playroom and at home. Dibs's school behavior also improved. His teachers reported that he responded in the classroom, occasionally initiated conversations, was "happy, calm, and showing an interest in other children." The temper tantrums ceased.

At the conclusion of the play therapy sessions, a standardized intelligence test was administered and Dibs achieved an overall IQ score of 168. The brilliant and gifted child that had been buried underneath such emotional turmoil had emerged in play therapy.

COMMENTARY: Dibs was offered a child-centered play therapy experience during a time when corrective and intrusive measures were often prescribed, including institutionalization. It is unlikely that this child, however, would have emerged had such severe measures been taken. Dibs was offered a safe place in which to explore and find himself, and having been given the opportunity, reclaimed his childhood. A child who had been written off as neurologically and emotionally damaged was able to establish positive relationships as a result of the healing power of the child-centered play therapy relationship.

SOURCE: Axline, V. (1964). *Dibs: In Search of Self.* New York: Ballantine Books.

POSSIBLE *DSM-IV* DIAGNOSES:

300.23   Social Phobia, Generalized
312.8   Conduct Disorder
309.9   Adjustment Disorder, Unspecified (Social Withdrawal), Chronic
313.89   Reactive Attachment Disorder of Infancy or Early Childhood

Index

Abuse and neglect, 1–14
   disclosure of, 7–8
   puppet play, 2–4
   self-concept and self-mastery, 9–11
   severe deprivation, dehydration,
      and coma, 5–6
   severely neglected emotionally
      abused child, 12–14
Academic Problem, withdrawn
   children, 260–261
Acord, L. T., 146–147
Acting out. *See* Aggression and
   acting out
Adjustment Disorder
   reading difficulties, 180–182
   social adjustment problems, 218–
      220
Adjustment Disorder, Unspecified,
   withdrawn children, 262–264,
   265–266, 267–269

Adjustment Disorder, Unspecified
   (Social Withdrawal), Chronic,
   withdrawn children, 260–261,
   270–272
Adjustment Disorder with Anxiety
   fear and anxiety, 116–118, 127–
      129
   hospitalization, 151–152, 153–
      155, 160–162, 163–165
   traumatization, 250–252, 256–257
Adjustment Disorder with
   Depressed Mood, social
   adjustment problems, 221–223
Adjustment Disorder with
   Disturbance of Conduct
   aggression and acting out, 33–34
   deaf and physically challenged
      children, 73–74
   social adjustment problems, 221–
      223, 224–225

Adjustment Disorder with Mixed
    Anxiety and Depressed Mood,
    traumatization, 245–247
Adjustment Disorder with Mixed
    Disturbance of Emotions and
    Conduct
    aggression and acting out, 30–
        32, 35–37
    deaf and physically challenged
        children, 73–74
    emotionally disturbed children,
        98–100
    grief, 136–138, 143–144
    social adjustment problems, 224–
        225
    traumatization, 248–249
Adolescence, dissociation and
    schizophrenia, group play
    therapy with adolescent
    hospitalized psychotic girls,
    90–92
Adoption, attachment difficulties,
    cognitive, reflective, and
    psychodynamic therapy in
    adopted boy, 45–47
Aggression and acting out, 15–40
    aggressive child, 16–18
    anger, fear, and control, 35–37
    developmental play group
        counseling, 28–29
    developmental therapy, 22–24
    institutionalized child, 33–34
    oppositional disordered
        children, video feedback,
        19–21
    psychoanalytic play therapy, 38–
        40
    social responsibility, group play
        rewarding, 25–27
    temper tantrums, brief therapy,
        30–32
Alexander, E. D., 112–113
Allan, J., 16–18, 81–83, 243–244

Anger, aggression and acting out,
    35–37
Anxiety. See Fear and anxiety
Anxiety Disorder Due to a General
    Medical Condition
    burn victims, 56–57, 58–59
    hospitalization, 146–147, 148–
        150, 151–152, 153–155, 158–
        159, 160–162, 163–165
Anxiety Disorder NOS
    aggression and acting out, 30–32
    autism, 50–52
    traumatization, 253–255
Armstrong, H. E., 25–27
Articulation disorders, speech
    difficulties, 235–236
Asthma, chronic illness, 62–64
Attachment difficulties, 41–47
    child-centered, long-term, 42–44
    cognitive, reflective, and
        psychodynamic therapy in
        adopted boy, 45–47
Attention-Deficit/Hyperactivity
    Disorder, Combined Type,
    dissociation and
    schizophrenia, 84–86
Attention-Deficit/Hyperactivity
    Disorder, Predominantly
    Hyperactive-Impulsive Type,
    aggression and acting out, 22–
    24, 25–27
Attention-Deficit/Hyperactivity
    Disorder NOS
    aggression and acting out, 22–24
    emotionally disturbed children,
        96–97
Autism, 49–54
    psychoanalytic play therapy, 53–54
    psychodynamic therapy with high-
        functioning child, 50–52
Autistic Disorder
    autism, 50–52, 53–54
    speech difficulties, 232–234

Axline, V. M., 180–182, 191–192, 259, 260–261, 270–272

Barlow, K., 114–115, 193–194
Barton, P. H., 148–150
Beers, P., 19–21
Behavioral approach
 cognitive-behavioral play therapy, enuresis and encopresis problems, 105–107
 as intervention with noneating child, withdrawn children, 267–269
 mother–daughter interactions, 130–132
Bentley, J., 62–64
Bereavement
 grief, 136–138, 139–140, 141–142, 143–144
 withdrawn children, 267–269
Berry, P., 243–244
Bilingual children, group play therapy, self-control development in, social adjustment problems, 224–225
Bills, R. E., 183–184
Birth, traumatization, traumatic birth symbolized in therapy, 256–257
Bixler, R. H., 185–187
Bligh, S., 235–236
Bloomberg, C. M., 214–215
Bouillion, K. R., 228–229
Brief play therapy
 aggression and acting out, temper tantrums, 30–32
 puppet therapy, cardiac catheterization, hospitalization, 151–152
 stammering, 122–124

Brody, V. A., 22–24
Bromfield, R., 50–52
Brown, K., 16–18
Burch, C. A., 2–4
Burn victims, 55–59
 multimodal treatment, 56–57
 preoperative play program, 58–59
Burton, C., 102–104
Butler, C., 90–92

Caldwell, M., 108–110
Cardiac catheterization, hospitalization, brief puppet therapy, 151–152
Carey, L., 136–138
Carlin, A. S., 25–27
Carter, S. R., 139–140
Cassell, S., 151–152
Caty, S., 156–157
Cerebral palsy, speech difficulties, group play therapy, speech, social skills, personality attributes, and intelligence improvement, 237–239
Chetnik, M., 195–197
Child abuse and neglect. See Abuse and neglect
Child-centered play therapy
 attachment difficulties, 42–44
 deaf and physically challenged children, preschool deaf children, 73–74
 dissociation and schizophrenia, 84–86
 grief, death of parent, 143–144
 group, self-concept and self-esteem, 208–209
 with mute, emotionally disturbed child, withdrawn children, 270–272
 reading difficulties, 183–184

Child-centered play therapy
  (*continued*)
  traumatization, with neglected,
    hospitalized child, 245–247
  withdrawn children, 260–261
Childhood Disintegrative Disorder,
  speech difficulties, 232–234
Child or Adolescent Antisocial
  Behavior
  aggression and acting out, 16–
    18, 22–24, 25–27, 35–37
  attachment difficulties, 42–44,
    45–47
  traumatization, 243–244
Chronic illness, 61–67
  asthma, 62–64
  filial therapy with families, 65–
    67
Clatworthy, S., 153–155
Clement, P. W., 262–264
Cognitive-behavioral play therapy,
  enuresis and encopresis
  problems, 105–107
Cognitive therapy, attachment
  difficulties, reflective and
  psychodynamic therapy in
  adopted boy, 45–47
Colbert, L., 42–44
Coma, abuse and neglect, severe
  deprivation, dehydration, 5–6
Conduct Disorder
  aggression and acting out, 25–
    27, 38–40
  attachment difficulties, 42–44,
    45–47
  deaf and physically challenged
    children, 75–77
  dissociation and schizophrenia,
    81–83
  emotionally disturbed children,
    96–97
  fear and anxiety, 133–134

grief, 139–140
  speech difficulties, 230–231
  withdrawn children, 270–272
Conn, J., 116–118
Control, aggression and acting out,
  35–37
Crow, J., 201–202

Daniel, C. A., 160–162
Deaf and physically challenged
  children, 69–77
  preschool deaf children, 73–74
  sand play with hyperkinetic,
    epileptic children, 71–72
  school-age deaf children, 75–
    77
Dehydration, abuse and neglect,
  severe deprivation and coma,
  5–6
Depta, J.-L., 141–142
Desensitization, fear and anxiety,
  behavioral approach, mother–
  daughter interactions, 130–
  132
Developmental therapy
  aggression and acting out, 22–
    24
  group play therapy, emotionally
    disturbed children, 94–95
  play group counseling,
    aggression and acting out,
    28–29
Disclosure, of abuse and neglect,
  7–8
Disorder of Written Expression,
  dissociation and
  schizophrenia, 84–86
Disruptive Behavior Disorder NOS
  aggression and acting out, 16–
    18, 22–24, 25–27, 30–32, 33–
    34, 35–37
  attachment difficulties, 42–44

deaf and physically challenged
     children, 71–72
emotionally disturbed children,
     98–100
social adjustment problems, 218–
     220, 221–223
traumatization, 243–244
Dissociation and schizophrenia,
     79–92
     child-centered play therapy, 84–
          86
     group play therapy with
          adolescent hospitalized
          psychotic girls, 90–92
     Jungian play therapy, 81–83
     regressed, hospitalized child, 87–
          89
Dissociative Identity Disorder
     dissociation and schizophrenia,
          84–86
     fear and anxiety, 112–113
Domestic violence, traumatization,
     intensive therapy with witness
     of, 248–249
Dupont, H., 230–231
Dysthymic Disorder
     attachment difficulties, 45–47
     deaf and physically challenged
          children, 75–77
     traumatization, 243–244, 253–
          255

Eaton, F., 90–92
Elective mutism. See Selective
     Mutism
Ellerton, M.-L., 156–157
Emotionally disturbed children,
     93–100
     group play therapy, 94–95, 98–
          100
     trichotillomania and mild
          microcephaly, 96–97

Enberg, S., 163–165
Encopresis
     enuresis and encopresis
          problems, 105–107
     grief, 136–138
Encopresis with Constipation and
     Overflow Incontinence, 108–
     110
Enuresis
     emotionally disturbed children,
          96–97
     enuresis and encopresis
          problems, 102–104
     grief, 136–138
     selective mutism, 193–194
     traumatization, 256–257
Enuresis and encopresis problems,
     101–110
     cognitive-behavioral play
          therapy, 105–107
     hide-and-seek and peekaboo
          games, 102–104
     psychodynamic play therapy,
          108–110
Epilepsy, deaf and physically
     challenged children, sand play
     with hyperkinetic children,
     71–72
Expressive Language Disorder
     autism, 53–54
     enuresis and encopresis
          problems, 105–107
     speech difficulties, 228–229,
          230–231, 235–236, 237–239

Fear and anxiety, 111–134
     aggression and acting out, 35–37
     behavioral approach, mother–
          daughter interactions, 130–
          132
     extreme anxiety in primary-
          grade child, 112–113

Fear and anxiety (*continued*)
  hair pulling, 114–115
  school phobia, brief play
      therapy, puppetry, 125–126
  separation anxiety, focused play,
      127–129
  Squiggle drawing technique,
      133–134
  stammering, brief play therapy
      for, 122–124
  structured play therapy for fear
      of kidnapping, 116–118
  toilet training, home play
      therapy for, 119–121
Feeding Disorder of Infancy or
    Early Childhood, withdrawn
    children, 267–269
Filial therapy
  with families, chronic illness, 65–
      67
  self-concept and self-esteem,
      203–205, 210–211
Flumen, A. B., 265–266
Friedman, D., 5–6
Fuchs, N. R., 119–121

Garot, P. A., 158–159
Gaulden, G. L., 28–29
Generalized Anxiety Attack, fear
    and anxiety, 116–118
Generalized Anxiety Disorder
  abuse and neglect, 2–4
  aggression and acting out, 38–
      40
  fear and anxiety, 112–113
  reading difficulties, 180–182
  social adjustment problems, 218–
      220
Gil, E., 79, 245–247
Glass, N. M., 203–205
Glazer-Waldman, H., 65–67
Goodban, M., 235–236

Gorman, J., 84–86
Gould, M. F., 206–207
Grief, 135–144
  child-centered play therapy,
      death of parent, 143–144
  group play therapy, death of
      parent, 141–142
  puppet play, homicide of parent,
      139–140
  sand play therapy, death of
      parent, 136–138
Group play therapy
  adolescent hospitalized psychotic
      girls, dissociation and
      schizophrenia, 90–92
  bilingual children, self-control
      development in, social
      adjustment problems, 224–
      225
  developmental play group
      counseling, aggression and
      acting out, 28–29
  emotionally disturbed children,
      94–95, 98–100
  grief, death of parent, 141–142
  individual play therapy and, for
      socially immature
      kindergarten children,
      social adjustment problems,
      216–217
  mentally challenged children,
      172–173, 177–178
  nondirective, to facilitate speech
      and language, 228–229
  operant conditioning, withdrawn
      children, 262–264
  for peer and sibling relationship
      problems, social adjustment
      problems, 214–215
  rewarding social responsibility,
      aggression and acting out,
      25–27

selective mutism, individual play therapy and, with enuresis, 193–194

self-concept and self-esteem, 206–207

social adjustment problems, for primary-grade boys, 221–223

speech, social skills, personality attributes, and intelligence improvement, 237–239

Guerney, B. G., Jr., 265–266

Gumaer, J., 94–95

Hair pulling, fear and anxiety, 114–115

Healy, M., 56–57

Hide-and-seek games, peekaboo games and, enuresis and encopresis problems, 102–104

Home play therapy, toilet training, fear and anxiety, 119–121

Homicide, of parent, puppet play, 139–140

Hospitalization, 145–165
  acute illness, 160–162
  cardiac catheterization, brief puppet therapy, 151–152
  child-centered play therapy, traumatization, with neglected child, 245–247
  dissociation and schizophrenia, 87–89
  effectiveness evaluation of play therapy program, 163–165
  hospital-induced anxiety, 153–155
  injection fears, 146–147
  intrusive procedures, 156–157
  lymphangioma, fear and stress, 158–159
  open heart surgery, 148–150

House, R. M., 208–209

Hyperkinetic children, deaf and physically challenged children, sand play with epileptic children, 71–72

Incarcerated parent, self-concept and self-esteem, filial therapy to improve parent–child relations, 210–211

Individual play therapy
  group play therapy and, for socially immature kindergarten children, social adjustment problems, 216–217
  selective mutism, group play therapy and, with enuresis, 193–194

Injection fears, hospitalization, 146–147

Institutionalized child, aggression and acting out, 33–34. *See also* Hospitalization

Intermittent Explosive Disorder, aggression and acting out, 25–27

Intrusive procedures, hospitalization, 156–157

Irwin, B., 87–89

Jackson, L., 232–234

Jensen, R., 108–110

Jungian play therapy
  aggression and acting out, 16–18
  dissociation and schizophrenia, 81–83

Kawai, H., 71–72

Kawai, I., 71–72

Kidnapping, structured play therapy for fear of, 116–118

Kirk, A., 108–110

Klem, P. R., 7–8
Knell, S., 105–107
Kot, S., 248–249
Kupperman, P., 235–236

Landreth, G., 65–67, 114–115, 193–194
Landsman, T., 230–231
Lanyado, M., 53–54
Lawton-Speert, S., 81–83
Learning-disabled children, 167–169
LeVieux, J., 143–144
Levy, D. M., 30–32, 122–124
Lobaugh, F. A., 210–211
Lymphangioma, hospitalization, 158–159

Machler, T. J., 125–126
Maclean, G., 250–252
Mehlman, B., 172–173
Mental Disorder NOS Due to a General Medical Condition, deaf and physically challenged children, 71–72
Mentally challenged children, 171–178
    group play therapy, 172–173
    individual play therapy, intelligence and emotional development, 174–176
    individual play therapy versus group play therapy, 177–178
Mental Retardation, Severity Unspecified
    enuresis and encopresis problems, 102–104
    mentally challenged children, 172–173
Microcephaly, trichotillomania and, emotionally disturbed children, 96–97

Mild Mental Retardation
    mentally challenged children, 177–178
    selective mutism, 191–192
Miller, H. E., 33–34
Milne, D. C., 262–264
Milos, M. E., 127–129
Milston, A., 45–47
Mixed Receptive-Expressive Language Disorder, speech difficulties, 228–229
Moderate Mental Retardation, mentally challenged children, 174–176, 177–178
Moore, D., 105–107
Morrison, T. L., 177–178
Multimodal treatment, burn victims, 56–57
Mundy, L., 174–176
Mutism, withdrawn children, child-centered play therapy with mute, emotionally disturbed child, 270–272

Naniwa, H., 71–72
Neglect. See Abuse and neglect
Neglect of Child
    abuse and neglect, 5–6, 12–14
    emotionally disturbed children, 98–100
    speech difficulties, 230–231
    traumatization, 245–247
Newcomer, B. L., 177–178
Nightmare Disorder, traumatization, 250–252
Norton, D., 65–67

O'Connor, K. J., 241n1
Open heart surgery, hospitalization, 148–150
Operant conditioning, in nondirective group play

therapy, withdrawn children,
    262–264
Oppositional Behavior Disorder
    NOS, traumatization, 243–244
Oppositional Defiant Disorder
    aggression and acting out, 16–
        18, 19–21, 22–24, 25–27, 38–
        40
    attachment difficulties, 42–44
    chronic illness, 62–64
    deaf and physically challenged
        children, 73–74
    dissociation and schizophrenia,
        81–83, 84–86
    emotionally disturbed children,
        96–97
    enuresis and encopresis
        problems, 102–104, 108–110
    fear and anxiety, 133–134
    grief, 139–140, 143–144
    selective mutism, 195–197
    social adjustment problems, 218–
        220
    speech difficulties, 230–231,
        232–234
Oualline, V. J., 73–74

Par, M. A., 35–37
Parent–Child Relational Problem
    abuse and neglect, 2–4, 12–14
    autism, 53–54
    enuresis and encopresis
        problems, 102–104, 108–110
    fear and anxiety, 112–113, 116–
        118, 130–132
    reading difficulties, 180–182
    self-concept and self-esteem,
        210–211
    social adjustment problems, 214–
        215
    traumatization, 245–247
    withdrawn children, 267–269

Peekaboo games, hide-and-seek
    games and, enuresis and
    encopresis problems, 102–104
Pelham, L. E., 216–217
Perez, C. L., 9–11
Perry, J. A., 96–97
Pervasive Developmental Disorder
    NOS
    selective mutism, 191–192
    speech difficulties, 232–234
Phonological Disorder
    dissociation and schizophrenia,
        84–86
    enuresis and encopresis
        problems, 105–107
    speech difficulties, 228–229,
        235–236, 237–239
Physical Abuse of Child
    abuse and neglect, 2–4
    reading difficulties, 180–182
    traumatization, 253–255
Physical and Sexual Abuse of
        Child, abuse and neglect, 7–8.
    See also Sexual Abuse of Child
Physically challenged children. See
    Deaf and physically challenged
    children
Pica, grief, sand play therapy,
    death of parent, 136–138
Posttraumatic Stress Disorder
    burn victims, 56–57, 58–59
    hospitalization, 146–147, 148–150
    traumatization, 245–247, 248–
        249, 250–252, 256–257
Preoperative play program, burn
    victims, 58–59
Psychoanalytic play therapy
    aggression and acting out, 38–40
    autism, 53–54
    with child suffering from
        traumatic neurosis, 250–252
    selective mutism, 195–197

Psychodynamic play therapy
  attachment difficulties, cognitive
    and reflective therapy in
    adopted boy, 45–47
  autism, high-functioning child,
    50–52
  enuresis and encopresis
    problems, 108–110
Psychotic Disorder NOS,
    dissociation and
    schizophrenia, 90–92
Puppet play
  abuse and neglect, 2–4
  brief therapy, cardiac
    catheterization,
    hospitalization, 151–152
  grief, homicide of parent, 139–
    140
  school phobia, brief play
    therapy, puppetry, 125–126

Quayle, R. L., 218–220

Racial differences, rejection in play
    therapy, traumatization, 253–
    255
Rae, W. A., 160–162
Reactive Attachment Disorder of
    Infancy or Early Childhood
  abuse and neglect, 5–6
  aggression and acting out, 22–24
  attachment difficulties, 42–44,
    45–47
  autism, 53–54
  enuresis and encopresis
    problems, 102–104
  withdrawn children, 270–272
Reading difficulties, 179–187
  behavioral problems and, 185–
    187
  child-centered play therapy,
    183–184

teacher use of play therapy, 180–
    182
Reading Disorder
  fear and anxiety, 116–118
  reading difficulties, 180–182,
    183–184, 185–187
  self-concept and self-esteem,
    201–202
Regression
  abuse and neglect, severely
    neglected emotionally
    abused child, 12–14
  speech difficulties, regression of
    speech in young child, 232–
    234
Reiss, S., 127–129
Rejection, in play therapy, racial
    differences, traumatization,
    253–255
Relational Problem NOS
  social adjustment problems, 214–
    215, 216–217, 218–220, 221–
    223, 224–225
  traumatization, 253–255
  withdrawn children, 260–261,
    262–264, 265–266
Relational Problem Related to a
    Mental Disorder or General
    Medical Condition, chronic
    illness, 62–64
Ritchie, J., 156–157
Rose, D., 90–92

Sand play
  grief, death of parent, 136–138
  hyperkinetic, epileptic children,
    71–72
  traumatization, 243–244
  water play and, aggression and
    acting out, anger, fear, and
    control, 35–37
Sanner, J. H., 160–162

Schaefer, C. E., 241n1
Schiffer, M., 98–100
Schizophrenia, Disorganized Type, dissociation and schizophrenia, 81–83, 84–86
Schizophrenia, Undifferentiated Type
  aggression and acting out, 25–27
  dissociation and schizophrenia, 87–89, 90–92
School adjustment problems, social adjustment problems, 218–220
School phobia, brief play therapy, puppetry, 125–126
Selective Mutism, 189–197
  individual and group play therapy, with enuresis, 193–194
  nondirective play therapy, 191–192
  psychoanalytic play therapy, 195–197
  speech difficulties, regression of speech in young child, 232–234
Self-concept and self-esteem, 199–211
  abuse and neglect, 9–11
  child-centered group play therapy, 208–209
  filial therapy, 203–205
  filial therapy to improve parent–child relations, 210–211
  group play therapy, 206–207
  reading problems, 201–202
Self-injurious behavior, aggression and acting out, psychoanalytic play therapy, 38–40
Separation anxiety, focused play, 127–129

Separation Anxiety Disorder
  abuse and neglect, 2–4
  autism, 53–54
  fear and anxiety, 127–129
  reading difficulties, 180–182
  selective mutism, 195–197
  traumatization, 250–252
Sexual Abuse of Child
  abuse and neglect, 7–8, 9–11
  dissociation and schizophrenia, 81–83
Sibling Relational Problem
  abuse and neglect, 7–8
  fear and anxiety, 116–118
  reading difficulties, 185–187
  social adjustment problems, 214–215
Siegel, C. L. F., 168–169
Smith, L. T., 221–223
Social adjustment problems, 213–225
  group and individual play therapy for socially immature kindergarten children, 216–217
  group play therapy, bilingual children, self-control development in, 224–225
  group play therapy for peer and sibling relationship problems, 214–215
  group play therapy for primary-grade boys, 221–223
  school adjustment problems, 218–220
Social Phobia, fear and anxiety, school phobia, brief play therapy, puppetry, 125–126
Social Phobia, Generalized, withdrawn children, 260–261, 270–272

Social responsibility, group play rewarding, aggression and acting out, 25–27
Sokoloff, M., 237–239
Specific Phobia, Situational Type, fear and anxiety, 119–121, 125–126
Speech difficulties, 227–239
    articulation disorders, 235–236
    emotionally based delayed speech, 230–231
    group play therapy, nondirective, to facilitate speech and language, 228–229
    group play therapy, speech, social skills, personality attributes, and intelligence improvement, 237–239
    regression of speech in young child, 232–234
Squiggle drawing technique, fear and anxiety, 133–134
Stammering, brief play therapy for, 122–124
Straughan, J., 130–132
Strother, J., 114–115, 193–194
Stuttering, fear and anxiety, stammering, brief play therapy for, 122–124

Tait, D. C., 141–142
Teachers
    play therapy provided by, withdrawn children, 265–266
    reading difficulties, play therapy, 180–182
Temper tantrums, aggression and acting out, brief therapy, 30–32
Terr, L., 241

Toilet training, home play therapy for, fear and anxiety, 119–121
Trauma, grief, puppet play, homicide of parent, 139–140
Traumatization, 241–257
    child-centered play therapy with neglected, hospitalized child, 245–247
    intensive therapy with witness of domestic violence, 248–249
    psychoanalytic play therapy with child suffering from traumatic neurosis, 250–252
    racial differences cause rejection in play therapy, 253–255
    sand play, 243–244
    traumatic birth symbolized in therapy, 256–257
Trichotillomania
    emotionally disturbed children, 96–97
    fear and anxiety, 114–115
Trostle, S. L., 224–225
Trust, hospitalization, open heart surgery, 148–150
Tung, M., 253–255

Ude-Pestel, A., 38–40
Upchurch, J., 160–162
Urban, E., 75–77

Valentine, M., 230–231
van Zyl, D. A., 256–257
Video feedback, Oppositional Defiant Disorder, 19–21

Walker, L. S., 56–57
Walls, D. L., 58–59
Warson, S., 108–110
West, J., 12–14

White, J. G., 267–269
Withdrawn children, 259–272
    behavioral learning theory, as
        intervention with noneating
        child, 267–269
    child-centered play therapy,
        260–261
    child-centered play therapy with
        mute, emotionally disturbed
        child, 270–272

operant conditioning in
    nondirective group play
    therapy, 262–264
teacher-provided therapy, 265–
    266
Worchel, F. F., 160–162

Ziegler, R., 133–134
Zilliacus, K., 163–165
Zimmerman, J., 65–67